THE MONOGRAPH SERIES

WOMEN IN MUSLIM RURAL SOCIETY

The Shiloah Center for Middle Eastern and African Studies
Tel Aviv University

The Shiloah Center is, with the Department of Middle Eastern and African History, a part of the School of History at Tel Aviv University. Its main purpose is to contribute, by research and documentation, to the dissemination of knowledge and understanding of the modern history and current affairs of the Middle East and Africa. Emphasis is laid on fields where Israeli scholarship is in a position to make a special contribution and on subjects relevant to the needs of society and the teaching requirements of the university.

The Monograph Series

The studies published in this series are the work of the Research Associates and Visiting Research Associates at the Shiloah Center. The views expressed in these publications are entirely the viewpoints of the respective authors.

Uriel Dann **IRAQ UNDER QASSEM**

* David Kim **THE AFRO-ASIAN MOVEMENT**

* Itamar Rabinovich **SYRIA UNDER THE BA'TH 1963—66**

* Aryeh Yodfat **ARAB POLITICS IN THE SOVIET MIRROR**

* Bernard Reich **QUEST FOR PEACE**

* Yaacov Ro'i **SOVIET DECISION MAKING IN PRACTICE**

* Titles distributed by Transaction Books

WOMEN IN MUSLIM RURAL SOCIETY

STATUS AND ROLE IN FAMILY AND COMMUNITY

JOSEPH GINAT

Transaction Books
New Brunswick, New Jersey

Library of Congress Catalog Number: 79-66432
ISBN: 0-87855-342-8 (cloth)
Printed in the United States of America

Library of Congress Cataloging in Publication Data
Ginat, J
Women in Muslim rural society.

Includes bibliographical references.
1. Women—Israel. 2. Women, Muslim. 3. Palestinian Arabs—Israel. I. Title.
HQ1728.5.G56 301.41'2'095694 79-66432
ISBN: 0-87855-342-8

Contents

List of Figures and Tables

To
Dalia, Na'ama and Iddo

Foreword

It is remarkable how homogeneous much of Arab culture is. A good example are the Arab's views about his own society; they consist of a set of stereotypes found all over the Arab world. Perhaps the most important and widely held stereotypes are that Arab society is divided into three discrete economic sectors: The peasants, the nomads and the townsmen; that political activities are for the most part conducted by men organized in corporate patrilineal descent groups; that women depend on men and cannot own property; that men prefer to marry their father's brother's daughter; and that men gain the esteem of their fellows by jealously guarding the honor of their women and by offering lavish hospitality. Most students of Arab societies have been influenced by these views and their accounts often illustrate these assumed patterns of culture.

Both Arabs and students of Arab society have tended to view the stereotypes as principles of social organization, and to interpret various aspects of social life as their manifestations. Thus the territorial organization of tribes, the political alliances of peasants or nomads, and the indigenous administrative order were all categorized as more or less inclusive corporate descent groups. Similarly, the preferred marriage of the father's brother's daughter became the paradigm for all marriages. The Arab sought to marry the closest available agnate; if he could not marry a first parallel cousin he married another agnate. Inconvenient facts were treated as exceptions or given special interpretations. A political faction in a village which cut across descent groups would be described as a temporary alliance of members of various descent groups. The marriage of a girl to a man from another village could always be explained on personal grounds: perhaps the girl's parents were afraid she might remain a spinster or she had been involved in a premarital affair, and no local boy would marry her. In short, both natives and foreign observers went to great lengths to keep the stereotyped view of Arab society intact.

In recent years there has been some uneasiness among students of Arab society about this state of affairs. This development can be attributed partly to the growing number of detailed studies of Arab communities of every kind, and partly to the accelerated pace of change in the region itself. In the oil producing states nomads are rapidly becoming townsmen, the state everywhere intervenes in village affairs and the cities grow in leaps and bounds. One can no longer treat nomadic tribes and villages communities as isolated, for they have become fully integrated into wider social fields. Furthermore, it has become clearer now that even in the past they were part of wider society. Nowadays even pastoral tribes and peasant villages are just specialized segments of a complex modern economy. That is not to say, however, that the Arab world is becoming another Western society. For it is "modernizing" in its own way, and at the same time it preserves some of its own traditions. Thus Western education and medicine exist everywhere side by side with Islamic learning and Oriental healing. And of course the native stereotypes about society shape the thinking and actions of people. Thus when a government tries to settle a "tribe" it usually acts on the assumption that the tribe is an alliance of related corporate groups. It may deprive the tribe of its territory, and thus of its identity, and yet treat it as a single unit, and its chief—as its legitimate representative. There is a growing awareness in the region that a more adequate view of society is needed, one that takes complex reality as its starting point, and which treats the older stereotypic view of society as only another factor affecting this reality. Two recent conferences attempted such a reassessment in two areas. One was devoted to *Rural Politics and Social Change in the Middle East* (Antoun & Harik 1972), and the other to the relations between *The Desert and the Town* (Nelson 1973). Concerted efforts to achieve new insights into Arab societies such as these, will not only lead to better individual studies, but will also contribute to anthropological theory in general.

On this background Dr. Ginat's study can be appreciated. It attempts to reassess several accepted truths about Arab village society. His main effort was directed at the position of women. He carried out very detailed, patient fieldwork, during which he established very good relationships with villagers of both sexes. He comes up with valuable and complete information about aspects of family life that have rarely been covered in such detail in the literature. The study shows first that one cannot speak about the position of women in general, for there is a great difference between women depending on the structure of their households and relationships. Women whose work contributes to the family's income, who have been able to acquire property, who exert control over their sons, and who have the quickness of mind to exploit suitable opportunities, such women often have their way in the economic and political affairs of their household and beyond. While women suffer legal and social handicaps, some of them can overcome these: they can manage and manipulate men who formally control their behavior and property, and other women, and crucially affect their actions. While their material and political resources may be limited, they have access to other forms of power, such as stratagem and the sanctions of withdrawal of cooperation. Yet it would be extremely hard for a woman to obtain the relative autonomy of movement and action that is the lot of so many men.

Dr. Ginat's analysis of marriage patterns dispels the common notion that men (or their fathers on their behalf) customarily seek the hand of their father's brother's daughter, and that this type of marriage illustrates a principle of endogamy in Arab village society. After carefully examining the numerous reasons for each marriage, he concludes that a combination of material and political considerations of the families involved, and not stated norm, determine the choice of spouses. Relatives are often in a position to coerce one another, and this leads to frequent matches between kin. The match, however, may not always serve the interests of the groom's family. A man may be forced to marry a father's brother's daughter against his wishes, because his father's brother has a hold over him. This is a far cry from the prevalent view that such matches are always initiated by the groom's father, and that they take place because custom demands so.

Dr. Ginat clarifies the notion of honor, which hitherto has had to "explain" so many things. in Arab society. Honor is essentially a person's capability to observe highly valued norms. In Arab societies a man's honor seems often to depend on the reputation of his women. Now it appears that his honor is gauged not by the actual sexual comportment of women for whom he is morally responsible, but by public attitude towards it. A woman may have been involved in reprehensible sexual behavior, a fact known to all the village, who may gossip about her. But her family's honor, claims Ginat, is touched to the raw only when the family is directly and publicly accused of her misbehavior. Such accusation is proof of the family's weakness: only a defenseless person can be accused to his face with impunity. It indicates that the family is so powerless that it cannot avenge the affront of the accuser, and so it turns its wrath aganst the member who "has brought shame on it." Ginat thus shows that honor is a symbolic aspect of power.

These examples show how Dr. Ginat's analysis adds to our understanding of some central themes in Arab sociology. There are many more interesting observations and insights to be found in his book which makes a significant contribution to reshaping Arab sociology, a process that will, one hopes, restore it to its former leading position in anthropology.

Emanuel Marx

Tel-Aviv University
March 1978

Preface

I have always been fascinated by the pattern of life, customs and traditions of the Arabs. I grew up in a cooperative smallholders' settlement (*moshav*) north of Jerusalem which was surrounded by many Arab villages, and in my childhood I came into contact with Arab peasants and learned to speak Arabic. During the War of Independence in 1948 we had to evacuate our settlement and from that time until I joined a kibbutz in the Negev in the late 1950s I had practically no contact with Arabs.

During my stay in the Negev I met Bedouin and soon became a frequent visitor in their tents, enjoying their generous and picturesque hospitality, and becoming familiar with their way of life and customs. I felt strongly attracted by this world, so close to the one in which I grew up, and yet so different in many ways. In 1964 I took up work in the Prime Minister's Office and was once again brought in close contact with Arab peasant communities. At this time I became acquainted with the rural settlements which are the subject of this book.

My first degree was in archeology and Middle Eastern studies. Later I turned to anthropology in order to concentrate on the social aspects of Arab society. After I had finished my fieldwork in the hamlets and the writing of my Ph.D. thesis, I decided to write the present book. Although the bulk of the data was collected in the years of my fieldwork, new insights suggested themselves and additional facts came to my knowledge which helped me deepen my analyses of the case histories presented, as well as focus them more precisely. In some instances I had the satisfaction of finding the theories presented here confirmed by subsequent events.

One of the reasons for writing this book is that if Arab society holds so much attraction for me, it must also arouse genuine interest and curiosity in others. I have tried to present scientifically established facts in a way that will make the text readable for any educated person. Successful anthropologists, whom I wish to imitate, discover facts that are fascinating to the general reader as well as to the social scientist. Scientific reports can make good reading because truth is often stranger than fiction, a truism that bears repetition.

This investigation of the role and status of the Arab rural Muslim woman is restricted to villages which possess sufficient land. It goes without saying that there are features in other rural communities, not in the same position regarding the ownership of fields, that bear comparison with the hamlets. However, the status and role of women in the village communities cannot be compared with those in places where girls and women are wage-earners or receivers of salaries, either employed outside their places of residence or within them in factories or workshops. There is little doubt that the definition of their role will be different and certainly the criteria of their status within their society. As these new situations in which girls and women find themselves have not, to the best of my knowledge, been made the subject of serious investigation, no valid comparison can be made.

There is one phenomenon which affects the status of female citizens of the State of Israel, Jewish and Arab alike. All of them receive monthly payments from the National Insurance Institute if they have two or more children, the rates increasing proportionately with the number of children. Since 1977 the cheques are made out in the names of the mothers, a fact which has contributed, in the absence of an investigation, to the heightening of their status. I have no reliable information on whether the women use the cheques as they see fit, or whether their husbands or other male members of the family force them to hand them over. Even if this happens, the very fact that the woman is the recipient of a substantial sum of money enhances her prestige and affects both her status and role.

The text refers to prices in Israeli Lirot of various goods and services. Because of the continuing devaluation of Israeli currency vis-à-vis the dollar, any comparison would be misleading. The absence of any comparison does not detract from any of the arguments presented.

The names of the characters in all the cases histories presented here have been changed, otherwise they are an accurate account of events in the hamlets.

In the text several Arab words and terms have been used. I have usually given the English translation, adding the Arabic in parenthesis, having only maintained those Arabic terms or words which are so widespread that I consider their use justified. These have been italicized.

Acknowledgments

The study on which this book is based, has been made possible by many institutions and individuals. The University of Utah Research Committee; the University of Utah Park Foundation; Mr. and Mrs. Benjamin Roe and the Harriet Travis Foundation, both of Salt Lake City; the Prime Minister's Office of the State of Israel; Emeq Hefer Regional Council; the Histadrut (Israeli General Federation of Labor) Research Committee; the Shiloah Institute for Middle Eastern and African Studies, Tel Aviv University; and the following departments in the University of Haifa: The Publications Department; The Research Committee; The Research Committee of the Faculty of Humanities and the Jewish Arab Center, have all contributed in the form of grants. I wish to thank Mr. Uri Thom of the University of Haifa and Mr. Aharon Harel of the Histadrut for arranging grants.

I owe deep gratitude to the chairman of the Department of Anthropology of the University of Utah, Dr. Seymour Parker, who never tired of guiding and advising me. Dr. Khosrow Mostofi, Director of the Middle East Center and Dr. Robert Anderson made insightful remarks, which helped me. I am also grateful to Dr. M. Bennet for her assistance in the early drafts of the manuscript. Dr. Moshe Schwartz has given much of his time to read the manuscript and has made helpful comments. Aliza Levenberg accompanied me on some of my visits to the hamlets, shared my impressions and met the persons involved. She often suggested additional interpretations, and for these I am grateful.

Mr. and Mrs. Benjamin Roe showed particular interest in my work. Their encouragement and personal involvement should be especially mentioned and acknowledged.

I feel very indebted to my teacher Professor Emanuel Marx without whom I might never have ventured into the field of anthropology and whom I first met in the black tents of the Bedouin. I took up a great deal of his time, especially when he went over the text of the book suggesting many improvements.

Anthony Grahame devoted much effort in preparing the manuscript for publication. He worked with characteristic intelligence, care and good taste.

I could never have undertaken this study without the patience and forbearance of my wife Dalia and our children, Na'ama and Iddo. Dalia assisted me by establishing contacts with the women of the hamlets. This was of particularly importance since it is not easy to obtain access to the female members of families in the society studied. Dalia also played successful hostess to the hamlet residents at our Tel Aviv home. The good relations my whole family entertained with the hamlet residents greatly facilitated my work.

Finally, I wish to extend my thanks to the villagers themselves. They were always ready to cooperate and help me comprehend much I found puzzling. They opened their homes to me with proverbial Arab hospitality. I always felt welcome though I plied them with questions and asked for explanations of much they took for granted. They were more than patient and understanding.

1

General Features of the Hamlets

This is a study of Israeli rural Arabs living in four adjacent hamlets, all offshoots of one village, Deir al-Ghusūn.[1] Geographical propinquity often makes it difficult to define where a hamlet begins and ends. Peters says that "where settlements are strung out in one line, one settlement merging with the next, the problem of defining a residential universe can be difficult."[2] For the purpose of this study, the hamlets are considered as one unit. Khirbet Yamma, Bir al-Sikke, Khirbet Ibthān and Marja lie within a radius of a few kilometers from the parent village Deir al-Ghusūn, in the mountains of Samaria (see figure 1). The parent village has not been studied, nor its two additional offshoots, Khirbet Masqūfa and Jarūshiyya for these villages were within Jordanian territory between 1949 and 1967, while the four hamlets investigated were within the boundaries of Israel during the same period.

Two related aspects of the total anthropological picture are emphasized – marriage patterns and the role of the Muslim Arab village woman. Attention has also been given to the changing economic and occupational situation in the hamlets. This study does not provide a self-contained introduction to the Arab world, nor even to the rural Arab scene within which the study population lives, though the reader may of course seek comparisons and contrasts with other peasant populations, especially with the rural Arab scene elsewhere. While it is not intended to give a comprehensive descriptive account of the population under study, a brief survey of the historical, geographical and ethnographic setting will serve as a supplement to, and a background for arguments presented later.

THE VILLAGES

At the time of the fieldwork Deir al-Ghusūn had a population of 4,200.[3] Its houses lie on both sides of a narrow, upward winding road that leads from North Samaria to the district town of Tul Karem. Olive groves are concentrated on the eastern slope, while Deir al-Ghusūn is situated on the rocky western side of the mountain. The fields are at a distance of approximately five kilometers to the west, since the poor terrain higher up does not permit the growth of crops. Many Arab villages are similarly placed, looking down on the plain so as to rule the approach to the settlement from the crest of a mountain. From this position they were better able to defend themselves against Bedouin raids that were frequent in the area until the turn of the twentieth century. The even greater insecurity in the plains prevented the systematic cultivation of the fields, and only when the Bedouin threat was greatly reduced, could permanent settlement replace the temporary encampments that were set up close to the lowland fields.

All offshoots of Deir al-Ghusūn, including the two in the mountains that were under Jordanian rule until 1967, are close to the property of their founders. The mountain villages are near the olive groves, from which they derive their main income. The women carry large barrels carefully balanced on their heads, their feet groping for a foothold on the stone strewn soil, while they carry a stick with which they beat the upper branches to make the ripe olives drop to the ground. These are gathered, first into the large pockets of special aprons, and later into the barrels.

In the offshoots up in the mountains, living conditions are simple. Water is drawn by women and children from wells adjacent to each house. There is no electricity, nor is there yet any in the offshoots in the plain, but there installations are complete so that linking them with the national electricity network remains an administrative issue. In the guestroom (*diwān*) of the head of the village (*mukhtār*) there are hand stools instead of the comfortable armchairs usually found in the homes of the four hamlets studied. The *tabūn*, a clay oven for baking and cooking, is much more in use here than in the plains. The donkey is still the main means of transport and its braying together with the bleating of the goats is a familiar sound. The landscape is picturesque, almost untouched by man, the ground uneven and rocky, the wind cool in summer and chilling in winter. The older residents continue to live the slow rhythm of

Figure 1
Relative Locations of the Parent Villages
'Attīl and Deir al-Ghusūn, and their Offshoots

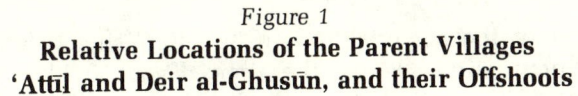

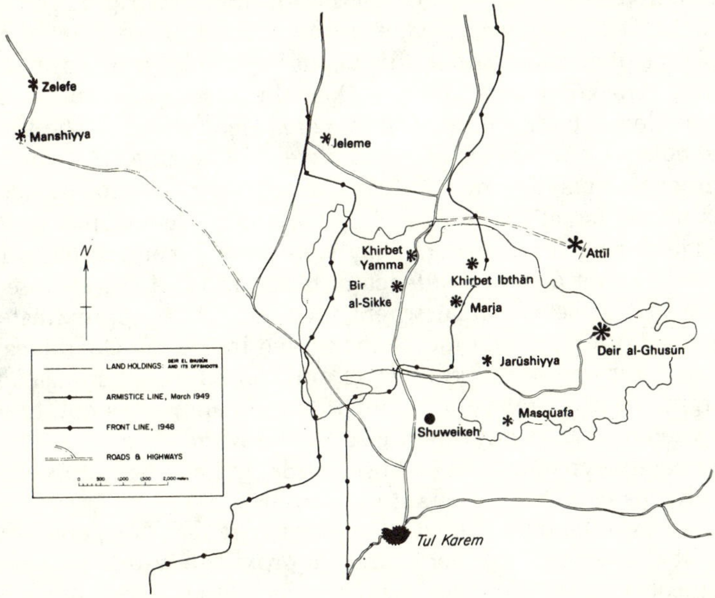

farm life while many of the younger generation leave the parental home to emigrate to other Arab countries where there are better job opportunities.

All six offshoots of Deir al-Ghusūn came into existence in the early decades of this century and maintained close links with the parent village. This contact was interrupted between 1949 and 1967, when no regular interaction between the four hamlets on the Israeli side of the border with the parent village and its two other offshoots in the Samarian mountains was possible because of hostilities between Israel and Jordan. What contacts were made tended to be sporadic and clandestine, people sometimes venturing across the border or meeting in adjacent fields. Under such circumstances, the residents being deprived of the possibility of meeting their relatives beyond the closed border, marriages could not be arranged. This estrangement intensified relations among the villages lying on the same side of the border. The four hamlets had to rely on each other for social, economic and political contacts while Deir al-Ghusūn and its two neighboring offshoots in Jordan were also drawn closer together.

The first of the six offshoots to be established was Khirbet Yamma, population 687 at the time of my fieldwork.[4] The population is not entirely composed of families originally resident in Deir al-Ghusūn. One group moved there from three offshoots of another parent village, that of 'Attīl, located approximately two kilometers north of Deir al-Ghusūn, and one of the few settlements in the plain in this area (see figure 1). The three offshoots of 'Attīl, Manshīyya, Zelefe and Jeleme, lie west of Khirbet Yamma. During the 1948 War of Independence this area was under Israeli control and the residents fled to the parent village during the fighting. They were later permitted to return to their former area of residence in Israel. Most of them chose to move to Khirbet Yamma, where they constitute approximately one third of the population. Some settled in Bāqa al-Gharbīyya, a village four and a half kilometers north of Khirbet Yamma. The merging of one Arab rural population with another is not, to my knowledge, found anywhere else in the Middle East.[5] Villages are usually separate units whose residents have been linked by family ties over many years if not centuries.

The next offshoot to be established was Bir al-Sikke, population 337 at the time of my fieldwork,[6] approximately one kilometer south of Khirbet Yamma. Then, Khirbet Ibthān (with 460 residents) two kilometers east of Khirbet Yamma was set up, followed by the two offshoots of Deir al-Ghusūn not included in the study. Finally, Marja (with a population of 334) came into existence, two kilometers southeast of Khirbet Yamma. The inhabitants of all four hamlets came from Deir al-Ghusūn, with the exception of the group living in Khirbet Yamma, and one other family that moved to Khirbet Ibthān directly from 'Attīl.

CHOICE OF RESEARCH LOCATION

The choice of research location was based on a number of considerations. The four hamlets have been under Israeli rule since 1949, unlike the parent village and its other two offshoots. To the best of my knowledge, no social or cultural anthropological study has so far been published on offshoots of a parent village that concentrates on one or on a group of such offshoots, though there have been a number of studies on Israeli and Palestinian nomad and rural communities.[7] Yet the interest in offshoots is evident. They have a relatively short history and their development can be traced to the very beginning. Some of my informants were among the first settlers and could provide information on the early years of the offshoots. It is always tempting for a researcher to view a settlement from the outset, for it puts data collected at a given moment into its proper perspective and leaves fewer lacunae than when the history of a place reaches back into the distant past.

The ties between the hamlets are of particular interest. First, the families (with the exceptions mentioned above) come from one and the same parent village; second, since they were cut off from normal contacts with the parent village and its two other offshoots due to a closed border, they had to fall back on each other and develop relations that compensated for the lost contacts. Their situation is so similar that they can be studied as one unit. The specific relations between them, and when circumstances permitted, with the parent village and the other two offshoots not included in the study, provide an interesting backdrop for an analysis of marriage patterns.

The distances between the hamlets, never forbidding, were further reduced when new roads facilitated quick travelling. The four offshoots in the plain are all linked with the parent village by paved paths or dirt trails. A major north-south highway connects Khirbet Yamma and Bir al-Sikke with access roads permitting vehicular travel east to Khirbet Ibthān and Marja from the highway (see figure 1). The same east-west road continues to Deir al-Ghusūn, while well trodden footpaths and dirt trails link the five villages in all directions. Cultural and other reasons combine with physical proximity to strengthen the ties among the hamlets and with the parent villages. Nevertheless, there were changes in the nature of associations, brought about by external and internal developments.

The parent village-offshoot relationship is especially close, a fact illustrated by the history of marriage patterns. The relations between the parent village and its offshoots are reflected in the frequency of marriages contracted during the early period of existence of the offshoots. The first inhabitants were still so attached to their former neighbors in Deir al-Ghusūn that the selection of marriage partners remained unaffected by distance. Later, the hamlets became independent and relations with the parent village changed correspondingly. This process was doubtless accelerated by the restricted contacts with Deir al-Ghusūn. When visits between the villages on both sides of the border became impossible, marriages could not be arranged.

Proper negotiations cannot be held during meetings in fields adjacent to the border, nor can the bride cross it. Only since the June 1967 War and the shift of the frontier, has the arrangement of marriages again become possible. It is probable, though this aspect has not been studied, that the relations between the parent village and its offshoot or offshoots are much closer than with other settlements, Arab and Jewish alike. This could be ascertained if comparative studies are undertaken, examining the relations of the four hamlets with Deir al-Ghusūn, and those of the other two offshoots never separated from it by a closed border.

Since the border fell, there has been a desire to reestablish former contacts. One means of doing so is by marriage. However, the fact that the four hamlets are now associated with the Regional Council in which the neighboring Jewish settlements are organized, sets them apart from the parent village and the two offshoots next to it. Prior to 1970 the population of each of the four hamlets was so small that no proper, individual council could be set up. The Israeli authorities decided to join the hamlets to the Regional Council since no significant development project could be undertaken without a functioning local government. For example, the implementation of the Israeli Bill of Compulsory Education is not possible without a local governing body.

The issue of membership in the Regional Council caused sharp controversies and the period preceding the final decision was one of intense political strife. Since existing factions could not evade taking sides in the controversy, other unresolved conflicts between the factions took on even sharper forms. The issue was such that members did not always accept the decisions of the heads of their factions and more than once changed sides. Until this time, political organization was mainly on *ḥamūla* lines.[8] In the issue of affiliation to the Regional Council, loyalty to one's *ḥamūla* was not always decisive. Since the decision about which faction to join was an individual one, the factions competed for membership on the basis of political views rather than appeals of kinship. Sides were switched so that members of one *ḥamūla* might, for the first time, find themselves in rivalling factions. Thus the *ḥamūla* was no longer the only conflict group. Factions were not formed according to whether affiliation to the Regional Council was desirable or not, but rather, the existing factions became more significant and influential, as well as more active, as a consequence of the debate. The admission of new members from other *ḥamūlas*[9] and the losing of members to other factions originally set up by other *ḥamūlas*, created a new dimension in political activity. Affiliation to the Regional Council also intensified interaction between the hamlets and neighboring Jewish settlements who demonstrated, among other things, the advantages of mechanization in agriculture. These contacts greatly influenced the life of the community.

Controversy did not come to an end when the representatives of the hamlets took their seats in the Regional Council. Political tension was kept high by full discussion of the Council meetings. Some of the most enthusiastic supporters of membership in the Regional Council were disappointed and defected to the other camp, while others became aware of the advantages that membership could bring and gave up their resistance.

RESEARCH METHODS

The fieldwork is divided into two distinct periods. The first lasted from October 1969 to March 1970 and was devoted to a preliminary investigation of the four hamlets. This was followed by collection of data between July 1972 and March 1974, with a two month interruption due to the October 1973 War. It was originally intended to conduct field studies for a period of twelve months only. However, the field work was extended to include the election campaign for both the Knesset (National Parliament) and the Regional Council, both scheduled for the end of October, 1973. The outbreak of war postponed the Knesset election until 30th December 1973 and the Regional Council elections were postponed indefinitely. The researcher expected an intensification of internal political struggle prior to the elections. There was reason to believe that there would be changes of political affiliation that would, in turn, reflect on the form the election struggle would take. The October War could not but affect the residents of the hamlets, a fact that was readily evident in daily conversations and in villagers' reactions to events.

The author usually spent four full days per week in the hamlets but often went there on other days in order to attend social functions such as weddings, circumcisions and funerals. The author also regularly visited the *diwāns*. There, exchange of information and current local gossip are the rule. The principal collection of data took place within the hamlets. Informant interview and participant observation together with standardized questionnaires were used to gain a view of their culture and traditions, and of the topics especially relevant to the study. The data was supplemented by routine library research and documentation from regional archives. Interviews with government officials whose work brought them into contact with the hamlets and their residents were a further source of significant information.

The interviews, based on the questionnaires, were conducted in April and May of 1973. Hamlet residents surveyed included both single and married men above the age of eighteen, and married women. Different questionnaires were used for males and females respectively (see appendix A). A total of 696 questionnaire interviews were completed—ninety-nine for single men, 283 for married men, and 314 for married women. These figures represent the total hamlet population members falling within the designated categories. The questionnaire-based interviews were conducted by five field research assistants. Three local male teachers who were also university students, interviewed the men; and female teachers of the local school undertook the women interviews. Of the female teachers one was a resident of Marja, while the other lived in Ṭaybe, eleven kilometers south of the hamlets. Some women preferred to give their answers to a co-resident, while others wished to speak to someone who was not part of their community. The answers of the questionnaires were used to cross-check the information obtained through participant observation, since this could not be relied upon exclusively. particularly where personal opinions were expressed.[10] One of the local dignitaries warned me not to accept the answers received through questionnaires uncritically. He also confessed that he had erred when he had argued in favor of affiliation. When I replied that eighty percent of the married and eighty-seven percent of the single males expressed support of the affiliation, he retorted that people often conceal what is in their hearts and answer what the researcher wishes to hear. He asked whether there had been marked differences between the results obtained through questionnaires and those received through participant observation and added that I should not take everything I heard in the *diwān* at face value.[11]

Similar warnings were given to me by others about the difficulties of evaluating statements made during interviews. However, I gained the impression that most of my informants were conscious of the implications of statements made in answer to direct questions. While the residents knew that they were providing information for a study, they were also on friendly terms with me so that interaction was usually informal. In some contexts they considered me a friend rather than a researcher. The comparative length and the nature of the contacts established in the hamlets has, I believe, helped me to properly assess the data gained through questionnaires.[12] Another context in which the residents were ready to comment and discuss their problems, were visits to my home in Tel Aviv. There, slides made in the hamlets were shown, and these often elicited interesting comments and information.

Since official population figures from various sources were not in agreement, the author conducted a census in the four hamlets. The most recent census undertaken by the Israel Central Statistical Bureau dated back to 1971, and only estimates were available for 1973. An example of discrepancies encountered occured when the Regional Council conducted two different censuses, one for taxation purposes, and the other in order to obtain the required details for the linking of the houses to the national electricity network. The figures from the first census were almost forty percent lower regarding the number of rooms. The interval between the two censuses was very short and the differences far from consistent with any actual housing changes that took place in the interim. In addition to making me wary of taking the results of my own census at face value, it also showed that the residents possessed enough familiarity with the working of the bureaucracy involved in the censuses to know that no cross-checking would be undertaken.[13]

Until I began the fieldwork, I was employed in the Prime Minister's Office as Deputy Adviser for Arab Affairs. This doubtless shortened the period required to become familiar with any informants, their living conditions, traditions, customs, values and beliefs, as well as with the political context within which the hamlet residents live. On the other hand, it meant accustoming myself and the villagers to another role. My former contacts had been in an official capacity and I had been known as the representative of the Administration. Now I was a researcher studying their way of life. They realized, however, that I had chosen my subject of enquiry because of my interest in Arab rural culture and organization, which had developed in the course of my official work. The preliminary fieldwork in 1969-70 was helpful in preparing the transition from one role to another. Even while at the University of Utah, I corresponded with several of my later informants, keeping track of developments in the hamlets and enquiring further into those aspects of their social organization which had originally aroused my interest.

As a government official, it had been my task to link the hamlet residents with the Administration and to represent them. At this time they had of course taken great care not to disclose any fact that might be detrimental to them. I was thus pleasantly surprised when, shortly after I had began the fieldwork, one resident told me of an incident that he would certainly have kept from me in my former role. He had fired a shot into the home of a neighbor with an unlicensed weapon, to create disunity between two lineages of a certain *ḥamūla* in order to recruit one of them to his political faction.

The residents discussed most intimate and personal matters with me and these discussions sometimes brought requests for intervention. When an old woman was distressed because her granddaughter seemed to be barren, I referred her to a gynecologist. The successful treatment by the physician made me the recipient of requests for similar advice. Such intervention greatly facilitated the obtaining of information from women, by no means an easy undertaking in Arab rural society. Evidence that the transition from one role to another was accepted by the inhabitants was that in only two instances did residents turn to me for the kind of intervention they had a right to expect from an official but not from a researcher. I refused to comply and allowed this refusal to be known. One of these cases however, could have been interpreted as an appeal for help made to a friend.

Beattie suggests that a researcher ". . . see the other culture and the whole social and cultural world of which it is part, as far as possible as it appears to the members of that culture themselves."[14] The researcher "must learn to think in the categories of the people he is studying as well as in his own, and this is never a simple task."[15] To perceive the world through the eyes of the subjects of the study through close contact with them and familiarity with their concepts and life style, combined with the necessity of not giving up one's own criteria, is no easy task. One may blunder through involvement. Williams rightly warns that "an anthropologist must avoid classification of observations in terms of his cultural experience."[16] Most anthropologists are more removed than I from the society they study and bring with them less preliminary knowledge of its background and value system. Yet I hope to have evaded the pitfall of taking too much for granted.

The research concentrates on the ethnographic present. The study is primarily synchronic, though marriage patterns have been dealt with diachronically, with historical insights adding depth and clarity to the interpretations given. A study concentrating only on those marriages contracted during the period of the researcher's fieldwork would be imperfect with respect to an understanding of marriage patterns in the hamlets.

ECOLOGY OF THE HAMLETS

Approaching the hamlets on a fine day, the visitor is struck by the beauty of the scenery of the fields and groves near Khirbet Yamma and by the quiet rhythm of life. Buses constantly pass on their way to Tul Karem and one after the other stops to let off passengers and accept new ones. The women, clad in their traditional garbs, chat happily by the roadside and enjoy the company of neighbors and relatives. Many remember the days when the only means of transport at their disposal was the donkey, a slow moving, lonely ride which could only be undertaken with a male member of the close family as escort. Now, most women travel unaccompanied in the comparitive security of public transport.

Khirbet Yamma was the earliest of the offshoots of Deir al-Ghusūn to be set up. Its first stone house was built between 1905 and 1909, another house followed before the outbreak of World War I and most of the buildings were completed immediately after 1918. The hamlet was set up on an ancient mound as its conical shape indicates. This distinguishes it from the natural elevation and is most evident when one looks down on the settlement from the top of the mountain. The hamlet consists of four clusters of buildings, of which the first cluster, the very center of the mound, is the oldest neighborhood.

Each house forms a rectangle around a courtyard where life is centered. There are many large old trees under which the children play or the women sit down for a chat. Two different types of stone have been used for building, undressed as well as dressed. The latter having been reused after being extricated from among the debris of the mound. Most of the structures dating to the early years of the hamlet's existence are no longer inhabited and serve today as enclosures for sheep. Though they are often derelict, some of the roofs are still more or less intact and reveal the original form, as well as the method of construction. Wooden beams and logs were placed across the tops of the walls over which a layer of soil mixed with stones was laid in order to protect the interior of the house against the vicissitudes of the climate.

The other three clusters of houses that make up Khirbet Yamma, together with the oldest, form a semicircle northeast of the center. Here, the houses are not of one and the same type. Some resemble the earliest buildings in the center of the mound, some are houses with domed roofs (*'aqed*), typical of the earlier days, while others look like modern housing projects constructed by the Israeli Ministry of Housing throughout the country (see figure 4). The houses of the new type are numerous. In some cases, a modern structure has been added to an old building, while in others an upper storey has been built on, the modern layout of which contrasts sharply with that of the older floor below. However, these two-storey buildings are fairly inconspicuous since their level is more or less the same as that of the newest houses, which are usually set up on pillars. The space this provides is used for storerooms or as a carport. The southern part of the hamlet is the modern neighborhood and closely resembles Jewish agricultural settlements founded in the 1950s when many new immigrants coming from the neighboring Arab countries had to be accommodated. The former residents of the offshoots of 'Attīl set up this neighborhood (*ḥara*) in the area between Khirbet Yamma and Bir al-Sikke to emphasize the fact that its residents are of slightly different origin. This *ḥara* fills almost the whole space between the two hamlets which makes them appear like one single village.

Bir al-Sikke literally means, "Well of/along the Path". The well that gives the hamlet its name still exists, but is presently closed up. The hamlet is subdivided into two distinct parts, the older section lying west of the road where most of the houses were built before 1948. The newer buildings are mostly situated east of the highway, most of them constructed after 1956 with a few interspersed among the older ones on the western side of the road. In the midst of the older part of the hamlet, a minaret rises steeply into the sky, looming above all other buildings.

Khirbet Ibthān is situated on a slope, with its newest buildings bordering on the fields of the 'Attīl plain. It is closest to the parent village and connected with it by an unpaved road leading directly to the highway linking 'Attīl and Deir al-Ghusūn. The hamlet consists of three distinct clusters of houses. The two oldest clusters are on the upper slope facing each other, with the saddle of a hill dividing them. Some of the earlier structures are actually modified caves which, until the turn of the sixth century A.D., had been used as dwelling places. Walls were erected to protect the entrances to the caves, turning them into safe shelters. Some of the buildings in the same part of the hamlet are of a newer type and are built on rock ledges, directly above the ancient caves which now serve mainly as storerooms. Most of the modern style housing is to be found in the lower section of the hamlet, though here and there a newer building also stands among the old-type houses. In the area between the old and new sections, there stands a mosque which lacks the usual minaret. The mosque is not conspicuous and can only be distinguished when one stands up close.

Marja, the last hamlet to be established, lies higher than the other offshoots of Deir al-Ghusūn, south of Khirbet Ibthān and east of both Khirbet Yamma and Bir al-Sikke. The hamlet is composed of two sections that are not directly connected and even have their separate access roads from the main highway. An additional small block of houses with yet another access path from the north leads to buildings situated between the two sections. The distance between the different entrances to the main parts of the hamlet is approximately five kilometers. Most of the houses in the northern sector were built in the early phase of the establishment of the hamlet. As in Khirbet Yamma, a mixture of styles prevails since structures have been continuously added. Most of the modern buildings are to be found in the southern part. The two access roads leading to the hamlet are steep; they pass through olive groves which fill the area between the housing sections. In 1973, the Regional Council laid a water line to this hamlet, but while farmers irrigate their fields according to the most up-to-date methods, they still take drinking water from cisterns.

As a rule, members of one *ḥamūla* are settled in one cluster of houses, though there are cases when two or even three *ḥamūlas* live in one *ḥara*, as in the parent village. New houses, located between the main groups of buildings, blur the dividing lines between the different *ḥamūlas* and this influences relations between members who live in the same neighborhood. It may also have contributed to the development where the *ḥamūla* is no longer a monolithic political unit, since relations with neighbors develop in daily intercourse with non-*ḥamūla*, co-*ḥara* residents, that may lead to political contacts outside the *ḥamūla*.

The sight of the hamlets actually tells a part of their history. The living habits of the past are perpetuated by those who inhabit the older buildings with their central courtyard within the walls. Here, they are inevitably less exposed to contact with others, even to those living in adjoining houses, just like in the past. The fact that the style of the buildings has been constantly modified and adjusted to current demands and needs, indicates awareness of outside changes and the will to adapt to a new form of living. The impression is that the hamlets are not islands where life stands still. They are open to what goes on in the wider environment and are willing to introduce alterations. If the influence of the break up of the *ḥamūla* as a production group is also taken into account (to be elaborated on later), several factors may be isolated that explain the change of role of the *ḥamūla* in the hamlets. These factors will be discussed within the context of the following section.

PUBLIC BUILDINGS AND SHOPS

The children of all four hamlets attend one elementary school, whose buildings stand on both sides of the road near the entrance to Khirbet Yamma. The meeting with members of one's peer group from the neighboring hamlets, offshoots of the same parent village, contributes to the preservation of the earlier close links that date back to co-residence in Deir al-Ghusūn. Relationships develop and in some ways the classroom serves as a *diwān* for the younger generation between lessons. In the school, age groups are much more distinct from one another than in the hamlets, where the children grow up together. As long as the children lived within their houses, either inside or in the courtyard hemmed in by walls, the outer world was almost nonexistent for them. Their universe was the *ḥamūla*, especially since the old type buildings usually accommodate the extended family. Simultaneously with the Bill of Compulsory Education (strictly observed in the hamlets, almost no child of school age being seen in the lanes in the morning), separate houses for the sons of the family were introduced and the nuclear family emerged as an independent group.

The older school complex, that dates back to the times when the British Mandatory Government ruled the country then called Palestine, stands on the eastern side of the road while the newer buildings are on the west. There is a playground in the space between the two complexes used mainly for soccer games that are very popular. This is another rallying point where pupils meet from different groups. Such affiliations inevitably weakens attachment to the *ḥamūla*, once the main and almost only ingroup for the rural Arab. The football field borders on the cemetery which provides a meeting ground for the female villagers who visit it every Thursday accompanied by their children. The women sit on the graves and pass on local gossip while the children play.

The kindergarten is part of the school building. It owes its existence not so much to the desire of women to see their toddlers taken care of as to the fact that the Compulsory Education Bill covers the pre-school age. The accommodation of the kindergarten in the school building is such that there is no strict division between children of school age and those below it. It would be interesting to study the relationships between the kindergarten children and those attending school classes, for the organization of children according to their age has its influence on their socialization. Unlike in the past, they do not grow up in a multi-generation group only. Their contacts with relatives of varying age are reduced and partly replaced by those with members of their peer group, not necessarily of their *ḥamūla* and not even of their *ḥara* or of their own hamlet. In 1970, an agricultural high school was established on the east side of the highway. This meant that students from the hamlets now had increasing contacts with students from villages in the surrounding area who also attended the high school. One rather unusual feature of the curriculum for girls is that the cookery classes are taught by a Jewish woman teacher. Since the academic year of 1974-75, graduating high school pupils can sit for the comprehensive government matriculation examinations.

Other public institutions include the offices of the liaison officer of the Regional Council and the representative of the Ministry of Welfare, both offices situated in the complex of public buildings next to the school. The mother-child care centre in Khirbet Yamma, set up in 1974, provides a meeting ground for women. This is especially important in a community where the older men prefer to 'free' their wives from duties that would lead them outside the walls of the home. "She makes the list of goods, she decides, but someone else goes to do the shopping," one man explained. Most of the younger women attend to their shopping by themselves, either in a local store or in the shops of the neighboring Jewish district town that caters to their needs and tastes, and sometimes in Tul Karem.

A nurse visits the hamlets three times a week. When there is need of hospitalization, women are usually sent to Bāqa al-

Gharbīyya which has a Histadrut Sick Fund Dispensary and a maternity hospital with a physician in constant attendance. The maternity ward is a new link with the outside world, for in the past women gave birth in their homes.

The mosque of Bir al-Sikke serves all four hamlets uniting the males in worship, particularly the older generation. Many of the younger males cannot attend daily services even if they wish to. Farmers who work outside the hamlets, cultivating their fields, sometimes interrupt their work to go to the mosque or pray wherever they are at the hour of prayer, but laborers and officials who work outside of their village tend to neglect worship. This is another center where the meeting between villagers has become more homogeneous in terms of age stratification.

Khirbet Yamma has two groceries and one store that sells building materials; Bir al-Sikke has one grocery and one store where agricultural implements may be purchased, while the other two hamlets have one grocery each. The groceries offer standardized, mass produced goods, mostly Israeli products. Typical Arab food such as *ṭḥīna* (a sesame seed dip) and *humūs* (a dip of chick peas or garbanzo beans) is produced in Jewish factories and sold in cans with Hebrew labels. It may be that the increased consumption of ready-made instead of home produced food is probably due to the fact that many women, especially the younger ones, are busy running the family farm, while their husbands work in Jewish towns or settlements.

In addition to packaged food, all kinds of commodities are displayed and sold in the groceries. The shops look rather like those in the Jewish towns in the earlier decades of this century, which also used to offer large varieties of goods before they became increasingly specialized. You can buy transistor batteries, glassware, china cups and cooking pots among other things. Since the hamlets have not yet been linked to the national electricity network, a refrigerator run by a generator stores dairy products, soft drinks (in great demand in the hamlets) and other perishable goods. The absence of refrigerators in the homes creates dependence on the local store and residents buy here what they might have preferred to purchase in larger, specialized shops in the neighboring towns.

The shops look clean and service is good though more leisurely than in the large towns. The owner is usually willing not only to discuss business but also local political affairs. The residents point out that prices tend to fluctuate, and on Friday, when most of the shops in the neighboring town are closed (because of the Muslim day of rest), the open shops in the hamlet allow prices to rise considerably. The stores are always full of customers who linger there, to exchange some words with the grocer or with a fellow customer. In this way, the store takes the place of the village well where women used to meet and chat in the past.

PRIVATE HOMES AND COURTYARDS

The newer houses are usually well kept and are often surrounded by carefully tended gardens abounding with flowers and shrubs. Sometimes there is an old tree, whose widely spreading branches provide shade. Looking down from one of the balconies of the houses higher up on the slope, the visitor can see the fields, with sprinklers swishing around. On Saturdays, when men do not work outside the village, families can be seen crowded on horse or mule-drawn carts on their way to picnics.

The courtyards echo to the sound of children who use whatever comes their way to play with—sticks, rocks and old pots. Rarely will a child have his own ball to play with. Inside the house there are neither toys or children's books, nor is there a special corner reserved for the children. Though kindergartens emphasize the special status and needs of the infant, this is not reflected in the organization of the home where the child is considered a miniature adult. The young are increasingly allowed to seek their own pleasures, and this may be due to the fact that their absence in the morning hours, and sometimes in the afternoon when activities are organized by the school, brings home the differences of age and in consequence a different approach to the young.

The courtyard is usually a space stretching between the house and the round brick *tabūn* (oven). The *tabūn* resembles a small, man-made cave and is used to bake bread or to prepare and keep warm various other dishes. It is often used together with a modern electric or gas oven. For example, there are dishes that require intense, well regulated heat in the initial phase of cooking and which are finished in the *tabūn* where the temperature is low. The women explain that a dish can be kept warm there for many hours. The woman of the house can be seen kneeling in front of the *tabūn*, while the children play around the space close by. This space is the domain of the woman, especially if she is a member of the older generation.

On entering a private home guests find themselves in the *diwān* behind which lie the other rooms. Until recently, each *ḥamūla* had its own communal *diwān*, where the male-members sat and discussed their affairs. Now each home has its own *diwān* and the nature of the visits has changed. Meetings in the home *diwān* are often casual and deal with personal matters since there are usually fewer guests than in the lineage or descent group *diwān*. The village dignitaries entertain more frequently than others who hold no office and this is reflected in the ceremonious conduct of both hosts and visitors. In recent years, local faction leaders have virtually turned their houses into social centers and their *diwāns* are often overflowing with guests.

Formerly, most of the *diwāns* of each descent group were located in houses of the *'aqed* type (dome-shaped roof), the older generation preferring this type to the more modern houses. These old buildings are relatively cool in summer and fairly warm in winter since they have thick walls constructed from heavy stones. There is usually only one large room, sometimes with a raised platform in the background that serves as a sleeping niche. The older type houses are often inhabitated by aging couples. Here there are no bedrooms, the mattresses are brought out every night and stored away in wall closets during the day. The toilet is usually just an outhouse without any seat facilities.

In the modern houses, the *diwān* is usually the best furnished room. Leather or imitation leather sofas and armchairs are arranged along the walls, where there are pictures of romantic forest and river scenes, or photos taken at marriage ceremonies. Sometimes there are class groups or pictures of national Arab leaders. Rarely are there curtains in this or any other room. In the middle of the *diwān* there is usually a long, low table on which cardamom scented Turkish coffee is served in small china cups. Here are placed ornamented ashtrays, cigarettes and perhaps some sweets. For the younger generation, the bedroom is very important. Often it is elaborately decorated in a Victorian style with a king-size bed and a pink or sky blue color scheme. Here too, sentimental paintings are the rule. Most houses have boilers or solar heated water systems installed on the flat roofs and next them the inevitable television antenna. Although both TV and the radio have to be operated with batteries or generators, their use is widespread. Sometimes brothers (who as a rule are neighbors) use one large generator jointly.

The many electric wires, newly strung between the houses, indicate that the hamlets are soon to be connected to the national electricity network. Light bulbs have even been inserted into their sockets in expectation.

PERSONAL CLOTHING

The same pastel shades that serve for the painting of the houses distinguish the clothing of the women. There are three styles of dress that are adopted, more or less consistently, by the members of the three generations. The oldest women wear long trousers, narrow at the ankles, and embroidered in bright colors around the lower edge. The top garment is a long, often white, dress. A long, white shawl, usually of sheer fabric, is thrown over the hair. The next younger generation preserves the combination of long trousers and a top-gown, but the dress is colored and no longer hides the outlines of the body as does the loosely falling garment worn by the older women.

Members of the youngest adult generation tend to follow western fashion though they are careful not to offend the feelings of their elders and try to conceal this adaptation to modern styles. At the time of my fieldwork trouser suits were the craze in Tel Aviv, Jerusalem and Haifa. The young women compromised by wearing tight stretch slacks, reminiscent of those worn by dancers, and a dress on top that was actually a long blouse. According to the fashion this was worn reaching the knees. The grandmothers were supposed not to notice the difference; the mothers having themselves somehow circumvented tradition, though less than their daughters, could not say much, and the young felt they were in step with the outside world. Incidentally, at that time dresses were worn at the length of the blouses worn over the slacks so that, had those been left out, they too would have been according to the fashion. Changes are made, but cautiously, so as not to create tension between the generations. High school girl students tend to wear modern slacks, with the dress clearly a blouse recognizable by everyone except their mothers and grandmothers.

The three generations of men also dress differently. The oldest residents put on the traditional, long, tight garb (*qumbaz*), usually in a dull color or sometimes striped, and cinched by a belt. Long trousers (*sirwal*), narrowing at the ankles, are visible beneath the *qumbaz*. The headgear consists of a heavy, white cloth (*ḥaṭah*) and a double, round cord (*'aqāl*) which holds the *ḥaṭah* in place. The second generation retains the traditional headgear, but wears Western-style trousers and shirts. The third generation dresses no differently from their European or American contemporaries; they wear trousers and shirts and, in winter, jackets. They never wear the *ḥaṭah* and have thus given up what marks them unmistakably as Arabs.

While status is not demonstrated by the women in their way of dressing, except that the wealthier choose finer and more expensive fabrics, it expresses itself conspicuously in the case of males. Dignitaries of the older generation like to wear a cream colored *ḥaṭah*, reaching down to the loins. This is much longer than that of their co-villagers who enjoy less status. Factors other than age or generation, however, dictate the choice of wardrobe in some circumstances, particularly in the case of the male hamlet dwellers. There are those who think nothing of laboring all day in the fields in Western trousers and a shirt, but who would never venture into the village so attired and would be laughed at by their fellows if they did. For them, the appropriate costume for nonworking hours is the more traditional *qumbaz* and *sirwal*. The second generation tends to dispense with the traditional headgear outside their own community, especially in the non-Arab environment. However, on ceremonial occasions the *ḥaṭah* and *'aqāl* are worn by middle-aged men in order to stress the fact that its wearer is an Arab.

The hamlets present a picture quite diffrerent from that of Jewish settlements in terms of clothing habits and in the layout and style of housing. There is a trend to minimize distinctive features and to renounce traditional clothes and housing conditions. This is especially displayed by the younger generation and may not be due to assimilatory tendencies but rather to changes in the wake of technological progress. The male Arab travelling by donkey is comfortably and suitably dressed in his ankle-long garb but this becomes a nuisance when he enters a bus or a car. Old and new thus blend in the clothing of the adult residents as may be expected in a period of transition.

The following chapter gives the historical background and environment of the parent village and facts relating to the establishment of the offshoots. The physical structure of the hamlets, the institutions within them and the services provided, are described. Problems of occupation and employment are analyzed as well as trade union affiliation (Histadrut). Agricultural methods are depicted and their influence on the pattern of life is shown.

NOTES

1. A distinction is made between *hamlet* and *offshoot*. Villages are referred to as "offshoots" in connection with the "parent village" and as "hamlets" in all other contexts. "Offshoot," is synonymous with the term "branch village" as used by other writers. See Abner Cohen, *Arab Border– Villages in Israel: A Study of Community and Change in Social Organization* (Manchester; Manchester University Press, 1965), p. 10; Gideon Golany, *Geography of Settlements of Eron Valley Region: Determining Factors In the Formation of Branch Villages* (Ph.D. disertation, Jerusalem; The Hebrew University, 1966) Vol. III. (Hebrew). It has been specifically applied to Khirbet Ibthān: ". . . a modern offshoot of Deir al-Ghusūn," Israel, Department of Antiquities and Museums, File No. 66.

2. See Peters' foreword to Jacob Black-Michaud, *Cohesive Force: Feud in the Mediterranean and the Middle East* (Oxford, Basil Blackwell, 1975) p. XXV.

3. Personal communication, (April, 1973) from Muḥammad Amin, a *mukhtar* (head of village; literally, "elected one") of Deir al-Ghusūn. The Jordanian census of 1961, including the two offshoots east of the Israeli-Jordanian armistice line, listed the total number of residents as 4,131. According to the census conducted by the Israeli Central Bureau of Statistics (1967), the number of inhabitants of Deir al-Ghusun (excluding the two offshoots) was 3,660.

4. From a census conducted by myself in April, 1973.

5. There was a similar case on the West Bank, where a group of refugees from Deir Yasın settled in Baytīn, the village studied by Lutfıyya. However, Lutfıyya only described the division of the village into different neighborhoods, without mentioning this group specifically. See Abdulla M. Lutfiyya, *Baytīn, A Jordanian Village* (The Hague, Mouton, 1966) pp. 27-29.

6. This and the following figures for the offshoots are taken from my 1973 census (cf. note 4).

7. Hilma Granqvist, *Marriage Conditions in a Palestinian Village* (Helsingfors: Societas Scintiarum Fennica, 1931 Vol. I, 1935 Vol. II); Hilma Granqvist, *Birth and Childhood Among the Arabs: Studies in a Muhammadan Village in Palestine* (Helsingfors: Söderström, 1974); Hilma Granqvist, *Child Problems Among the Arabs: Studies in a Muhammadan Village in Palestine* (Helsingfors: Söderström, 1950); Richard R. Randolph, *The Social Structure of the Qdiraat Bedouin* (Berkeley: Ph. D. dissertation, University of California, 1963); Henry Rosenfeld, *They were Peasants: Social Anthropological Studies on the Arab Village in Israel* (Tel Aviv: Hakibbutz Hameuchad,1964, (Hebrew); Emanuel Marx, *Bedouin of the Negev* (Manchester; Manchester University Press, 1967);

Subhi Abu Gosh, *The Politics of an Arab Village in Israel* (Princeton: Ph. D. dissertation, Princeton University, 1969); Gideon M. Kressel, *The Dynamics of Israeli-Arab Community in a Process of Urbanization* (Tel Aviv, Ph.D. dissertation, Tel Aviv University, 1972, Hebrew); *Shifting Patterns of Conflict in Selected Arab Villages in Israel* (Bloomington: Ph.D. dissertation Indiana University, 1973); Arlette Goldberg, *Le Changement Social dans un Village Musulman d'Israel* (Paris: Doctoral thesis, Sorbonne, 1974); Joseph Ginat, *A Rural Arab Community in Israel: Marriage Patterns and Woman's Status* (Salt Lake City: Ph. D. dissertation, University of Utah, 1975); Gideon M. Kressel, *Individuality Against Tribality: The Dynamics of a Bedouin Community in a Process of Urbanization* (Tel Aviv: Hakibbutz Hameuchad, 1976, in Hebrew). Reference is made only to studies conducted in Israel (or Palestine) and the West Bank. Additional research on *The Druze: Living in Israel* has recently been completed by Jonathan Oppenheimer, Haifa University. Gillian Lewando-Hundt, a British scholar, has also concluded field research on selected Bedouin populations in the Negev. Reports of both studies were not available at the time of writing.

8. The term *ḥamūla* has been used through out as an equivalent for lineage, see Cohen, pp. 2-3; or as an equivalent for clan, see Richard T. Antoun, *Arab Village: A Social Structural Study of a Trans-Jordanian Peasant Community*, (Bloomington: Indiana University Press, 1972) pp. 44-45, but neither adequately translates *ḥamūla*. In this study "lineage" refers to a descent group up to five generations (see Chart 1). A "descent group," in turn, is composed of a number of lineages. However, the terms "lineage" and "descent group" are occasionally used interchangeably. The villagers conceptualized the term "extended family" as part of a lineage. The *ḥamūla* is the patronymic group, whose members adopted its surname for a number of reasons. In addition to the members of a descent group, that is the offspring of one ancestor, the *ḥamūla* includes individuals who have voluntarily joined the core of the descent group. Together, all these constitute the patronymic group called *ḥamūla* (see Chart 2).

9. The correct plural form of *ḥamūla* is *ḥamāyyil*, but for convenience's sake the term *ḥamūlas* is used.

10. In his conclusion to interviews conducted with Israeli Arabs, Landau notes that "...sociologists such as Professor Morroe Berger... and David Lerner... have already pointed out the difficulties of conducting interviews in countries of the Middle East." Landau adds that "...most of those interviewed refused point blank to cooperate; this applied to practically all farmers (who, when they agreed to answer, were obviously insincere, giving standard replies expressing loyalty to the State, etc.), as well as many of the townspeople. Those who agreed to reply were highly suspicious, despite the fact the interviewing was manifestly sponsored by the Hebrew University in Jerusalem and that

the interviewers were students—Jews and Arabs alike. . . Even in 1961 the population and housing census of the Israel CBS ran into several difficulties among the Arabs, despite capable pre-census propaganda on a country-wide basis." Jacob M. Landau, *The Arabs in Israel: A Political Study* (London: Oxford University Press, 1969) p. 261.

11. For the analysis of emic and etic data, see Marvin Harris, *The Rise of Anthropological Theory: A History of Theories of Culture* (New York: Thomas Y. Crowell, 1970) pp. 568-604.

12. The use of questionnaires, particularly with female residents, has been influenced by Bott's ideas. Elizabeth Bott, *Family and Social Network: Roles, norms and external relationships in ordinary urban families* (London: Tavistock Publications, 1964) pp. 231-237.

13. Data from Regional Council files, courtesy of Y. Shamash, Liaison Officer to the hamlets.

14. John Beattie, *Understanding an African Kingdom: Bunyoro* (New York: Holt, Rinehart and Winston, 1965) p. 2.

15. Ibid.

16. Thomas Rhys Williams, *Field Methods in the Study of Culture* (New York: Holt, Rinehart and Winston, 1967) p. 24.

Manshiyya
Zelefe
Masqūfa
Jarūshiyya
Khirbet Yamma
Bir al-Sikke
Khirbet Ibthān
Marja
Deir al-Ghusūn
'Attil
Jeleme

2

Historical Background and Environment

ESTABLISHMENT OF OFFSHOOTS

Deir al-Ghusūn, (literally, The Monastery of Branches)[1] is like most of the Arab villages in the area, situated on a mountain. Security reasons, as already explained, combined with the threat of malaria in the lowland swamps explain the setting up of settlements high in the mountains. However, it seems that malaria deterred prospective settlers less than the fear of Bedouin raids.[2]

Deir al-Ghusūn consists of three neighborhoods (*ḥara*), each neighborhood not necessarily inhabited by members of one *ḥamūla*. The southern quarter is called Jabeliyya[3] after the *ḥamūla* that settled there originally; the name of eastern quarter is Amīn, called after the largest *ḥamūla* residing in it; and the third *ḥara*, Kharīta, lies in the west. Kharīta is inhabited by several *ḥamūlas* but its name is not derived from any *ḥamūla* living in it. Several of the residents of this *ḥara* have chosen to adopt its name as their own and were officially registered under it. Their identity cards bore this surname although it represented no patronymic affiliation. One member of the Abū Bader *ḥamūla* had an identity card issued in the name of S'adī 'Āref Abū Bader, while his brother held an identity card with the name Dhib 'Āref Kharita.[4] In some villages the *ḥaras* are simply termed western, eastern, southern or northern,[5] such as in 'Attīl where the two main *ḥaras* are named 'Eastern' and 'Western'.

The early residents of Deir al-Ghusūn did not constitute one homogeneous group. Some came from neighboring Arab countries while others from villages in the Samarian or Hebron mountains. The last group to join Deir al-Ghusūn was that of Masārwa (literally, "Egyptians"), whose ancestors arrived with a large immigration wave from Egypt in the 1840s, after Ibrāhīm Pasha's conquest of Palestine.[6]

The first offshoots were established in the last quarter of the nineteenth century and the last at the end of World War I. During the Ottoman Period farmers found it impractical to cultivate their fields located more than two hours walking distance from their villages for fear of Bedouin marauders. Nor were farmers in the habit of "sleeping overnight in the distant fields."[7] Travellers in the days of the Ottoman rule tell of frequent Bedouin raids on the villages which the government could not prevent.[8] Records dating back to the middle of the sixteenth century state that the Palestinian Bedouin were not subjugated by Sultan Salīm. In the seventeenth century the presence of a tribe south of Mt. Carmel in the vicinity of the hamlets was reported whose members did not consider themselves subjects of the Sultan and refused to obey his orders.[9] Due to lack of political stability the security situation further deteriorated in the last decades of the eighteenth century when Bedouin raids (*ghazzū*) were a frequent occurrence.[10]

Travellers were advised to keep at a safe distance from the Bedouin, whom Volney defined as "enemies of security."[11] When Ibrāhīm Pasha occupied the region in 1831, he set up a more effective administration than his predecessors and put an end to the raids. Robinson and Smith stress the submission of the popular Bedouin Chiefs by the Egyptian government and the fact that the "district was quiet and safe, like the rest of the country."[12] But a strong rule also meant interference with the daily life of the villagers and they rebelled against it. Ibrāhīm Pasha, according to Robinson and Smith, took personal command of the troops quelling a peasant rebellion in the area. Subsequently, the whole district submitted without further resistance.[13] However, peace and order did not last long, and it was only in the late 1860s that peasants began to plough land further away and spend the night in the fields, at least during the agricultural season.[14] These stays in the low land, at first fairly short, led to the establishment of various permanent offshoots.

The survey of Western Palestine undertaken by Conder and Kitchener in 1871-7 makes no reference to the offshoots of Deir al-Ghusūn, although it does show two of the offshoots of 'Attīl. This is what is said about the parent village.

> Deir al-Ghusūn—A village of moderate size, on a hill, with a well (Bir el 'Aharibeh) to the west. On the north is open low

> ground. It is surrounded with magnificent groves of olives occupying an area of about three square miles towards the south.[15]

While 'Attīl is described as:

> A considerable village on a hill at the edge of the plain, with open ground to the north and a broad valley to the south. It has round it a small olive grove, and is supplied by cisterns.[16]

The 'Attīl offshoots are each accorded one line only.

> "Jelamah—A small mud hamlet on the side of the knell. Zelafe—A very small hamlet, with springs on the south."[17]

This shows that these two 'Attīl offshoots were already permanent settlements in the seventies of the nineteenth century and that the residents lived in houses. Only Manshīyya, the third offshoot of 'Attīl, was established after World War I. During the period from the second part of the nineteenth century to the establishment of permanent housing, the peasants were not accustomed to spending more than two or three months a year in the plains. The agricultural seasons were autumn, when sowing took place, and spring, when harvesting was completed. The period when housing in the plain was of a temporary character is known as *'izbe* (seasonal dwelling).[18]

The offshoots were often erected on sites of ancient settlements, (as for example Yamma, Ibthān and Jeleme) whose remnants are called *khirbe* (literally "ruin"). Non-Arabs, including government officials in the region thought that *khirbe* was Arabic for offshoot and they wrongly attached this word to the names of the hamlets. The Arabs distinguish two types of villages—those built on the ruins of an ancient settlement and those set up on natural hills. The term *khirbe* is used only in names of villages in the first category. Another frequently used prefix for village names is *nazle* ("to go down" in Arabic). Golany explains that it refers to a settlement transferred to the plain from the mountains but adds that the villagers themselves claim it means "encampment."[19] The latter explanation is convincing since the word *manzal* which is derived from the root *nzl*, is used for a temporary Bedouin camp.[20] *Nazle* therefore, is parallel to *'izbe* but the latter was dropped once a seasonally occupied site became a permanent settlement. However the former term has survived as part of the name.

The first peasants to move to the plain may be divided into three categories. The first settlers were residents of the parent village whose land was farthest away from Deir al-Ghusūn in the direction of the plain to the west.[21] The second consisted of landless immigrants, mostly from Egypt, who joined the offshoots as *ḥarrāthin* (ploughmen) and were mainly employed by the owners of large tracts of land. They were usually paid in kind, keeping part of their own produce, an arrangement known as sharecropping. The third category was made up of owners of herds and flocks who were attracted by the good pastures at the foothills and along the coast. The herders and shepherds came to live in the village in two separate stages. First, in 1934 as a result of an epidemic that killed many of their cattle and sheep; and second, in 1947-8, with the outbreak of the War of Independence. This second group had previously lived close to the coast, in Ghabāt al-Ṭaybe,[22] nineteen kilometers southwest of Yamma.

DIFFERENT TYPES OF DWELLING

Both the hamlet residents who originated from Deir al-Ghusūn and the Egyptian immigrants immediately started building houses, while the herders and shepherds preferred tents because they had to be mobile. These tent dwellers were peasants by origin and were used to living in stone houses although their children and some of their grandchildren were born in tents. When the offshoots were set up, the shiftless life of the tent camp turned into the routine existence of a rural settlement. The herds could graze safely in the fields and yielded a greater profit than did the cultivation of the land. This meant a measure of economic security and physical safety. Yet in order to increase the herds and flocks, new pastures had to be found which made semi-nomadic life inevitable. This was not necessarily considered a hardship since:

> Nomadism had many advantages. Nomads paid no taxes, were not conscripted to the army, were armed (while the peasants were prohibited from keeping arms). . .[23]

The herding camps were set up to provide maximum security, and in winter, protection against the inclements of the weather. Usually, the tents were placed from south to north in two parallel lines, each consisting of no fewer than four tents. The space in the center was reserved for the animals. In summer, the tents were scattered and usually set up close to the fields where the farmers worked.

Tent camps arranged in one line are found both in the Negev and Northern Sinai, though the two-line pattern belongs to the past. The older residents explain that even the now extinct two-line arrangement is fairly new. In more distant days, a rectangular, circular or semicircular camp defense system was generally adhered to, as it provided maximum protection for the livestock.[24] This system with its minor variations was only discarded in the late twenties. Marx reports that the guest-tent (*shiq*) is usually in the southeastern corner of the camp.[25] In the south of the country, the *shiq* stands at the northern end of the line. The tents are constructed according to the pattern developed by the Bedouin in the vicinity. In the northern part of the country, the roof and the upper portion of the sides are made of strips of woven goat hair, while the walls rising to a height of two to three feet, are of reeds. In the south of the country, the Bedouin lead a more nomadic existence and their tents are constructed of goat hair strips so as to be easily dismantled and repitched. Reed walls are only used by those Bedouin who do not often strike camp, since they are harder to dismantle. Tents are sometimes also found in permanent rural settlements, as for example in Ghabāt al-Ṭaybe. One group of peasants of a lineage of the Yazīd *ḥamūla*, only moved out of their tents in about 1948. However, they no longer adhered to the defensive structure in arranging their camps and the tents were dispersed in the fields after their inhabitants had attained security through marriage alliances with powerful Ṭaybe residents. Once the Bedouin learned that the Yazīds were related to the strongest *ḥamūla* of the Ṭaybe village on whose land the Yazīds were camped, they no longer resorted to aggression.

Yet it would be wrong to assume that the hamlet residents felt safe in their houses, otherwise they would not have erected the high rectangular walls with their narrow entrances and gates that were clearly designed to keep away outsiders. The rooms faced an open courtyard, which was used by all nuclear families living in the house though each family occupied a separate room. The walls, made either of limestone or mud brick, were too thin to allow for genuine privacy. Buildings erected before World War I look even more like fortifications. They have a double wall, an internal plastered one and another external wall built without mortar and held together by the sheer weight of the stones. Small holes placed close to the roof provide a minimum of ventilation. Villagers claim that the double-walled structure is a necessary precaution against robbers, for any drilling or digging leads to a collapse of the outer wall burying any intruder under the debris. An architect confirmed the effectiveness of the measures taken against possible robbers or enemies.[26] Thus even permanent rural communities took precautions against marauders and did not relax their vigilance.

SITUATION AFTER RHODES AGREEMENT

The war in 1947-8 put an end to tent dwelling in the Maritime plain. During the fighting the hamlets turned into military bases for the Arabs, while Israeli positions were established in the plain. According to the Rhodes Agreement, a narrow strip in the foothills with its twenty-seven Arab villages was transferred to Israel.[27] The offshoots were not only cut off from their parent village and its two other offshoots, but also from the Nablus—Samarian mountains, until then their economic, political and cultural hinterland. This strip of land, widening the bottleneck of Israel between the Mediterranean Sea and the Jordanian border, is known as the "Triangle."[28] As a result of the war, part of the land owned by the hamlet residents was taken over by newly established Israeli border settlements.[29] The fields in the plains did not, however, belong to the offshoot residents alone. Parts of the fields were owned by residents of the parent village, while others were owned jointly by brothers and cousins, who might or might not live on the same side of the border.

After the transfer of the Triangle to Israel, some Arab peasants who had participated in the 1936-39 riots against the Jews, preferred to leave for Jordan, together with their close relatives. Many of them moved to Deir al-Ghusūn.[30] Sometimes Arabs in Israel changed their names so as not to be identified with relatives known for anti-Jewish activities. The Yazīd family for example, adopted the name of the Amin *ḥamūla*. So, brothers and their offspring might not have the same surnames, while persons born into different families and not linked by kinship suddenly carried the same *ḥamūla* name,[31] a state termed "fictional kinship."

LAND OWNERSHIP

Before 1948, Deir al-Ghusūn's residents owned 27,700 *dūnams* of which 11,700 were in the plain and 16,000 were hilly terrain

Figure 2

Distribution of Land Holdings among the Offshoots of Deir al-Ghusūn

(Map redrawn from Government of Israel, Department of Survey, 1:10,000 series, Sheet 551. Data compiled with the assistance of hamlet representatives to the Regional Council.)

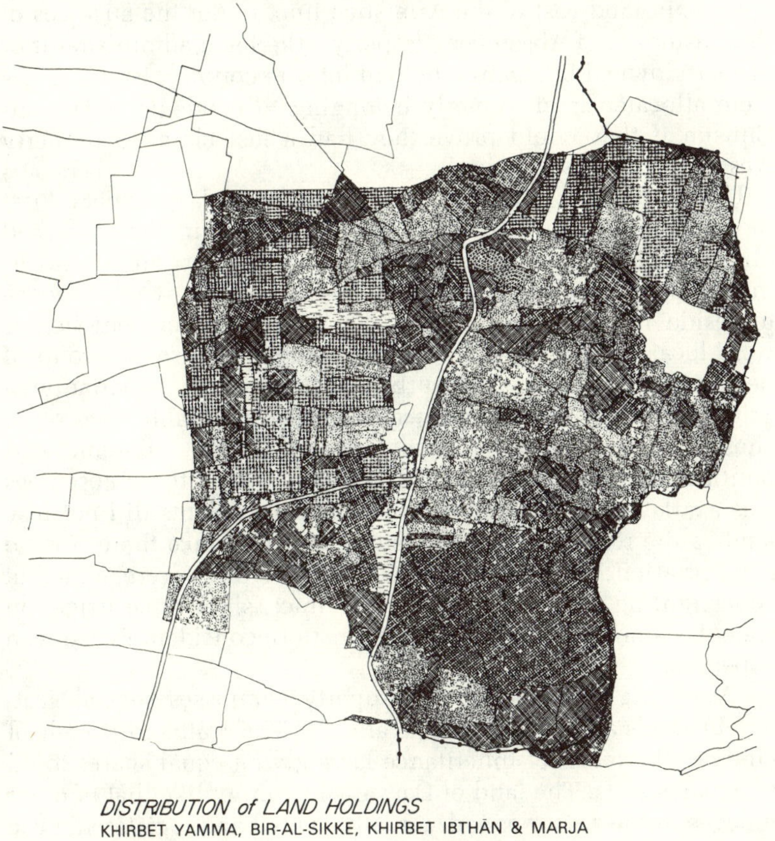

on which olive and almond orchards had been planted.[32] The Armistice line left only 1,200 *dūnams* of plain land with Deir al-Ghusūn in Jordan while the remaining 10,500 were in Israeli territory. The parent village retained 12,500 *dūnams* of hilly terrain in Jordan, while 3,500 *dūnams* were on the Israeli side of the border (see figure 2).

Part of the plain was occupied by new Israeli settlements, but some hamlet residents owned land west of what used to be known as the "Iraqi position," that is an army entrenchment in part of the Triangle prior to its transfer to Israeli administration.[33] These landholders received an equivalent compensation of Deir al-Ghusūn land east of the Armistice line, under the auspices of the Custodian of Absentees' Property—the legal administrator of property owned by Arabs who had left the country. Israeli Arabs were allocated land formerly belonging to residents of Deir al-Ghusūn if they could prove they had a just claim to property west of the Armistice Line.

There were two other categories of absentee landowners. First those who owned a small area of land in the plain and possessed olive orchards east of the Armistice Line or olive presses in the parent village. Obviously, such persons would choose to reside in the parent village where their permanent homes were located. The second category comprised a small group of persons who had moved to urban centers in the Samarian area prior to the war, preferring town to village life. Nablus was often chosen as the new residence since it is the economic and political center of the area. The land owned by these absentees was available for transfer and the hamlet residents did not lose land as the result of the war (see figure 2),[34] since there was no expropriation in the region. What transfers there were, aimed at concentrating property into a single tract, since once irrigation water became available in 1958, this pattern considerably reduced expenses.

"As a rule" says Granott, "property comprises several scattered parcels all over the village area."[35] The scattered parcels of land are the result of inheritance laws giving equal shares to all of a man's sons. The land of Deir al-Ghusūn, unlike that of other villages in the area, was individually owned and registered, even prior to 1948. The 'Attīl property on the other hand was *mush'a*, a system Granott describes as follows:

> *Mush'a* is a relic of joint ownership of land. Under it the properties are regarded as owned by the community, which is always a village community—but are in the actual possession of several owners, each of whom has a certain share of the joint property, though his ownership of any special area is not fixed. Usually, the fields are redistributed periodically among

Figure 3
Agricultural Distribution Map Showing Lands Farmed by Hamlet Residents
(Map redrawn from Government of Israel, Department of Survey, 1:10,000 series, Sheet 551. Data compiled with the assistance of hamlet representatives to the Regional Council.)

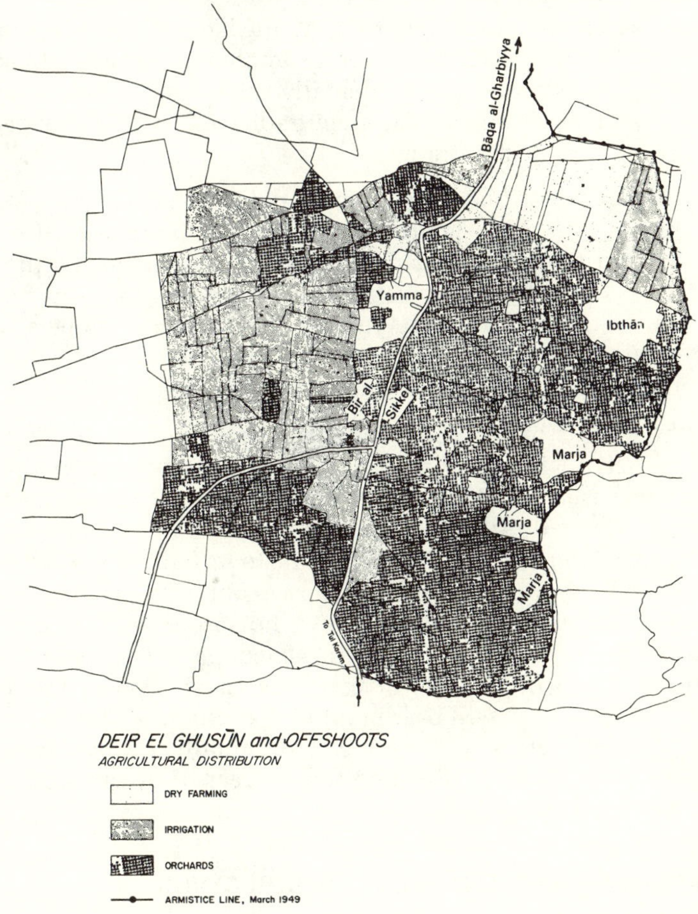

the members of the community according to some generally accepted plan.[36]

This form of ownership creates economic interdependence in the village and may lead to closer interpersonal relationships, but individually owned territories that do not change hands ensures relative independence, and this form of ownership is more conducive to long term investment.

Two of the 'Attīl offshoots were established on *mush'a* property of their parent village while the third was set up on individually owned land. In 1943, 'Attīl's *mush'a* property was divided and every male inhabitant received an equally parcelled share,[37] about one eighth of 'Attīl's plain area being *mush'a*.[38] There were variations in the handling of *mush'a* land, the inhabitants of Zelefe and Manshīyya, for example, never undertook any annual redistribution. Incidentally, the establishment of the two hamlets on *mush'a* land contradicted the rules concerning ownership of such terrain:

> No houses or buildings may be erected and no trees may be planted on these lands without special permission from the highest Imperial Treasury authorities. . . The *mish'a* [mush'a] lands of a village are distributed or apportioned each year for cultivation during that year to the various members of the community who desire to and who are able to cultivate them—that is to plough and sow them with grain.[39]

If the land is built upon, redistribution is impossible. Thus, the two parent villages differ in their system of ownership. The method used in Deir al-Ghusūn was less common than that chosen by 'Attīl.[40] It goes without saying that a man who occupies land temporarily, will relate to its cultivation differently than if he were in permanent possession. Unless the sense of solidarity with his co-villagers, who are equally eligible for allotment of the land for a stipulated period of time is very strong, a peasant will not invest a great deal of effort and money in cultivation. He will bear in mind that others will reap what he has sowed. Where the land is individually owned, initiative, energy and funds for the land will be reaped by members of his immediate family.

HOUSING PROJECTS AND NEW BUILDINGS

After the March 1949 Rhodes Agreement, residents of the offshoots of 'Attīl were allowed to return to Israel. The area where they had lived before was already occupied and cultivated by new settlements. The solution suggested by the authorities and accepted by the group was that the former inhabitants of 'Attīl's offshoots be settled in other Arab villages and alloted land

Figure 4

Plan of Khirbet Yamma Housing Development,
(Redrawn from Ministry of Housing plan; original courtesy of Mr. Z. Guzman, Department of Minorities, Israel Ministry of Housing.)

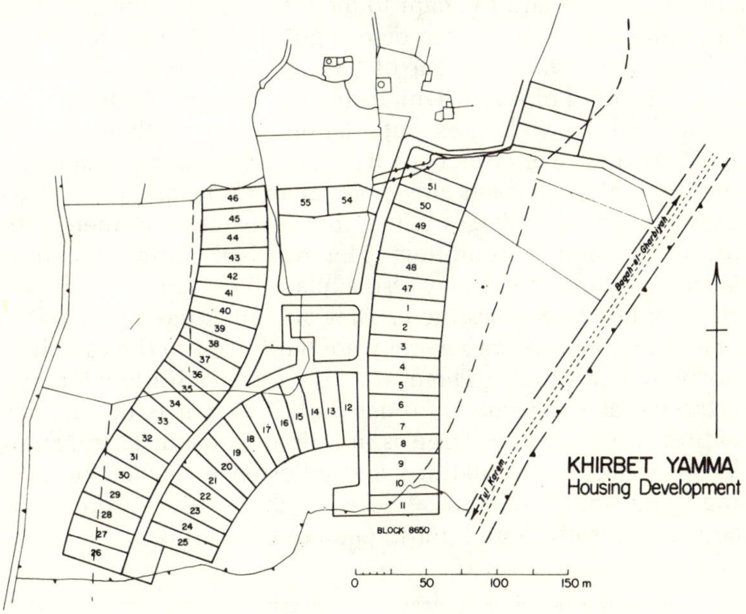

in those villages. The Israeli administration provided housing projects for these residents but they were not completed before 1961. Up to this time the future occupants lived in deserted buildings whose former residents had moved to Jordan. The Ministry of Housing built the dwelling units to allow for possible future expansion (see figure 4).[41] Only twenty-one out of close to 100 families opted for apartments in the housing projects. Those prefering to build their own homes were compensated by a plot within the housing project and a sum of money. The future tenants formed a cooperative and were granted long-term mortage loans by the Ministry of Housing at low rates of interest on the basis of their membership (4.5 percent over a period of twenty-five years).[42] The contracted stipulated repayment of the loan was to be made in Israeli pounds at the current dollar rate of exchange. Due to the repeated devaluation of the Israeli currency, the monthly payment increased considerably and this slowed down liquidation of the debt. The bank has chosen, therefore, to link the loan with the cost-of-living index instead of with the dollar rate of exchange.

The peasants are by no means unwilling to give up their traditional habits and to adapt to modern, technological society. This readiness to change can be recognized by the casual visitor to the hamlets. Only ten out of 283 interviewees (six percent) still live in the houses in which they were born. Residents did not just build new houses but planned them with a view to making the best use of modern living ideas. It may of course be that the hamlet residents are more inclined to accept changes than inhabitants of villages with a longer history, but there is no evidence for this assumption. The relatively brief period of existence of the hamlets may also explain the comparatively low number of domed houses there. They are much more frequent in the parent village where several were built prior to the establishment of the offshoots. There are also fewer additional rooms constructed as extensions of older buildings, nor is the number of entirely new wings as large as in Deir al-Ghusūn. There, many older buildings were modified and adjusted to newer forms of living. The small windows close to the ceiling were often enlarged to permit more light to penetrate into the house.

Table 1

Changes in Housing Type (in percentages)

Period	*Moved to Stone House from:*		*Moved to Concrete or Cinder Block House from:*						*Total Families*
	Tent	*Aqed*	*Tent*	*Aqed*	*Mud Brick House*	*Stone House*	*Mud Brick and Stone*	*Other types*	
Before 1948	25.0	14.3	3.5	14.3	7.2	35.7	–	–	10.2 (28)
1949-1956	–	–	4.4	43.5	–	34.8	13.0	4.3	8.5 (23)
1957-1965	0.6	–	4.8	17.0	6.1	66.1	4.8	0.6	60.5 (165)
1966-1967	–	–	8.3	8.3	83.4	–	–	–	4.3 (12)
[1957-1967]	0.5	–	5.1	16.6	11.4	61.9	4.5	–	[64.8 (177)]
1968-1973	–	–	2.2	31.1	–	62.3	4.4	–	16.5 (45)
%	2.9	1.5	4.4	20.9	3.7	60.4	5.1	1.1	100
Total Number of: Families	(8)	(4)	(12)	(57)	(10)	(165)	(14)	(3)	(273)

Note that the period [1957-1967] comprises figures relating to the periods 1957-65 and 1966-7. While there are a total of 283 married men in the hamlets, only 273 gave answers to questions on changes in housing.

Table I provides figures relating to these changes. Some of this building activity may well have been stimulated by the sight of more modern buildings in the towns, both Arab and Jewish. Most of the changes in the houses of the hamlets occurred in the sixteen years preceding my field work, not in the years immediately following the setting up of the hamlets. At the time of the establishment of the offshoots, preferences regarding housing varied. About twenty-eight percent of those who moved to the offshoots took up residence in tents, while twenty-percent moved immediately into the houses in which they still lived at the time of my fieldwork. The other eight percent first moved into temporary housing and only later entered the buildings they had constructed for themselves. Only twenty-three families (8.5 percent) built their homes during the period 1949 till 1956. This may be explained by the feeling of uncertainty that prevailed in the hamlets after the establishment of the State of Israel. The villagers preferred to watch developments, they did not show initiative during these years. When the political situation stabilized in the period between 1957 and 1963, the atmosphere changed and so did the conduct of the residents. They undertook building houses at a much greater rate, not only as a result of the changed political atmosphere but also because nuclear families increasingly preferred separate residences. Table I (see item six, questionnaire for males, appendix A) reveals one important feature—married sons wish to move away from their parental home, but prefer to build nearby. This means that interaction

Table 2

Place of Birth

	Informant's Birthplace				
Father's Birthplace	*Yamma, Ibthān, Bir al-Sikke, Marja*	*Deir al-Ghusūn, 'Attīl*	*Jeleme, Zelefe, Manshīyya*	*Other Locations*	*Total Married Men*
Yamma, Ibthān, Bir al-Sikke, Marja	46%	46%	—	8%	100% (200)
Deir al-Ghusūn, 'Attīl	4%	88%	—	8%	100% (28)
Jeleme, Zelefe, Manshīyya	—	28%	61%	11%	100% (39)
Other Locations	7%	47%	—	46%	100% (16)
TOTAL	33% (94)	48% (135)	8% (24)	11% (30)	100% (283)

between close family members is not significantly reduced, the parents retain the advantage of living close by (and vice-versa), while the house of the young couple is considered a unit by itself and the consequent benefits of privacy enjoyed.

In order to assess the changes in the types of housing, and the reasons for such changes, the birthplace of those interviewed should be borne in mind as well as that of their fathers. The respective data are shown in Table 2. Two hundred out of a total of 283 married men (seventy percent) were born in the hamlets. Forty-six percent of the fathers of those born in the hamlets were also born there. Another forty-six percent of the fathers were born in the parent villages, and the rest elsewhere. Twenty-eight men were born in the parent villages and the fathers of eighty-eight percent of these were born there too. Thirty-nine male residents were born in the 'Attīl offshoots, twenty-eight percent of their fathers were born in 'Attīl; and sixty-one percent of the fathers were born in 'Attīl's offshoots. The table thus indicates that the 'Attīl offshoots were established earlier than those of Deir al-Ghusūn.

The size of the house and the average number of rooms occupied by a family[43] is indicated in Table 3.[44] Out of 270 houses, 124 have been constructed without the legally required license since 1948. Thirty-two offenders were taken to court, of whom twenty-two were served demolition orders and ten others fined. Only one of the demolition orders was actually carried out. All thirty-two buildings whose owners were sued are outside the built-up area. It seems that no permits were applied for by those who built in the permitted building areas mainly because some of the plots were not their sole property. Sometimes, a co-owner no longer lives in Israel and his share is

Table 3

House Size and Number of Occupants

Distribution of Residents	*House Size (number of rooms)* 1	2	3	4	5+	*Total*
Number of Families	25	139	79	18	8	269
Percentage of Families	9	52	29	7	3	100
Number of Persons	85	544	440	166	87	1,322
% of Population	6	42	34	12	6	100
Persons per House (average)	3.4	3.9	5.6	9.2	10.9	4.9
Persons per Room	3.4	1.9	1.9	2.3	2.0	2.1

administered by the Custodian for Absentee Property. No plans can be submitted to the Regional Building Committee, the proper authority, without legally established ownership. An additional reason for building without permission is that according to regulations the house should not cover more than sixty percent of the plot, so that many sites are too small to build on if the legal requirements are respected.

LOCAL GOVERNMENT AND INSTITUTIONS

Until April 1949 the hamlets were part of Deir al-Ghusūn in terms of local government, the *mukhtār* being responsible for the offshoots.[45] In addition, hamlets had honorary *mukhtārs*, usually one in each, except in Khirbet Ibthān which had two. These men dealt with minor issues and intrafamily relations, perhaps because such matters are best arranged by a co-resident. The honorary *mukhtārs* also had limited official contacts with the District Commissioner's Office in Tul Karem but unlike the *mukhtār* in the parent village, they received no remuneration for their services.

The term *mukhtār* (literally, "the one elected") indicates that the holder of the office is elected. This is misleading for he is not chosen by his *ḥamūla* but usually appointed by the authorities, though recommendations are taken into account. In 1964, the office of the *mukhtār* was abolished in Israel and the official holding the same post was called *mu'atamad* (literally,"trustee"). Another innovation was that candidates were required to be literate. These arrangements were cancelled when the four hamlets joined the Regional Council of Emeq Hefer, negotiations for which were initiated by the Ministry of Interior in 1966.[46] The reasons were obvious: in Israel, essential services such as the supply of electricity and piped water are provided by government-controlled companies. These companies prefer to deal with local authorities which are legally entitled to receive grants and loans and may be held responsible for their use. Furthermore, such a local body can collect taxes. The number of residents of the hamlets has at no time exceeded 1,600 so that there cannot be an effective local body, not even for all four hamlets together. Once they became attached to the Regional Council, in which mainly Jewish *moshavim* (smallholders' cooperative settlements) and *kibbūtzim* (communal settlements) were represented, the Ministry of Interior appointed local committees in each of them. These consist of five members, except in Marja where there are only three. One member of each local committee is delegated to the Regional Council till elections for the Regional Council take place. Tax collection lagged behind considerably, until the Regional Council turned to the District Court in 1971-72 after which almost the total sum assessed was quickly paid up.[47]

EDUCATION

The implementation of the Bill of Compulsory Education,[48] like that of any other law, depends on the existence of an authority to implement the law. Once this authority existed, the school population grew rapidly since parents readily cooperated. After affiliation to the Regional Council, two buildings were added to the elementary school. Table 4 shows elementary school attendance.[49] Until 1963-64 not a single girl reached the seventh grade of elementary school, most dropping out at the end of the fifth grade,[50] though graduation was at the end of the eighth form. At that time no girl qualified for high school. Cohen points out economic reasons behind the discontinuance of school attendance by girls, mentioning the role they play in the running

Table 4

Elementary School Attendance

Scholastic	*Attendance according to Sex and Grade*									
	4th Grade		*5th Grade*		*6th Grade*		*7th Grade*		*8th Grade*	
Year	M	F	M	F	M	F	M	F	M	F
1954-55	14	10	13	7	16	6	15	–	9	–
1957-58	13	8	12	5	13	1	13	–	9	–
1960-61	15	12	13	12	12	2	12	–	13	–
1964-65	22	16	21	8	18	3	16	3	13	1
1967-68	18	16	20	16	20	15	19	6	20	–
1968-69	29	28	25	16	25	17	16	12	16	6
1969-70	33	24	31	23	27	17	25	14	16	9
1970-71	31	33	32	31	32	29	28	15	20	10
1971-72	34	32	33	30	31	28	29	26	18	13
1972-73	33	42	32	35	29	32	30	25	29	25

of the household and in the fields[51]; while Granqvist lays stress on the prevention of 'sin' as a reason for keeping girls at home.[52] Co-education has become the norm in Israeli Arab schools, but it is still a prohibitive factor in Arab female education on the West

Bank. When the local authority resorted to fines for drop-outs before the termination of the legally stipulated age, the girls continued to study to the eighth grade, but punitive measures were not the only and perhaps not even a decisive reason for this development. The members of the local Education Committee responsible for the implementation of the Bill are parents of the pupils. They are much better suited to persuade co-citizens to let their children study, than non-resident officials.[53]

The influence exercised in this way is demonstrated by the data in Table 5 which shows that eight girls who finished elementary school in 1970-71 continued at the local high school and only one girl had dropped out by the tenth grade.[54] In 1972-73, twelve of thirteen female elementary school graduates, who

Table 5

Agricultural High School Attendance

Academic Year	Residence and Sex of Students: Hamlet Residents M	F	Total	Non-hamlet Residents M	F	Total	Total
1971-72 (9th Grade)	26	8	34	21	—	21	55
1972-73 (9th Grade)	17	12	29	28	4	32	61
1972-73 (10th Grade)	28	7	35	21	1	22	57

had finished school a year before, continued with high school studies. In talks with parents of some of the female students who attended the high school, almost all of them stressed that they would not have permitted their daughters to attend a high school in another village. Nevertheless, five girls out of twenty-nine students who were residents of the four hamlets, attended high school in the district (in Ṭaybe and Bāqa al-Gharbīyya) in 1972-73. They were in the eleventh and twelfth grades.

Among those included in the study only one girl received education beyond high school level. She was the first female student to graduate from elementary school (1964-65), and went on to a teacher training college.[55] Today she is a teacher at the local elementary school. Four of her male colleagues have similar post-secondary education and are preparing for an academic degree. The woman teacher does not study at the university since this would mean travelling relatively long distances and perhaps even staying overnight in the large city.

There were nineteen post-high school students in the year 1972/73, five of whom attended a teachers college, the level of which is lower than that of the university. Another five studied at European universities, three of them in Eastern Europe. Four of the students abroad attended medical school, while the fifth prepared for an engineering degree.[56] So far, only one resident has graduated from an Israeli university—a mechanical engineer.

Table 6

Formal Education: Male Hamlet Residents
(in percentages)

Level of Formal Education	*Married Men (Age)* Up to 30	31-50	51 and over	*Single Men* 18 and over	*Combined*
No schooling	—	6.0	58.5	—	16.2
Grades 1-3	—	4.5	15.5	—	5.6
Grades 4-6	20.9	45.9	16.9	3.4	31.7
Grades 7-8	61.7	35.4	1.5	58.0	35.6
Grades 9-10	11.6	2.2	—	4.5	4.6
Grades 11-12	3.5	4.5	1.5	18.2	3.5
University, College, or Teachers' College	2.3	—	—	15.9	0.7
No information	—	1.5	6.1	—	2.1
TOTALS	100	100	100	100	100
	(86)	(131)	(65)	(85)	(283)

Table 6 reflects the changes in the level of formal education in the hamlets. In the age group fifty-one and over, more than fifty-eight percent of the married males never attended school, while there is no male in the age group up to thirty who did not study for at least three years. Only twenty percent did not finish the seventh or eighth grades and sixty-two percent graduated from elementary school; fifteen percent went on to high school, although less than four percent actually graduated. A special difficulty encountered by Israeli Arabs should be borne in mind. They grew up in an environment where they heard only one language—Arabic. Their parents, especially their fathers, were often in touch with the authorities and usually knew Hebrew, a language easily learned by speakers of Arabic, and a *sine qua non* for study at an Israeli university. English, equally essential for academic studies since most textbooks are in that language is however, a major obstacle. It is the second foreign language for Arab children and not the first as for Hebrew speaking Israelis. This presents special difficulties in the passing of matriculation and university entrance examinations.

Single males have a better formal education than married ones. Almost sixteen percent of single males went on to universities and colleges, while about eighteen percent were high school graduates.[57] It may be assumed that married males concentrate more on earning a living than single ones. Table 7 shows a steep increase in the number of years of formal education for girls. The younger they are, the longer they attend school and this affects their status within the family. The knowledge and understanding they gain from formal education help them to deal with problems they may have to solve while the males of the family work outside the village. Illiteracy is no longer widespread in the hamlets, not even among women. High school education has turned into the norm and it looks as if higher education for girls will follow.[58]

Table 7

Formal Education: Married Female Hamlet Residents (in percentages)

Woman's Age	*Number of Years in School* 0	1-2	3-4	5-6	7-8	9-10	*Total*	*Average No. of Years in School*
Up to 20	–	16	38	23	–	23	(13)	5.1
21-25	54	12	9	14	5	5	(56)	2.1
26-30	59	14	16	7	4	–	(56)	1.5
31-40	95	3	1	1	–	–	(78)	0
41-50	95	5	–	–	–	–	(43)	0
51 or over	99	1	–	–	–	–	(71)	0
All Ages	78	7	6	5	2	2	(317)	0.6

Since Hebrew is taught from the third elementary school grade on, many read newspapers in that language. In answer to the question 'do you read the newspaper', ninety-eight males and one female answered in the affirmative, a discrepancy between the sexes that also exists in western society, though on a smaller scale. Seventy-seven read papers in Arabic and twenty-two in Hebrew. Forty-six buy the paper every day, and fifty-three only once or twice weekly. Among the forty-six daily readers, fourteen read in Hebrew. Among the second group, forty-seven preferred an Arabic paper and only six a paper in Hebrew. It is interesting to note that although the Hebrew press provides more information on regional affairs, papers in Arabic are preferred. It is probable that the Hebrew readers comprise students who attended Jewish high schools before the Yamma high school was opened.

TRANSPORTATION AND COMMUNICATIONS

The hamlets are located between two Jewish urban centers—Natanya and Hadera, both towns about twenty-three kilometers away. Hadera caters to the needs of the Arab rural population and is the preferred shopping center. Many of the shopkeepers speak some Arabic since most of the women are not fluent in Hebrew, unlike their males who have much more contact with the Jewish environment. Frequent buses, running in both directions, stop at the entrances to the hamlets. The buses are especially full in the early morning when the laborers leave for work and in the late afternoon when they return. The description of remote and isolated Arab villages found in literature certainly does not apply here. There is a bus to Haifa every morning and two cab-owners in the hamlets are kept busy by the residents.

Table 8 shows the vehicles owned by hamlet residents. Possession of a private car is a symbol of mobility and prosperity, and every fourth family in the hamlets owns one. There are thirty-three trucks in the hamlets and twenty-six tractors are used to cultivate the land, some of which are rented to peasants from other villages. The trucks and pick-up trucks are mostly used to transport vegetables to Tel Aviv market.

Table 8

Vehicles Owned by Hamlet Residents

Type of Vehicle	*No. of Vehicles*	*% of Families*
Private car, Pick-ups, Jeep	65	23
Large Truck (over 4 tons)	33	12
Taxicab	2	1
Motorcycle, Moped	7	3
Tractor	26	9

A great deal of the shopping is done in local groceries (already described) and there are also two cafes selling cigarettes and other minor items. Mail is delivered daily by a mobile post office van and four residents distribute it in their respective hamlets. Two of my informants, however, prefer a postbox in Natanya since they suspect that the local postmen are not efficient enough and might also read their letters. Once a month the mobile post office distribues the Social Insurance checks, when a long line may be seen waiting well ahead of the time when the van is due to arrive.[59] Twenty-one telephones have been installed since 1968, before which there were none.

Other data collected in the hamlets is as follows: There are twenty-one generators in operation which provide light for ninety-seven houses (thirty-four percent of the households), all of which possess TV sets. Most of the generators are insured, though insurance business is otherwise far from lively in the area, except of course for the obligatory car insurance. Only twenty percent of the population have taken out life insurance and no more than nine families have insured their homes. It should be remembered that the concept of insurance is alien to Arab society everywhere and insurance brokers point out that the Jewish population did not usually insure their property and life in the not too distant past. Western and central European immigrants have popularized the idea.

The annual average temperature is between 19-21^0 Celsius, less warm than in the coastal strip. The air is usually dry and even during hot summer days the breeze makes the heat bearable. There are about six to nine days of hot and dry winds per annum.[60]

CONTACTS BETWEEN HAMLETS

The four hamlets are treated here as a single unit due to their similarity. The inhabitants originated from the same parent village (with few exceptions), left it for the same reasons, and settled in close proximity. Their children attend the same elementary schools and together the hamlets joined the Regional Council. All these facts account for their functioning as a unit and set them apart from their wider environment. Contacts between the hamlets would have been close, even if they had not been cut off from their natural hinterland for almost two decades. The closed border doubtless promoted rapprochement because it increased mutual dependence, the residents seeking in each other what they had lost. Circumstances forced them to become autonomous and create their own institutions. At one time they shared the *mukhtār* with the parent village, now they have their own officials and have to find or accept substitute administrative frameworks. They have developed shopping habits adapted to the new situation, making purchases in the neighboring Jewish towns of Hadera and Natanya, instead of Tul Karem where they can once again visit if they wish.

Geographically and demographically, the hamlets are very similar. Even when the border was removed in 1967, and when clandestine and of necessity irregular contacts turned into open and regular ones, it was evident that changes had taken place which could neither be undone nor disregarded. The same process of drawing close together took place between the parent village and the other two offshoots. They too felt united by a common fate, just as the four hamlets. Now these two units have had to relearn cooperation and neighborliness in a new setting.

When the hostile border separated the hamlets from the other villages, they developed on different lines and required different services and means of transportation. The influence of the Jordanian monarchic rule, its institutions and norms, political, social and economic, was quite unlike that exerted on the four hamlets by Israel. The Israeli Arab villagers are neighbors of Jewish agricultural settlements whose methods of cultivation and social organization are sophisticated and who have established flourishing industries processing farm products. The hamlet residents encountered a highly advanced farming population whose influence may partly explain a certain estrangement between the parent village and its offshoots after normal relations were reestablished.

The four hamlets have learned to live within the State of Israel whose citizens they are, organizing politically to meet the demands of their wider environment and reinforcing the political structures within the hamlets through marriage unions. During the enforced hiatus with the hamlets, the parent village and the two offshoots east of the armistice line, relied on the wider Arab hinterland. Many from the parent village are salaried workers in Arab states other than Jordan, such as Kuwait, while others lease land in Northern Lebanon. Since June 1967 they have been able to visit relatives and neighbors in Israel, for it is here in their native villages that they have their roots. Nevertheless, exposure to a different reality and new contacts has broken up the formerly fairly monolithic structure of rural society, of which the parent village and its offshoots used to be part. When the reunion with the hamlets took place, differences were noticeable and the villagers who had been under Jordanian rule, often call the hamlet residents 'Israelis' when pointing out dissimilarities.

The differences between the villages on both sides of the former border are easily discernible. They may partly be explained by different topographical conditions, the parent village and its other two offshoots are mountain settlements while the hamlets are situated on the plain. The shops in the Israeli hamlets offer a considerable variety of commodities, and sell the kind of goods usually consumed in an urban and fairly sophisticated society; the store in the parent village is accommodated in the depth of a mountain cave that is dark and cool, where seeds and agricultural implements are sold side by side with basic grocery wares, quite unlike the hamlet shops which are typical of any to be found in a rural settlement in Israel. The rhythm of life is also different. In Israel all but the most essential tasks are suspended on Saturday (Sabbath). Since many male residents work 'outside', usually in Jewish villages and towns, Saturday has of necessity become a day of rest in the hamlets. The elementary school serving the four hamlets is closed and families usually spend the time together. Neighbors pay social calls, excursions may be arranged and those farming activities for which the help of the males is desired or needed, are performed. In the parent village the day of rest is Friday, according to Muslim tradition. This affects interaction between the mountain residents and those of the hamlets in the plain.

The influence of the Jewish environment on the hamlets increased after they were incorporated in an organization of predominantly Jewish character such as the Regional Council. New channels of communication with this wider environment have developed, but the very fact that contacts with Jewish Israelis have intensified, brings with it an increased consciousness of the minority situation of the hamlet residents. The Regional Council provides equal services to all settlements affiliated to it, including the hamlets. This further enhances the differences between the hamlets and the parent village and the other two offshoots. While Jordan, Kuwait and other Arab states influence life in the mountain villages, the hamlets exist within a modern industrial society, with a highly developed network of communications. Although differing in some ways from their wider Jewish environment, in spite of growing administrative and economic links, the hamlets are quite unlike the parent village and the other two offshoots.

In the hamlets, women are given considerable responsibility regarding the administration of the family property because of the men's absence through work outside the village. This affects women's status and role, and is discussed in later chapters. These chapters will describe in detail the power women exercise, especially in those cases where they contribute to the family income.

NOTES

1. Arab village names in the Middle East frequently begin with the word *deir* (monastery).

2. Fifty years ago malaria was frequent in the lowland swamp region, while less common in mountain settlements. See Yaacov Shimoni, *Arabs in Palestine* (Tel Aviv: Am Oved, 1947) p. 158 (Hebrew). This did not necessarily deter settlement in the plain as indicated by the establishment of the two 'Attīl offshoots around the turn of the century when the plains were certainly not malaria free.

3. While villages are called by their correct names, pseudonyms are used for individual residents and the *ḥamūlas*.

4. The full name of an Arab is generally composed of his first name, as well as that of his father and his family name. He will often state his first name, that of his father and grandfather and only then, his family name.

5. Gabriel Baer, *Population and Society in the Arab East* (London: Routledge and Kegan Paul, 1964) p. 169.

6. Abner Cohen, *Arab Border Villages in Israel: A Study of Community and Change in a Social Organization* (Manchester, England: Manchester University Press, 1965) p. 11.

7. David H. K. Amiran, "The Pattern of Settlements in Palestine," *Israeli Exploration Journal* 3, (1953) pp. 72-3.

8. Itzaq Ben-Zvi, *Eretz-Israel, Under Ottoman Rule: Four Centuries of History* (Jerusalem: Bialik Institute, 1955) p. 37 (Hebrew).

9. Ibid.

10. Amiran, p. 5.

11. Constantin François Volney, *Voyage en Egypte et en Syrie pendant les annêes 1783, 1784 et 1975* (Paris: Desenne, 1787) Vol. 2, p. 411.

12. Edward Robinson and Eli Smith, *Biblical Researches in Palestine, Mount Sinai and Arabic Petrea: A Journal of Travels in the year 1838*, Vol. III (London: J. Murray, 1841) p. 135.

13. Ibid., pp. 135-36. Informants, having been told the story of events by their elders, state that Bedouin tribesmen were among the peasants who mutinied.

14. Amiran, p. 73.

15. Claude Reignier Conder and Horatio Herbert Kitchener, *The Survey of Western Palestine, Memoirs* (London: The Committee of the Palestine Exploration Fund, 1882) Vol. 2, p. 152.

16. Ibid., p. 152.

17. Ibid., p. 152.

18. See Gideon Golany, "*Geography of Settlements of Eron Valley Region: Determining Factor in the Formation of Branch Villages*." Ph.D. dissertation. Jerusalem: The Hebrew University, 1966, p. 9 (Hebrew). The verb *'azab* means, literally, "go far away." Its noun is *'azbah* (plural: *'azāb*), that is "hamlet" or "farm", see *Hava*, Arabic-English Dictionary, Catholic Press, Beirut, pp. 469-70. The singular of the noun is pronounced *'izbeh* by the inhabitants of the region and means "seasonal camping in fields."

19. Ibid. His interpretation also applies to another term used as an affix to the proper names of the offshoots—*ṭahta*, meaning "low" or "under." In the Galilee and in Judean mountain villages as well, a parent village name is often suffixed by the word *fōqa* ("upper"), while the offshoot, bearing the same primary name as the parent village, receives the suffix *ṭahta*. Some of the elders of Yamma say that when Bir al-Sikke was first established it was called Yamma Ṭahta. This would be a rare usage of the term in this region since Yamma Ṭahta is actually the "granddaughter" village. In the Bible, offshoots are called "daughters." For example, "Beth Shean and its daughters, and Ibleam and its daughters and the inhabitants of Megiddo and its daughters." (Josh. 17:11). (The English version uses "towns" rather than "daughters"). Other examples are found in Judges 1:27 and 2 Chron. 28:18.

20. The dictionary definition of manzal ("inn", or "lodging") fits the modern usage of the term for a temporary nomad's camp.

21. The distance between the parent village and the fields in the western plain is roughly seven to nine kilometers. Golany, *Eron Valley*, gives the average distance between the parent village and the fields to the west as seventeen and a half kilometers in the Samaria region.

22. The literal meaning of *ghaba* is "forest," since the area was previously covered with trees. The offshoots along the strip of the Sharon added the prefix *ghaba* to their name (compare the use of the prefixes *nazle* and *khirbe*). See Shimoni, p. 162. Golany, p. 8, believes that the term *ghaba* indicates abundance of vegetation.

23. Cohen, p. 7.

24. Gustaf Hermann Dalman, *Arbeit und Sitte in Palastina; Zeltleben* (Hildesheim: Geory Olms, 1964) pp. 27-28, shows a photograph of a rectangularly shaped camp from the first decade of the 20th century. The author explains that for security reasons a Bedouin will never pitch his tent far away from the group camp. The camps of the camel-raising Bedouin are usually built in two lines, while those of the sheep and goat herders have a semicircular shape. Conder, describing camps in the same area, says that "among the Arabs of the Judea desert the largest

tent in one camp contained some thirty families or over a hundred persons." As to the arrangement of the tents, he adds that "among the Ta'amireh and Jāhalīn the usual form is a rectangle," Claude Reigniers Conder, *Tent Work in Palestine* (London: R. Bentley and Son, 1879) Vol. 2, p. 275. On speaking of a semicircular camp, Barth emphasizes that

". . . with some justification every herd owner feels that outside his camp he is surrounded by a hostile world full of sheep thieves and robbers. At night even adult men are afraid to go far outside the circle of tents and no one pitches his tent alone at any distance from the others for fear of night isolation and consequent vulnerability to thieves." Frederick Barth, *Nomads of South Persia: The Basseri Tribe of the Khamsheh Confederacy* (Boston: Little, Brown and Little, 1961) p. 47. Strong tribes have no need for defensive camp structures, as Musil writes when speaking of the Rwala Bedouin of the Syrian desert: "The Rwala do not pitch camps in the shape of an ellipse as do some other tribes. Each one may pitch his tent where he likes, for his tribe is strong and can withstand any enemy." Alios Musil, *The Manners and Customs of the Rwala Bedouins*, (American Geographic Society, Oriental Explorations and Studies, No. 6, 1928) p. 77.

25. Emanuel Marx, *Bedouin of the Negev* (Manchester, England: Manchester University Press, 1967) pp. 82, 178-80.

26. Verified by Moshe Lauffenfeld, designer of the new housing project in Yamma.

27. The armistice agreement between Israel and the Hashemite Kingdom of Jordan was signed on the island of Rhodes in April 1949. For the full text of the agreement, see United Nations, The Rhodes Agreement: Armistice Agreement between Israel and the Hashemite Kingdom of Jordan. Security Council, Official Records: Fourth Year, Special Supplement No. 1, 1949, New York.

28. The term "Triangle," does not fit here since the area is actually a narrow strip of land, although the three towns in the area, Tul Karem and Jenin form a triangle on the map. At the time of the British Mandate, the three towns and the adjacent strip of land were one single district known as "The Triangle."

29. See Cohen, p. 1. He also points out the importance of a line of border settlements, ibid. p. 17.

30. In Article VI, Section 6 the Rhodes Agreement stipulates that "...in the event any of the inhabitants should decide to leave their villages, they shall be entitled to take with them their livestock and other movable property. . ." United Nations, Rhodes Agreement, p. 4. In the course of terrorist activities, one of the inhabitants of Yamma, a member of the Ibn Hajar family, was sentenced to death and hanged by the British authorities. His partner, the commander of the Yazīd underground group escaped to one of the Arab countries. This man's report to the High Commander of the Arab rebellion about his terrorist activities (primarily of mining roads, railways and electrical or telephone poles)

was translated into Hebrew and published by the "Haganah" from the Arab Underground archives of the 1936-39 activities. The book was edited anonymously [Ezra Danin] *Documents and Figures* (Tel Aviv: Hamagen Haivry, 1944, Hebrew).

A British intelligence report gives the names of those active in the rebellion in the region. It refers to the commander of the Yamma group of the Yazīd saying that he was "responsible for the landmine terror around Tul Karem and that his house was subsequently demolished. "Said to be now in Syria," see Hagana Archives, file No. AA 143. From information dated October 15, 1939, it is learned that 'Abd al-Qādir Yazīd returned together with some of the men under his command, among them members of the Amīn and Ibn Sinai families—Hagana Archives, file No. TA 191, 8/2.

31. In 1953, the greater part of the Yazīd *ḥamūla* reverted to the name of Yazīd, after a member of the Amīn *ḥamūla* had killed a man with the dead man's wife, his mistress, acting as accomplice.

32. One *dūnam* equals 0.25 acre. Out of the 27,770 *dūnams*, 710 were listed under railways, roads, rivers and lakes. Palestine Government Village Statistics, Jerusalem, 1945; see also Abraham Granot, *The Land System in Palestine: History and Structure*, (London: Eyre and Spottiswoode, 1952) p. 192.

33. General 'Abd al-Karīm Qāem, who became ruler of Iraq after the overthrow of the monarchy, commanded the unit stationed south of the parent village. The Iraqi Army who assisted the Jordanians, were stationed in this area during the War of Independence.

34. In only two cases did residents in these hamlets not come to an agreement with the Custodian concerning the reparcelling of property. One was the case of two brothers of the Asad family who claimed ownership of twenty-six *dūnams* and refused to accept an exchange. The other was that of a member of the 'Arishī family, who asked for fourteen *dūnams*. The Custodian, however, recognized only eight *dūnams* as the man's property. The man unsuccessfully argued his case for twenty years, without reaching final settlement.

35. Granott, p. 197.

36. Ibid., p. 213. For further information on the *mush'a* system, see ibid., pp. 213-248. See also, Palestine Government Village Statistics, p. 31.

37. Granott, p. 226.

38. Ibid., p. 192.

39. Samuel Bergheim, "Land Tenure in Palestine: Answers to Questions," *Palestine Exploration Fund Quarterly Statements*, 26 (1894) pp. 191-99.

40. The term *mush'a* is not always correctly applied. As mentioned above, Deir al-Ghusūn land was individually owned. When brothers did not divide land inherited from their father, officials applied the term *mush'a* to this cooperative system. After the Israeli-Jordanian Armistice

Agreement there were several cases where members of one family who had previously jointly cultivated their land now lived on opposite sides of the hostile border. As they had not registered their parts of these fields under individual names, the Custodian of Absentees' Property arranged for the partition using the percentage of land each individual would have inherited as a criterion. The land was then registered in the name of one person. There were two instances when hamlet residents (who crossed into Israel in 1949), laid claim to their father's property. Again, the Custodian only confirmed the right for that part of the property the farmer would have inherited if he had been an Israeli citizen. In 1954, before irrigation was introduced in the area, these farmers decided not to remain in Israel since their property was too small to provide for a living and returned to the parent village.

41. Israel Ministry of Housing, *For Better Living* (Tel Aviv: Japhet Press, 1964) p. 11.

42. Those married after 1949 received only loans, since they did not own homes prior to the war.

43. According to Gertz, the average occupation per room in the hamlets in 1968 was 3.28. Abraham Gertz, "The Settlements and their Inhabitants." In *Emeq Hefer: A Historical Demographic and Emeq Hefer: A Historical Demographic and Economic Survey*, (Kefar Vitkin: Emeq Hefer Regional Council, 1970) p. 150 (Hebrew). However, (see Table 1) forty-five families (16.5 per cent of the total number) have exchanged their homes for new ones since 1968. They were mainly young couples, none of these homes having less than three rooms. The approximate density in the homes of the newly married couples is three persons per room. Gertz uses statistics from Jewish settlements for comparison. The number of dwellers per room for the Jewish population was 1.12 as opposed to 2.1 in the hamlets.

44. There are no data for fourteen of the families. Some reside with their parents, while others did not answer the question.

45. During the British Mandate there was only one *mukhtār* in Deir al-Ghusūn in charge of the hamlets but the Jordanians appointed another.

46. Personal communication from Mr. Erez, Ministry of Interior. In larger villages in the area, local councils were set up in 1959 — see Cohen, p. 94. Regarding legal procedure, Cohen says that "according to the law, it is the Minister of Interior who can decide on the recommendation of the District Commissioner, which village should have a council. The first council is appointed by the Minister after he (or his representative) holds adequate consultation with persons who, in his judgement, represent public opinion in the village. After this council is set up, at least six months should elapse before free elections for a new council be held." Cohen, p. 95.

47. The Council's taxation system for the hamlet residents was organized as follows:

Property Owned	*Annual Tax*
1 *dūnam* land, unirrigated	IL 1
1 *dūnam* land, irrigated	IL 2
One room house	IL 40
Two room house	IL 90
Three room house	IL 140
Four room house	IL 200

The Council's resolution regarding taxation was published in the Official Gazette. See Government of Israel, *Official Gazette* (Jerusalem: The Government Press, 1969) No. 2353. In 1969-70 the Council succeeded in collecting only IL 7,956 of the IL 31,000 debt incurred by the hamlet residents (the fiscal year starts on 1 April). The corresponding figure for the year 1970-71 was IL 11,000 out of IL 30,000. However, in 1971-72, after the Local Council turned to the District Court, the inhabitants quickly paid the debt and the Tax collection amounted to IL 27,500 out of a debt of IL 28,000. Figures have been taken from the files of the Emeq Hefer Council or are based on a personal communication from Mr. Yaacov Shamash, the Council's liaison officer to the hamlets.

48. Compulsory education in Israel covers kindergarten and nine grades of elementary school. The Regional Council is responsible for implementation.

49. Figures in Table 4 rely on local school records of attendance.

50. Hilma Granquist, *Marriage Conditions in a Palestinian Village Vol. I* Commentationes Humanarum Litterarum Vol. 3, No. 8. (Helsingfors, Finland: Soceitas Sciantiarum Fennica, 1955), pp. 43-4.

51. Cohen, p. 36.

52. Granqvist, *Marriage Conditions Vol. I*, p. 45.

53. My thanks to Mr. Yaacov Shamash, liaison officer to the Regional Council, for pointing this out.

54. Numbers of students according to school records.

55. The period of study at the Teachers' College is two years.

56. Admission to medical schools in Israel is difficult, as is admission to the Engineering Department of the Haifa Technion. High marks are required and there are competitive entrance examinations.

57. About eighty to eighty-five percent of the single males under twenty-five are high school graduates. This is in keeping with the findings of Mar'i and Binyamin. They report that parents, pupils and teachers alike are in favor of high school education. They stress its educational and practical value in a transitional society such as the Israel Arab society. See Sami Mar'i and Abraham Binyamin, *The Attitude of Arab Society in Israel towards Technological-Vocational Education* (University of Haifa, School of Education, Research Institute for Arab Education and its Development, 1975) p. 5. Mar'i and Zāher state that a significant rise in the percentage of Arab high school

students occurred in 1970. Sami Mar'i and Nabiyya Zāher, *Facts and Trends in the Development of Arab Education in Israel* (University of Haifa, School of Education, Research Institute for Arab Education and its Development, 1976) pp. 55-64.

58. Generally speaking, the female residents of West Bank villages received a higher level of formal education than those in the hamlets. The reason for this was that there was not suitable employment for girls in the West Bank villages due to a shortage of arable land. It was left to the Israel Ministry of Agriculture to help introduce intensive cultivation of the soil and modern agricultural methods after the Six Day War.

Some farmers leased land under irrigation in the Jordan Valley and even in northern Lebanon, and stayed in these areas throughout the entire agricultural season. As high school education is free in Jordan and since parents would not send their daughters to other countries or distant places to work for wages, they let them go to school instead. After June 1967, more than a few of the parents stopped their daughters attending high school. Instead, they obtained employment for them in adjoining Israeli settlements and towns.

In other words, the scholastic achievements of girls in the West Bank villages adjacent to the hamlet area were a function of socioeconomic and ecological factors. In addition to the influence exerted by the Local Education Committee, school attendance in the West Bank villages also encouraged parents in the hamlets to permit their daughters to attend high school. The example set by the West Bank villages sparked efforts of the Local Education Committee to induce parents to let their daughters continue in school.

59. The recipients of social insurance payments fall into two categories — the aged and mothers of three or more children. To encourage large families, the Israeli government pays a special allowance from the third child on.

60. Annual average precipitation in the years 1931-61 (measured at a station two miles north of the hamlets) was 558 mm. There follow examples of rainfall in more recent years:

Year	*Total Rainfall*	*Heaviest Rainfall*
1968-69	917 mm	January
1970-71	581 mm	January
1972-73	471 mm	December
1973-74	638 mm	January

There are about 200 to 240 nights when dew is in evidence in the plain.

In the hottest month the temperature is between twenty-two and twenty-four degrees Celsius, and in the coldest, between twelve and fourteen degrees. The dominant wind directions are southwest, west, and northwest. In the plain, where the hamlets are located, there is little danger of frost. Data on climatic conditions are based on information from the Meteorological Service of Israel.

3

Economic Structure

OCCUPATION

Until the termination of the British Mandatory Government the Arab farmer tilled his land without the help of modern technology, making a living from subsistence agriculture.[1] From 1948 employment began to take place outside the villages, increasing substantially after 1956 when military restrictions no longer obstructed movement from one place to another. The introduction of irrigation freed manpower and intensified this trend to leave the villages in order to earn wages. Modern methods of farming made it possible for the women to run the farms with minimal male help and the result was that farming was no longer the principal occupation for many males.

In order to analyze the distribution of employment, it is first necessary to present facts regarding the age stratification within the hamlets (see Tables 9 and 10 overleaf).[2] According to the official 1931 census of Palestine, eighty-six percent of the Muslim villagers were engaged in agriculture.[3] Figures relating to Arab villages in the State of Israel for 1971 show that sixty-five percent of the males aged twenty-two to thirty-three were fully employed outside the villages, while thirteen percent cultivated their own fields either as a full or part time occupation. Of those between thirty-two and forty-one years old, fifty-nine percent worked full-time outside their villages, while twenty-two percent cultivated their own land. The situation was very different regarding the age group of fifty-one to sixty-three, where forty-three percent tilled their own land; and the age group sixty-two to seventy-one, where seven percent of the males worked outside their villages and fifty-one percent did not work at all.[4]

In 1922 the rural Arab population of Palestine amounted to 66.8 percent of the total Arab population in the country; as

Table 9

Age and Sex Distribution of Hamlet Residents

Age	*Male*	*Female*	*Totals (% Age)*
0-4	167	152	319 (17.2)
5-9	138	125	263 (14.2)
10-14	144	139	283 (15.3)
15-19	110	145	255 (13.8)
20-24	76	79	155 (8.4)
25-29	64	76	140 (7.5)
30-34	56	40	96 (5.2)
35-39	48	44	92 (4.9)
40-44	31	35	66 (3.5)
45-49	18	28	46 (2.5)
50-54	18	15	33 (1.8)
55-59	7	13	20 (1.1)
60-64	8	10	18 (1.0)
65-69	15	17	32 (1.7)
70-74	9	10	19 (1.0)
75-79	7	4	11 (0.6)
80-84	3	0	3 (0.2)
85-89	1	1	2 (0.1)
90-94	0	0	0
95-99	1	0	1 (0.1)
TOTALS	921	933	1,854 (100)

against 67.4 percent in 1931. Until 1941 there was a slight trend toward urbanization. The percentage of the Arab urban population grew from 32.6 to thirty-five percent, while the rural population decreased from 67.4 to sixty-five percent. According to Abramovitz and Guelfat, the percentage of those fully occupied on farms (of the total number of Arab breadwinners) was about fifty-eight percent in 1941, as against sixty percent in 1931.[5] Up to the 1940s there were not many changes in the employment structure outside the villages.

In order to demonstrate the difference between the occupational distribution of hamlet residents during the Mandatory period and 1973, a diachronic summary of the data is presented in Table 10. The data shows that about one hundred heads of nuclear families, representing thirty-five percent of the employed married men have cultivated their land as a full-time job for more than twenty-six years. About the same number of hamlet residents were salaried employees outside the village, ninety-

Table 10

Occupational Data: Married Male Hamlet Residents

Major Occupation(s)	*Number of Years Employed in Present Occupation* Up to 5	6-10	11-25	26 +	Unspecified	TOTALS
Farmer (on own farm)	9.1%	19.2%	27.4%	32.3%	2.0%	35.0% (99)
Farmer (on own farm), also employed outside hamlets	37.9%	17.3%	37.9%	6.9%	–	10.2% (29)
Farmer (on own farm), also self-employed	20.0%	30.0%	30.0%	10.0%	10.0%	3.5% (10)
Salaried employee only	39.8%	37.8%	21.4%	1.0%	–	34.7% (98)
Self-employed only (non-agricultural	44.9%	24.2%	17.2%	10.3%	3.4%	10.2% (29)
Other or unemployed	–	–	–	–	–	6.4% (18)
Total	32.5%	25.1%	27.2%	13.8%	1.4%	100% (283)

eight persons representing 34.7 percent of the total group; to this must be added a second category of those not engaged in agriculture, the twenty-nine self-employed representing 10.2 percent of the total group. Altogether then, nearly forty-five percent of hamlet residents derived no income from farming in 1973.

The self-employed occupy themselves by opening stores or coffee houses, or by doing small-scale contracting work. They are mostly comprised of those too young to have inherited land from their fathers. They define themselves as "only employed" in the sense of not being engaged in farming. These young men help less on the farm than those employed outside the village who have already received their property. When they do come in possession of land they will join the category of farmers who also work outside the village. The dramatic increase in self-employed, non-agricultural work, indicated in Table 10, in the five years preceding the field study, can be mainly attributed to the 1966 economic recession in Israel. Residents realized that as salaried employees they were more vulnerable to national economic trends than if they were self-employed. A number of residents lost their jobs as salaried employees at this time and the lesson seems to have been learned by others as the figures indicate.

An additional 37.9 percent of the total group has done farm work for eleven to twenty-five years as well as working outside the hamlets. The changes in the division of occupation in the decade preceding my fieldwork were due to the transition from extensive to intensive farming. Also important was that housekeeping became facilitated through gadgets, freeing women for farm work.[6] The older sons began to work outside the village but none of the hamlet girls and women were gainfully employed outside as this negatively affected family status. But this was not the accepted view in the neighboring villages where women started going out to agricultural work in nearby Jewish settlements in the late 1950s and early 1960s, due to lack of nearby land.[7]

With the help of irrigation, two or even three successive vegetable crops may be grown instead of one wheat or barley crop, so that the female members of the farmers' families are busy most of the year. For sowing and harvesting, the hamlet residents not only recruit all hands available in their families, but also employ women from villages east of the 1949 Israel-Jordanian Armistice line—preferably from Deir al-Ghusūn and its two other offshoots, and from 'Attīl. Both married and single hamlet women used to work in neighboring Jewish settlements in the 1950s but ceased when intensive methods of cultivation were introduced. Now they work in the hamlets.

Rosenfeld claims that Arab villagers "have been transformed from a village dwelling peasantry to a proletariat living in villages."[8] This is not true of the hamlet residents who work outside and yet live in the village. They take on salaried employment as long as they do not possess any land of their own. Once they inherit their fields, they cultivate them, either full or part-time. Even those who cannot come home every evening, do not relate to their villages as dormitory towns. Their absence has economic reasons. They continue to be concerned with village affairs and consider it their home. While Rosenfeld's description may fit those Arab villages in regions which have lost most of their land, it does not apply to the hamlets.[9]

Table 11 indicates the annual duration of employment for married male residents. Almost all the residents are fully employed throughout the year. Most of the thirty-seven percent working less than ten months per year are either elderly or sickly. Three of them are self-employed, selling olives for preservation. Table 12 shows that more than three-quarters of the residents are satisfied with their present occupation. This is

Table 11

Annual Duration of Employment: Married Male Hamlet Residents (in percentages)

Major Occupation(s)	*Months Employed Per Year* 0-3	4-6	7-9	10-12	Uncertain
Farmer (on own farm)	1.0	2.0	—	61.5	35.5
Farmer, also employed outside hamlets	—	17.2	13.8	37.9	31.1
Farmer, also self-employed	—	—	—	80.0	20.0
Salaried employee only	1.0	2.0	12.0	75.0	10.0
Self-employed only	—	6.2	9.0	78.3	6.5
Other or Unemployed	100	—	—	—	—
Total (283 men)	6.3	3.9	6.7	63.7	19.4

Table 12

Job Satisfaction: Married Male Hamlet Residents

Job Satisfaction	*Number of Men (%)*
Satisfied with present occupation	227 (80.2)
Dissatisfied	
1. Would prefer to be engaged in trade	10 (3.6)
2. Present income insufficient	8 (2.9)
3. Other reasons	22 (7.7)
No information	16 (5.6)
TOTAL	283 (100)

Table 13

Present Occupation: Unmarried Male Hamlet Residents (aged 18 or over)

Occupation	*% of Men*
Farmer	17
Employed outside hamlets	48
Student, not gainfully employed	26
Self-employed	9

perhaps due to the well placed location of the hamlets in relation to work opportunities. Residents do not have to stay overnight near their places of work but can return to their own homes in the evening. Table 13 (overleaf) illustrates the occupational categories among the 101 unmarried men aged eighteen and above, seventy-seven percent of whom are satisfied with their work. Most of them work outside the village in addition to helping their parents in the fields. Five of the twenty-six percent listed as students live abroad, while nine others are accommodated in university or teachers' college dormitories in Israel and only return to their villages during vacation. The remaining twelve are high school students living in their parents' homes.

HISTADRUT MEMBERSHIP

The Histadrut is a trade union roof-organization as well as the owner of industrial and commercial enterprises. After the State, it is the second largest employer in the country, providing health services through a Sick Fund, organizing cultural and social activities, and building large housing projects. At the time of my field work 60.48 percent of the total population of Israel were members of the Histadrut. The percentage for the entire Arab population in Israel was 38.67 percent.[10]

Table 14 shows Histadrut membership in the hamlets according to age groups. Older residents are not inclined to join the organization because few of them are employed outside the village. They are also reluctant to enter any framework that is alien to them in conception and character. There are no

Table 14

Membership in the Histadrut

		Membership Status (in percentages)					
			Non-members				
Informant's Age	*Number of informants*	*Member*	*Not interested*	*No Sick Fund Clinic*	*Health services inadequate*	*Have not thought about it*	*Would like to join but haven't yet*
18-31	86	16	27	34	7	21	11
31-50	132	16	20	35	16	24	5
51 or over	65	–	21	13	10	50	6
All Ages	283	14	21	28	12	30	9

Histadrut members among those over fifty-one years old, while the corresponding figure for those between eighteen and thirty is sixteen percent. About half of the residents in this age group explain this either by indifference to the organization or say that they are not familiar with its functions and role. Some point out the absence of a youth club in the hamlets as a reason for not joining the Histadrut. Also, the Sick Fund arrangements are not to the liking of many residents. They have to travel to another village, Bāqa-al-Gharbīyya, at a distance of about five kilometers. It is not so much the time wasted as the 'loss of face' that is resented. To travel so far is not 'becoming'. It is felt to be humiliating to have to wait to be treated until the staff has finished treating the local residents (of Bāqa al-Gharbīyya). Being forced to wait indicates a lack of social prestige.

The meaning of status in terms of distances that have to be covered is described in a case history in chapter four which shows that the less a wedding party moves away from its residence to meet the other group in exchange marriages, the higher its standing. Still, what the hamlet residents say about the Histadrut should not be taken at face value. Other reasons, not easily disclosed, doubtless exist even if they are not spelled out. As the Histadrut does not restrict its services to employed persons, the self-employed might have been attracted by the guidance provided for farmers and cattle breeders. However, no more than six hamlet residents have joined the Histadrut since October 1975, two of them being Histadrut officials anyway.

LAND LEASES

Details of land leases in the hamlets are given in Table 15 (overleaf). Most contracts were made either with the Land Authority of the Ministry of Agriculture or with local residents. Twenty-one farmers leased a total 245 *dūnams* from the Land Authority, that is about one-third of the entire area leased in the villages; while twenty-four residents leased 201 *dūnams* (twenty-seven percent of the leased area) from non-relatives. Only two villagers leased land from Jewish farmers, one of them a relatively large area of over 100 *dūnams*. The entire area leased from Jewish farmers amounts to twenty-one percent (155 *dūnams*) of the total leased land. About one half of the farmers made contracts with co-residents. Table 16 (overleaf) shows the distribution of leased land according to the size of the area per farmer. Of all peasants leasing land, 77.4 percent hold less than ten

Table 15

Land Leased by Residents

Leased from:	*No. of Persons Leasing*	*Area in dunams*	*Percent of Leased Land*	*Average Size of Landholding*
Government	21	245	33.1	11.7
Related hamlet resident	7	56	7.6	8.0
Hamlet resident, non-relative	24	201	27.3	8.4
Arab from another Israeli village	5	44	8.8	5.9
Arab, West Bank resident	2	23	3.1	11.5
Jewish landowner	2	155	21.0	77.5
No information available	1	15	2.0	15.0
Totals	62	739	100	11.9

Table 16

Distribution of Leased Agricultural Land

Amount of Land Leased (in dūnams)	*Residents Leasing Land (%)*
Up to 5	19 (30.6)
6-10	29 (46.8)
11-20	8 (12.9)
21-50	5 (8.1)
51 or more	1 (1.6)
TOTAL	62 (100)

Table 17

Annual Cost of Leased Agricultural Land: Payment in Currency

Cost Per Dūnam	*Number of Residents (%)*
Less than IL 50	12 (29.3)
IL 50-90	5 (12.2)
IL 100 or more	17 (41.5)
No information	7 (17.1)
TOTAL	41 (100)

Table 18

Annual Cost of Leased Agricultural Land: Payment Partly in Kind

Annual Cost	*Residents Leasing Land (%)*
Less than 33% of produce	3 (14.3)
33% of produce	3 (14.3)
40% of produce	3 (14.3)
50% of produce	9 (42.8)
No information	3 (14.3)
TOTAL	21 (100)

dūnams. The amounts and kinds of payment involved are shown in Tables 17 and 18. Traditionally, Arabs used to lease not for money but only to receive in kind. Land leased from the Authorities and Jewish owners is paid for in money and this is influencing land lease arrangements between Arabs. Farmers in both categories leased the land together with the water supply required for cultivation.

Cohen says that "the almost complete absence of tenancy and leasehold, which featured highly in the pre-1949 village economy," is characteristic of the new agriculture in most Triangle villages.[11] He ascribes this to the liquidation of large landholdings. It is probable that increased employment opportunities outside the villages played a part in the change, often providing better income than could be obtained from cultivating land. Cohen argues that farmers find it difficult to give up the independence that goes with working the land and thus prefer leases though they may work harder than salaried employees. Also, they like to be close to their nuclear family and their *ḥamūla*. Although farming may not always provide a high income and the vicissitudes of the climate may play havoc with one's efforts, a minimum income is at all times ensured. Wage earners, on the other hand, are inevitably much more dependent on the general economic situation.[12]

DISTRIBUTION OF IRRIGATION WATER

Irrigation was introduced in 1958 and has especially helped those whose land holdings are small. Until then, they often worked outside the village; now they lease land from those who have land to spare. Irrigation means that less soil is required to support a family than with extensive farming. Some farmers do not have a large enough water allocation for all their fields, so they lease their surplus, either for cash or payment in kind. Preference is usually given to farm produce from the leased land. Where there is a shortage of water, intensive agriculture is not possible. The majority of farmers in the hamlets are allotted less water than they need. As a result land can be leased at fairly low rates, as farmers want to make at least some profit out of land they cannot cultivate intensively. Sometimes a man who takes out a lease does not have a high enough water quota for the additional land and turns to yet another farmer to lease water; the soil is leased from one source and the water from another.

Table 19

Irrigation Water Quotas

	Land Area Under Intensive Cultivation (dūnams)						
	0	*1-2*	*3-5*	*6-10*	*11-15*	*16+*	*Total*
No. of Persons	9	4	9	26	10	36	94
	(9.6)	(4.2)	(9.6)	(27.7)	(10.6)	(38.3)	(100)
Water Allocation	45	16	42	125	56	290	574
(in 1,000 cubic meters)	(7.8)	(2.7)	(7.3)	(21.7)	(9.7)	(50.5)	(100)
Average Allocation per Person (in 1,000 cubic meters)	5.0	4.0	4.7	4.8	5.6	8.0	6.1
Estimated Allocation per *dūnam* (in 1,000 cubic meters)	—	2.7	1.2	0.6	0.4	0.4	—

Table 20

Irrigation Water Allocations

Area Under Intensive	*Water Allocation (in 1,000 cubic meters)*								
Cultivation (dūnams)	*0*	*1-2*	*3-4*	*5-6*	*7-8*	*9-10*	*11-15*	*16+*	*Total*
0	—	1	1	6	—	1	—	—	9
1-2	3	1	—	3	—	—	—	—	7
3-5	9	—	3	6	—	—	—	—	18
6-10	8	2	4	17	1	1	1	—	34
11-15	—	—	1	7	1	1	—	—	10
16 or more	3	—	1	18	3	6	5	3	39
TOTAL	23	4	10	57	5	9	6	3	117

The average quantity of water required per *dūnam* in one season is 500 cubic meters for intensive cultivation. If this area is sowed twice annually, only 400 cubic meters are needed each time. Greenhouses, which are becoming a common feature in the hamlets, require 1,000 cubic meters per *dūnam*.[13] Table 19 indicates the number of landless peasants allotted water and should be compared with Table 20, showing the number of landowners not receiving any water. Nine peasants were allotted 45,000 cubic meters of water in 1972-3 without possessing any land suited for intensive agriculture though they might own olive orchards on hilly terrain. Four farmers who have between one and two *dūnams* of land each received 16,000 cubic meters. Peasants possessing between three and five *dūnams* were allocated 42,000 cubic meters. Table 20 shows that twenty-three hamlet residents received no water allocation at all, though they own considerable areas of land. Three of them have more than sixteen *dūnams*; eight have between six and ten *dūnams*; nine have between three and five *dūnams*, while three possess no more than one or two *dūnams*.

Some of the farmers receive a water allocation though they do not own land, while others own land but have not been allocated a water allowance. The following case histories illustrate arrangements residents made between themselves. One member of the Ibn Sina *ḥamūla*, with a water allocation of more than 20,000 cubic meters, leased twenty-one *dūnams* from someone residing outside the hamlets whose fields are adjacent to those of the hamlet residents. A member of the Abū Bader *ḥamūla* lives in one household with his three wives, their ten children and his mother. He secured 6,000 cubic meters of water from another resident in return for one fourth of his total agricultural produce. Ahmad leased seven *dūnams* from a neighbor paying IL 150 (Israeli Lirot) per *dūnam*, and secured water from another hamlet resident. He took out a three year lease from a Jewish settler who pays half of the expenses of cultivation. Ahmad retains the sole right to work the land, giving one half of the produce to the landowner.[14] His wife and teenaged children undertake the farm work while he works as a tractor mechanic in a neighboring Jewish settlement. He considers himself a farmer though he rarely does agricultural work. Rashīd 'Attīlī leased ten *dūnams* for two years, paying IL 150 per *dūnam* in advance every year. Such leasing arrangements have advantages for both sides and allow the leasee to plan his cultivation programme.

The plain north of Ibthān has not yet been connected with the general irrigation system. Until June 1967, the plain was cultivated without irrigation. After the Six Day War the inhabitants of Ibthān purchased water from the village of 'Attīl which had, until then, been outside the Israeli borders. Four wells in the vicinity of fields lying close to Ibthan were owned by 'Attīl villagers charged their Ibthān neighbors IL 14 per hour for their water, permitting sixty sprinklers to be operated simultaneously—using ninety cubic meters per hour. Each sprinkler used up to 1.5 cubic meters per hour, thus, they had to pay IL 0.15 per cubic meter of water from the 'Attīl wells, as contrasted with the cost of IL 0.06 for water from the national water line. Nevertheless, the peasants found that it was worth their while to pay almost three times the official price for irrigation water in order to be able to cultivate their land intensively.

With the availability of water, the economic situation of the hamlet of Ibthān greatly improved for almost all residents. Although the elimination of the border prevented smuggling which had, until the War, been one of the sources of income for a few hamlet residents, irrigation now made possible the raising of two or three vegetable crops every year. Without intensive cultivation methods only wheat and barley had been planted, yielding just one crop a year. The development of the plain north of Ibthān after the Six Day War may be compared with that of the western plain in the late 1950s and early 1960s when irrigation water first became available in the hamlets.

Once it had been decided to make irrigation water available to the hamlets, the Ministry of Agriculture conducted a survey to be used as a basis for the distribution of water resources among the peasants.[15] The Ministry defined a farmer as someone deriving his livelihood only from agriculture and possessing at least thirty *dūnams* of land and those so defined were eligible for a water allocation of 5,000 cubic meters. This policy caused a large number of complaints to be addressed to the authorities. It was argued by some of the residents that they had to live on incomes derived from agriculture even though they owned less than thirty *dūnams*. In addition they pointed to the fact that some of the residents had been granted a water allocation even though their land ownings were below the stipulated area of thirty *dūnams*. Some of these farmers, who had received a water allocation, also earned good money outside the hamlets. They were self-employed construction contractors or owners of businesses. Others worked for wages at well paid jobs. Also the introduction of cultivation under plastic ground coverings (see plates) required an adjustment of the water allocation policy. Those farmers who owned thirty *dūnams* or more could not utilize all of the area they possessed, since this new agricultural technique did not allow them to make use of more than eight or ten *dūnams*.

As a result the Ministry of Agriculture had to modify its policy and change the criteria of eligibility—reducing the area required for water allocation from thirty to fifteen *dūnams* per unit of 5,000 cubic meters of water, increasing the number of recognized farmers considerably. The stipulation that no farmer should take on paid employment was dropped. By 1971-72, even peasants owning less than ten *dūnams* possessed full water rights. In addition, the previously stipulated rate of 5,000 cubic meters per *dūnam* was increased to 6,000 and the authorities were contemplating a quota of 8,000 cubic meters per *dūnam* to encourage farmers to cultivate fields and increase agricultural produce.

A member of the Abū Bader family was the first to build a greenhouse for cucumbers and tomatoes in the area. He realized that this method was more profitable for growing certain crops than that of covering the vegetables with plastic material (for details see appendix B). The quantity of vegetables raised on an area of four *dūnams* in greenhouses could only be obtained by working ten *dūnams* with the method of covering the vegetables with plastic material.

The importance of water distribution cannot be overestimated. In Israel, water is a scarce commodity, especially in rural settlements. Whoever controls the water supply possesses power, both economic and political. The quantity of water put at a man's disposal determines the profitability of his fields. Any excess supply of water will enable him to 'help' others who have not received a sufficient quota, political support being gained from those who require this scarce commodity essential to their economic success.

WATER COOPERATIVES

The application of modern agricultural methods depends to a large extent on the availability of water. Where water is not abundant, distribution must be organized. Cooperatives seemed the right method, especially as the Arab rural population is familiar with this way of providing services and commodities since the days of the British Mandatory Government.[16]

Cooperatives proliferated after 1948 and even more so after 1956. Then, as now, the motivation was not to implement Socialist ideology as in the Jewish sector, but mere expediency. Cooperatives were judged an effective method of providing services. There are about 120 Arab cooperatives registered with the Ministry of Labor. They are supervised by the Arab Department of the Histadrut, operate in more than seventy villages and have over 12,000 members.[17] Organization of water supplies though cooperatives offers many advantages. Water is obtained at more favorable rates than for the individual and contacts with the authorities are smoother.[18] Furthermore, cooperatives reduce the number of outlets from the central water line. This is important since numerous outlets tend to reduce the water pressure.

There are four drinking and four irrigation water cooperatives in the hamlets. In addition, five outlets from the central pipeline are used by farmers who are not members of any cooperative. These private outlets are very much in demand and cause a great deal of rivalry among the residents, and among cooperative members in particular. It also happens that applicants are refused membership, usually after they have criticized or opposed heads of cooperatives.

The first three irrigation water cooperatives were organized on the lines of *ḥamūla* affiliation. Non-members are sometimes supplied with water if the heads of the cooperatives expect them to join the organization at a later date. This creates a 'debt', to be discharged later through support of the sponsors who in this way are helped to retain their key positions in the cooperative. These sponsors possess considerable political power. They have access to the water resources and dominate part of their distribution, enjoying both status and political power. Any resident with a private outlet is a threat to the leaders of the cooperatives for he can muster political support through the supply of water and in this way reduce the power of the heads of the cooperative. There is one significant difference between elected cooperative heads and suppliers who have a private outlet—the latter do not have to be elected, their power depending entirely on the needs of people for water. There is almost no limitation to the exercise of this power since they do not have to stand for election.

The cooperatives have known a great deal of internal strife and political tension which has led to splits. In 1967 the weaker section of the Yazīd *ḥamūla* decided to establish its own cooperative called *'Adel* (justice) and successfully canvassed for members among the dissatisfied of other cooperatives. The existence of *'Adel* touched off further requests for private outlets from the general water line. A member of the Qarūm family received an outlet from the central pipe. In turn, he undertook to provide several families with the water they required. This action resulted in an accumulation of political power to the extent that he could compete with the heads of the cooperatives, whose sway over others had the same basis. An additional outlet means that the farmer who has secured it, can supply water to whoever he sees fit and on his own terms. This makes possible the setting up of factions held together by economic interests.

The significant role that the distribution of water plays in the region is evident. Control over the supply of water is a powerful weapon that may cause dissension bringing with it a new foci of political power. Internal political strife within the *ḥamūla* increases and the power of factions not organized on *ḥamūla* lines grows. This trend is also due to changes of occupation. When numerous members of the *ḥamūla* work outside the hamlet, its functions do not remain the same, for it no longer organizes mutual economic aid. There is growing opposition to cooperatives organized by *ḥamūlas*. Some think it preferable to entrust the Regional Council with the task of regulating water supplies and collecting fees. Inevitably, the heads of the cooperatives do their best to discourage any move to liquidate their organization.

There is also a cooperative producing olive oil. It operates only during the picking season and is poorly managed. The Registrar of Cooperatives in the Ministry of Labor has repeatedly considered liquidating it because of its bad management but so far no decision has been made.[19]

LIVESTOCK

Eight hamlet farmers own a total of 260 sheep, while three farmers collectively own forty-eight cows. Only one farmer raises chickens and ducks, and there are no more than seven horses and two mules in all four hamlets. As intensive agriculture has replaced traditional methods of farming, pasture for livestock is no longer available. There is an acute shortage of shepherds in the hamlets. The job of shepherd is not only badly paid but ties a person to his flock for long hours. In the past, children worked as shepherds in addition to handicapped or old persons who lacked the physical strength for farming before modern methods of cultivation were introduced. Now the Bill of Compulsory Education keeps children in the classroom most of the day and provides additional frameworks for them after the lessons and in the vacations.

It is interesting to note that nomads accord a higher status to shepherds than rural populations. Sedentary groups depend chiefly on the fields for their livelihood, while flocks only provide a supplementary income. For the nomads they are a valuable possession which they can take along from one site to another. A Bedouin will invest in flocks whenever he possesses the financial means. In the hamlets, full employment further reduces the number of persons who are prepared to work as shepherds.[20]

A case history illustrates the situation. One of the farmers in the hamlets owns more than thirty head of cattle and sixty sheep, but is unable to act as shepherd since he is physically handicapped, walking with a heavy limp. Both his sons refused to undertake the care of the livestock. They are building workers employed in Tel Aviv and not inclined to forego their wages. Their motive, however, is not only financial. They are simply not prepared to take on work that is considered humiliating and which would lower their status. The head of the family finally solved the problem by hiring a shepherd from one of the West Bank villages. In the light of this difficulty it is not surprising that thirty-eight farmers no longer keep any cattle or sheep while eleven others had sheep in the past which they were forced to sell because of the lack of available manpower.

OCCUPATIONAL CHANGES AND ATTITUDE TO VILLAGE

Two thirds of the population no longer work in the hamlets, or at least not only there. Of this group, one half depends entirely on agriculture, and the other half works for wages outside the village but help in the fields after their outside work.

Salaried employees such as teachers and officials have many informal and formal contracts with non-villagers. Their view of the world outside and their relations with it are different from those of the farmers whose life is entirely village centered. Even a teacher employed in the local school meets numerous outsiders and unlike the other residents, belongs to a bureaucratic organization with a well defined hierarchy. The younger, qualified men, often enter into social relations with their Jewish Israeli co-workers and become familiar with the basic values and customs of a modern non-agrarian society. They encounter stratified communities, encompassing political and social structures hitherto unknown to them, and this exposure is reflected in their changing living habits. All this is in sharp contrast to the older residents employed (usually in unskilled work) outside their village. They have limited formal contact with non-villagers and almost no informal relations with them.

Those most exposed to outside influences are inevitably the best educated. Formal education makes it easy for them to keep up informal contacts with persons outside their narrowly confined village community. The numbers of young men (and women) who possess a high school education are on the increase. universities attract many students and once a person is trained to take on a well paid job, he often prefers it to farm work. The students do not, however, become estranged from their rural environment but use their new knowledge to help it. For instance, many acquire teacher training qualifications and later work locally. Such an attitude indicates that the younger generation will not desert the villages but adjust to changing conditions.

The interviews and informal talks the author has had with Arab white-collar workers indicate that their work outside the village, in the services or professions, has not led to an alienation from rural society. They feel close to the hamlets and see no reason why they should desert their homes and heritage. It is natural that they seek work for which they are qualified through education and this means working outside the village. Their economic independence has greatly modified their pattern of life. No longer do they depend on their fathers' for a choice of marriage partner but choose with an eye to achieved rather than ascribed status. Perhaps the most important change that the new conditions have brought to the hamlets is that the *ḥamūla* is no longer the only framework for economic and political activities on which the loyalties of the residents are concentrated.

Changes in the economic situation bring about changes in the social structure of society. It is to these changes that the following chapters are devoted. Marriage patterns, the relationship with the nuclear family, and the status and role of woman which is the focus of this work, will be the main areas of discussion.

NOTES

1. Abner Cohen, *Arab Border Villages in Israel: A Study of Community and Change in a Social Organization* (Manchester England: Manchester University Press, 1965), p. 19.

2. All data in Table 9 are based on my census, February 1974 (see chapter 1).

3. Zev Abramovitz and Itzhak Guelfat, *The Arab Economy* (Tel Aviv: Hakibbutz Hameuhad, 1944), pp. 29-30. Of the Christian villagers, seventy-three percent were farmers, while twenty-seven percent were otherwise employed.

4. Israel, Central Bureau of Statistics, Census of Agriculture, 1971 (Jerusalem, 1973, Manpower Employment Series, No. 2).

5. Abramovitz and Guelfat, pp. 24-30.

6. Cohen, p. 22.

7. Ibid., p. 39.

8. Henry Rosenfeld, "From Peasantry to Wage Labor and Residual Peasantry: The Transformation of an Arab Village," in *Process and Pattern in Culture: Essays in Honor of Julian Steward*, ed. Robert A. Manners (Chicago: Aldine, 1964) p. 229.

9. See Cohen, p. 20.

10. See Executive Body, Histadrut Budget Proposal for 1974 (Tel Aviv: Va'ad Hapo'el, 1974) p. 6.

11. Cohen, p. 33.

12. Ibid., pp. 33-34.

13. Data concerning water allocations (Table 19 and 20) were obtained through questionnaires (see appendix A) and personal statements from each peasant, verified by the *mu'atamads*.

14. Regarding payment in kind for the leasing of land in the Negev, Marx says: "When the landowner supplies the land, implements and draught animals, the sharecropprs as a rule get fifty percent of the grain. If the owner has provided the seeds as well, he first subtracts the quantity supplied from the net harvest and the grain is then measured out in equal shares." Emanuel Marx, *Bedouin of the Negev* (Manchester, England: Manchester University Press, 1967), p. 197.

15. Personal communication from Yoel Shohat, Ministry of Agriculture in Hadera.

16. Viteles gives a detailed description of Arab cooperatives during the British Mandatory Government. See Harry Viteles, *A History of the Cooperative Movement in Israel* (London: Vallentine and Mitchell, 1966) Vol. 1.

17. Michael Fadidah, *Arab Cooperation: Socio-Economic Study* (Tel Aviv: Israeli Institute for Research and Information, 1972) p. 32.

18. My thanks to Yair Yaqir, Office of the Registrar of Cooperatives, Ministry of Labor, for explaining the organization of water supplies in the hamlets.

19. Letter from Registrar of Cooperatives, dated November 21, 1972 (Israel Ministry of Labor, File No. 1689), addressed to all nineteen members of the cooperative "El Baraka" stating the Registrar's intention to liquidate the cooperative. At a general meeting in Bir al-Sikke on 21 November, members persuaded the Registrar and the Histadrut representatives to allow its operation to continue.

20. Cohen observes a similar situation. See Cohen, pp. 36-37.

4

Marriage Patterns

Special attention has been paid to marriage patterns in the hamlets. The data presented here however, does not confirm the findings of other studies of Middle Eastern societies that marriage between first patrilateral parallel cousins, that is the father's brother's daughter (FBD), is preferred and serves as a paradigm for all marriages. I have found it advisable to observe and analyze other patterns of marriage, as I believe that choices are determined by numerous factors combining to form various configurations.

Two main categories may be distinguished: in-group and out-group marriages. The term 'in-group marriage' is used for unions within the descent group. Accordingly, FBD is classified as a sub-category of in-group marriage. Findings in the present study indicate that FBD should be viewed as being part of a wider framework, that of the entire descent group. The second category, out-group marriages, includes unions between different descent groups within the village as well as with residents of other communities. My fieldwork points to the existence of a further sub-category, that of marriage between members of different descent groups whose parents own adjoining fields. This marriage pattern is really a variation of the sub-category mentioned above, husband and wife are members of different descent groups but possess an additional characteristic. They share economic interests due to the vicinity of their property. This has become particularly significant since the introduction of irrigation which encourages cooperation between owners of neighboring fields.

Marriage patterns will be analyzed on the assumption that they are much more complex in character than is usually claimed, and that they must be categorized. The main categories used by other researchers are not adequate enough to classify the data collected here. It is common in Arab villages for brothers to live close to each other, or more precisely, in the vicinity of their parental home. More often than not, they inherit adjoining fields. Thus, a marriage may have been contracted that belongs to the sub-category of children of owners of adjoining fields, but the bride and the groom may at the same time be patrilateral parallel cousins. Yet being cousins has not been decisive in determining their marriage, though statistically it will be classified as FBD. Most scholars take the view that FBD marriage is preferred but their explanations as to why this is so vary. Before presenting an analysis of the marriage patterns in the hamlets it is first necessary to briefly review the literature on this topic.

ALLEGED RIGHT TO MARRY FBD

The author agrees with Keyser that FBD marriage is of "inconclusive nature", to be explained by one factor or by a combination of several factors as part of a wider range of marriage patterns or as an independent phenomenon.[1] Scholars living at the turn of the century usually emphasized the right of a man to marry his FBD (bint 'amm).[2] Baldensperger writes that the first cousin has rights against which all other claims cannot be upheld[3]; and Granqvist quotes a proverb according to which a cousin may take down a girl already sitting on the bridal camel so as to marry her.[4] Canaan, Musil and others refer to the same proverb to support the argument that FBD marriage is preferred.[5]

Scholars of the 1950s, such as Patai and Barth take this view for granted.[6] Patai claims that preference and right go together, pointing out that preference may exist without right, but right (in this context) depends on preference. Some writers, such as Luṭfīyya, Khuri and Kressel, define FBD marriage as a preferred pattern, as do Murphy and Kasdan. Others, such as Rosenfeld, Peters, Abou Zeid, Cohen, Marx and Barth refer to the right to marry one's FBD.[7] Cohen points out that FBD marriage is "regarded as axiomatic" in the culture, though de facto it is often avoided.[8] Black-Michaud's remarks may explain the point at issue. He speaks of "the potential flexibility of systems which, at the ideological level, appear perfectly rigid and predicate clean cut distinctions," but "portend a wide discrepancy between the stated norm and the observable fact."[9] It is easy to be hoodwinked about the actual situation for informants always tend to stress norms and insist on ideology, disregarding deviations. Black-Michaud goes on to explain that there is a "familiar dichotomy between the folk image and the model constructed by the anthropologist," a warning to be heeded.[10]

EXPLANATIONS FOR ALLEGED FBD PREFERENCE

A much disputed point is the alleged economic advantage the family derives from FBD marriage. The Quran (4:12) stipulates that a daughter has the right to one half of the share inherited by her brother upon their father's death. This property, Granqvist says and Rosenfeld agrees, would be lost to a woman's natal family upon marriage to a non-relative.[11] It should be noted that in most Arab rural communities daughters only inherit land when no sons are available. The Quran Law is thus irrelevant.

Barth's explanation, gives priority to political rather than economic factors. He maintains that FBD marriage solidifies "the minimal lineage as a corporate group in functional struggle . . . and serves to reinforce the political implications of the lineage system."[12] Aswad claims that "the closest alliance one can have is with one's brother against a rival brother."[13] Her claim seems rather inconclusive as there is no reason to assume that there is always strife between brothers.

Murphy and Kasdan stress the social structure and functional considerations in the non-political sphere. Their attitude is best summed up in their statement that "parallel cousin marriage contributes to the extreme fission of agnatic lines . . . and . . . encysts the patrilineal segments."[14] Peters, in observing the Bedouin, quotes the saying: "Marry your paternal cousins and both your paternal and maternal relatives will be one."[15] An agnate who is also a mother's brother cannot be compared to one to whom one is not otherwise related.[16] Randolph, explaining FBD marriages by a theory of Bedouin endogamy, notes that "a man who is both a patrilateral and a matrilateral uncle to a boy, is very likely to give him a daughter."[17]

Antoun cites four functions of the FBD type of marriage, one of which he considers specifically "structural":

> If the dispute be within the lineage, this complication serves to define the lines of division; if the dispute involves other lineages the complication serves to intensify the bonds among close patrilineal kinsmen . . .[18]

Goldberg, whose study deals with a Jewish immigrant community settlement in Israel, the residents coming from Tripoli in Libya, explains FBD marriage with that expected "by chance alone, taking into consideration demographic characteristics of the community." He then compares the results by applying the formal mathematical model of Gilbert and Hammel.[19] Goldberg indicates that the rate of FBD marriage would be higher if a larger number of suitable female candidates were available.

Khuri chooses to explain FBD marriage psychologically, as a contribution to "harmonious family relations."[20] Nakhleh finds this argument plausible, because FBD marriage, by not adding new relationships, decreases the prospects of conflict. He quotes his own father who said that in FBD marriage the son's wife would behave like a daughter rather than like a daughter-in-law.[21] Khuri also mentions the Oedipus complex theory in explanation of FBD marriage.[22] Westermarck holds the opposite view and insists on the element of "sexual shame . . . in the presence of a member of his (or her) own family circle."[23] He goes as far as to conclude that marital relationships between cousins in the close-knit Arab family are contrary to human nature. This is an interesting discrepancy of views, for while Khuri assumes that close family ties make relations between husband and wife more harmonious, Westermarck thinks that familiarity reduces mutual sexual attraction and causes indifference to the partner who is almost taken for granted. In a marriage union between close relatives, the young woman is not usually separated from her family of origin and need not part from her accustomed environment. This continuity of existence gives the woman a sense of emotional security in her family of reproduction. Keyser argues that exogamy, being "insecure and undefended is to endogamy which is secure and defended, as endogamy which is insecure and undefended (incest) is to security maintained by virtue of nonexogamy or marriage to the nearest non-incestuous kin."[24]

Some scholars have chosen the cultural approach to explain alleged preference for FBD marriage. Patai considers FBD a "cultural" phenomenon, implying that no further explanation is required.[25] Goldberg explains that preference for FBD marriage is only one element in a system of "cultural rules" relating to the selection of a marriage partner.[26] He adds that this includes both kinship orientated and nonkinship rules. Kressel, in his study of a sedentarized Bedouin community, concludes that FBD marriage is a cultural symbol of prestige.[27] He claims that in the Middle East, endogamy is no more than a tradition, a man might point out that his grandfather and father were married to their FBD's, and his son as well. Kressel defines this as a cultural trait and elaborates on its significance.[28] Another aspect suggested by him is that endogamy is "connected . . . with the general conception of sexual relationships in which the male is the active partner. . . The sexual act is grasped symbolically as an offensive act. Sex is violence in the understanding of intra-communal, inter-groupal relationships of marriage."[29] Marriage does not, Kressel thinks, automatically harmonize family relations. He also believes that "the mere use of a cultural symbol" . . . is an "expression of intra-communal aggression."[30]

Peters, in choosing an ecological approach which does not aim at explaining FBD preference only, shows how cousin marriage, like all other patterns of marriage, helps "weaving ties" in different directions.[31] In other words, marriages build alliances which are especially important in desert and rural societies. Marx distinguishes between groups living on the plain and others residing in hilly regions, noticing that these two types of population show different frequencies for FBD marriage.[32] He also analyzes marriage pattern data on other levels such as Bedouin versus peasant populations living among the Bedouin; large versus small groups, and population segments defined by political interests. He correlates these with geographical locations of residence and concludes that Bedouin and peasants differ in respect of FBD marriages as do large and small groups. He finds that "in some cases sections deliberately refrained from contracting possible [FBD] matches."[33]

A variety of explanations have been given for FBD marriage, ranging from Luṭfīyya's belief that marrying a close relative promises more understanding husbands,[34] to Patai's argument that economic and psychological factors lead to FBD marriage.[35] Antoun proposed a combination of economic, political and structural functions,[36] and Nakhleh explains FBD marriage by various factors, including property control and psychological reasons, as well as religious and legal ones.[37]

So far, different opinions have been cited on two planes, that of right and that of preference. Most authors agree on preference for FBD but as stated earlier, the causes vary and are almost never identical. Right is an option to be taken or rejected. One need not make use of it but one is free to claim it. The question is, whether this right exists only on the plane of ideology or whether it can be translated into fact whenever desired. This can be investigated. If preference is shown by a high percentage of FBD marriages, it may be said that the right is realized. It will be seen later, however, that this is not the case, indicating that both right and preference exist in terms of ideology. (Lévi-Strauss prefers the term "prescriptive" to that of right). As to preference, he says "it has long been known that societies which advocate marriage between certain types of kin adhere to the norm only in a small number of cases."[38] He uses the term 'preferential' "to describe any system in which . . . the proportion of marriages between a certain type of real or classificatory relative is higher than where it is the result of chance, whether the members of the group are aware of this or not."[39]

The very variety of explanation is in itself proof that no simple and unambiguous answer exists. Ayoub considers FBD marriage one of many manifestations of a preference for in-group marriages. She argues that anyone 'naturally' prefers to marry within the kin group. This would make preference for FBD marriage an epiphenomenon of marriages in the wider range of the total kin group. Accordingly, Ayoub redefines the term *ibn 'amm* to suit her theory and her claim that it covers "all age peers in the kin group."[40] Gilbert and Hammel agree with Ayoub and stress that "high rates of FBD marriages . . . derive from preference other than a specific one. . ."[41] Hammel and Goldberg emphasize that FBD marriage is no more than "one variety of a set of marriages."[42] The FBD then is turned into a sub-type of in-group marriage. Rosenfeld has constructed a scale of degrees of preferences. He lists them in the following order: ". . . within one's clan, if possible to one's first paternal cousin . . . otherwise . . . a villager or a stranger bride. . ."[43] According to Rosenfeld, FBD has top priority and only when it is ruled out, will another choice be contemplated.

There is no proof that FBD marriage is preferred to one with second or third cousins. Hamlet residents gave specific reasons for each marriage. No case was identical with another, though there were of course, common features helping to categorize the marriages according to patterns. The same situation suggests itself with regard to out-group marriages. If out-group marriage was selected, there was no evident preference for marriage partners living within the same village over those living elsewhere, or *vice-versa*. It is expedient, for the purpose of analysis, to divide marriages into two broad categories, in-group and out-group, and to further subdivide each. The out-group marriage category consists of those involving partners from the same village and those with partners from different villages or towns. In-group marriages include, as already stated, FBD marriage.

PROPOSED EVALUATION OF MARRIAGE PATTERNS

The analysis of data on actual marriage partner selection made by the hamlet residents is based on a two-part approach. The results of each part are subsequently correlated. The first part involves a descriptive model derived, in part, from the work of Winch, Goode, Peres and Schrift.[44] The second part involves a methodological innovation in the handling and tabulating of marriage pattern data: marriages are divided according to carefully determined time-period units. This method, unlike that used in most other studies in this field, does not treat the entire chronological sequence of marriage patterns as a single statistical block, but is based on a new approach with regard to time-period subdivisions.

Before presenting methodological details, additional interpretive bases and background data will be noted. In Arab rural society it is not the individual (neither male nor female) but the family that is responsible for the marriage choice. Furthermore, the male's relatives usually open the marriage negotiations. Considerable influence is also exerted by the descent group and the village community. The ideological norms, as well as actual behavior, of the individuals involved in an Arab hamlet marriage are not entirely "individually" determined. The entire cultural context in which the couples live must be recognized.

THE MODEL

The model is based on the assumption that a partner in marriage is chosen from a "pool"[45] of suitable candidates.[46] The process of selection begins by considering all candidates available as possible marriage partners for the person in question. This "field of possibilities"[47] is then narrowed, until a list of *bona fide* candidates (the pool of candidates) emerges. One or more families are often approached with a proposal of marriage for one of its members. The elimination process takes place in three distinct phases, each on the strength of different criteria. The "field of possibilities" is defined by laws and regulations and other non-personal factors such as hostile borders, geographical distances and movement restrictions imposed by military governments. Each of these comes into play in marriage partner selection among the Arab hamlet population.

The "field of eligibles" is formed according to personal (primarily culturally determined) preferences. It consists of candidates

Figure 5
The "Field of Eligibles"

A — Persons with elementary education
B — Persons aged 17 to 23
C — Residents of same village
The FIELD OF ELIGIBLES

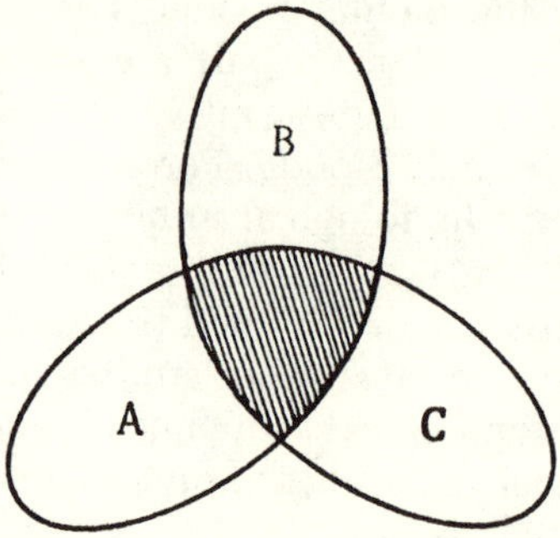

from the "field of possibilities" who possess the resources, qualifications and character traits required. Incest taboos and prohibitions of marriage with a partner not belonging to one's religious community must also be taken into consideration. If, for example, a family expects a candidate to have a full elementary school education (a relatively recent addition to selection criteria in the hamlets) as well as to be in the age group of seventeen to twenty-three, and a resident of the same village, the "field of eligibles" may be conceptualized as the area of overlap of three criterion-based population segments (see figure 5). Taking into consideration only the demands of the individual who seeks a marriage partner, the "field of eligibles" represents the final list of all suitable candidates. One additional selective factor must also be accounted for in the model. Since marriages can officially only be contracted with the mutual consent of

a — The "Field of Possibilities"
b — The "Field of Eligibles"
c — The "Field of Consenters"
The POOL OF CANDIDATES

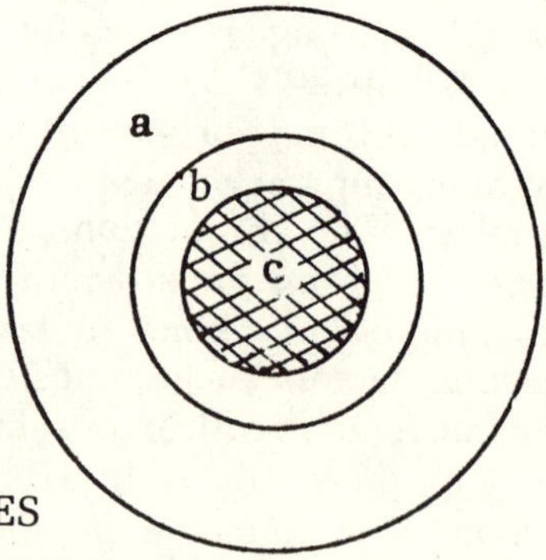

Figure 6
The "Pool of Candidates"

both parties, "the field of consenters" narrows the range even further.[48] Stated simply, the potential candidate has to be willing to marry the individual in question. The pool of candidates is the result of the process of elimination and represents the list of actual marriage candidates. It corresponds with the "field of consenters," represented by the smallest of three concentric circles (see figure 6).

The structure of the three sets of fields determines which will influence the field of candidates most. Prospects depend on who ultimately enters the pool of candidates, rather than who falls within the "field of eligibles." Actually, only the composition of the pool of candidates is relevant regarding the prospect of marriage. The model assumes that the population under study is constant with regard to distribution of the relevant attributes, though there is a possibility of modifications as a result of changes in one or more fields.[49] Changes in the pool of candidates may occur due to changes in the "field of possibilities" and/or eligibles, and/or consenters, or as a result of laws and restrictions, or the removal of hostile frontiers and subsequent renewed contacts. All these affect the three fields including the pool of candidates.

Most researchers show the frequency of first patrilateral cousin marriage by presenting gross statistical data. That is they collect all data on marriages up to a specified point in time, usually beginning with the oldest living person in the society under study, and divide the total numbers into different marriage pattern categories. Generally, this then illustrates the proportion of FBD (and/or all in-group) marriages versus out-group marriages. Marx presents details on five different Arab communities where the highest percentage of first patrilateral parallel cousin marriage is fourteen percent and the average approximately twelve percent.[50] The highest percentage in Marx's example of total in-group marriages is 33.7 percent, and the average approximately thirty percent.[51] Khuri reports that FBD marriage among Muslims in the community studied by him amounted to eleven percent,[52] while Antoun reports a percentage of fifteen.[53] Similar figures are presented in Table 21 (overleaf). The percentage of patrilateral cousin marriages for the hamlets is 14.2 percent; that of the total of in-group marriages 38.9 percent; and 61.1 percent for out-group marriages.

The system of analyzing marriage pattern data synchronically cannot be applied satisfactorily to data referring to the past. The circumstances in which marriages were contracted in the past

Table 21
Distribution of Marriages by Category

Category	In-group		Out-group		
	FBD	*Other*	*Within Hamlets*	*Outside Hamlets*	*Total Marriages*
No. of Marriages	45 (14.2%)	78 (24.7%)	97 (30.7%)	96 (30.4%)	
Totals	123 (38.9%)		193 (61.1%)		316 (100%)

differ significantly from those contracted in the hamlets at the present time, and this significant fact should not be overlooked. In the course of an extended period changes occur within any given society which will, in turn, influence the "field of candidates" and the "field of possibilities." Such changes inevitably influence the "field of eligibles" and of course, the actual pool of candidates.

In a number of studies, variations of the traditional statistical approach have been attempted. Cuisenier was the first to arrange marriage pattern data according to periods. He divided the total period of his study into three sub-periods determined by external events. The first sub-period was from 1938 to 1944; the second began after the Second World War and ends when the parcelling of the territory into plots was undertaken; while the third terminated with the introduction of the Protectorate in the North African community he studied. Cuisenier initiated a new methodological approach while at the same time remaining faithful to the traditional practice of emphasizing changes, or their absence, in the frequency of FBD marriages. A conspicuous characteristic of his approach was that he deemed the external changes, used to divide the total time span into periods, not specific to the one group under study but felt, instead, that they were shared by other communities in the same region. He then analyzed the pattern of parallel cousin marriages and found no changes in the proportion of such marriages in the different sub-periods.[54] It is argued here that the time period divisions should be specific to the community under study and determined by events that are of importance to it.

The system employed by Chelhood is based on a division of his sample into generations: above the age of sixty-five, between forty-five and sixty-five, between twenty-five and forty-five, and below twenty-five.[55] Aswad applies the same divisions but concludes that the results do not correspond with those of Cuisinier or Chelhood, since "polygny and parallel cousin marriage are directly correlated according to status, yet within a status level, there is no necessary direct relationship."[56] She adds ". . . that one of the highest periods of parallel cousin marriage followed a period of feuding over the division of lands during the sedentarization period."[57] Aswad thinks that divisions should be according to generations, but her own results emphasize the importance that should be attributed to events in determining sub-periods. The date of sedentarization in Aswad's study should have been used to define a significant sub-period. Events which exert a powerful influence on the society in question and affect marriage patterns should determine sub-periods. The criterion of generations is especially hard to apply in societies with large families and certainly where polygyny is practised.

Rosenfeld and Kressel advocated a division into particular sub-periods which were not optimally suited to the purpose. Rosenfeld stipulates one period lasting from 1954 until June 1963, while the second begins in July 1964 and ends in 1969.[58] The years 1956 and 1967 should have been used as dividing lines between sub-periods. In October 1956 the Sinai Campaign took place and the Six Day War broke out in June 1967. Both wars influenced the life of the Israeli Arabs, including their marriage patterns. It may well be that, due to "micro" events in the village studied by Rosenfeld, the divisions of 1954, 1963 and 1969 are important locally, but the "macro" events of 1956 and 1967 and their impact cannot be neglected.

Kressel chooses to divide the period from December 1965 to December 1971 into small units: December 1965 to December 1967; December 1967 to April 1969; June 1970 to December 1974.[59] Again, June 1967 suggests itself as dividing line. Kressel states that six men married women from the occupied territories during the period December 1967 to June 1970. The change in the "field of possibilities," as well as in the "pool of candidates," took place in June 1967, in the middle of a sub-period as determined by Kressel, though the marriage ceremonies were held later. The June 1967 War and the subsequent change of international boundaries caused changes in the field of marriage candidates. It must be remembered that negotiations between families have to start well before the actual wedding date. Following the Six Day War such negotiations involving a family living in the occupied territory would likely have taken even longer since there had been no direct contacts possible for a period of almost twenty years. With all these factors taken into consideration, June rather than December 1967 seems the appropriate dividing line between sub-periods in a study of marriage patterns in the settlement studied by Kressel.

MARRIAGE PATTERNS IN THE HAMLETS

Table 22 gives the distribution of the total number of marriages of male residents, according to the determined sub-periods.[60] The marriages have been analyzed according to the proposed system of sub-period divisions. Five sub-periods are introduced between the end of World War I and 1974, beginning with the sub-period 1918-1930. It is during this time that the hamlets were established. The first two houses in Yamma were built at the turn of the century but the main influx of settlers from the parent village began after World War I. The memories of some of the oldest inhabitants provide direct information on the early years of existence of settlement. Many of the settlers were accustomed to commuting to the plains until the clusters of temporary dwellings turned into the nuclei of permanent settlements. Yet even then, there were close contacts between the hamlets in the plain and the villages in the Samarian mountains.

The beginning of the 1930s ushered in another sub-period in which it became possible to live permanently in the plain, so that the hamlets lost their temporary character. Their location made them important stopovers for residents of the parent village and other mountain settlers en route to the Coastal Strip and this added to the social, economic and political significance of the hamlets. After the 1948-49 war, the Israeli-Jordanian frontline passed between the parent village and the offshoots, cutting off the mountain villages with the commercial and industrial centers of the coastal town. The new border left the hamlets without the possibility of regular contacts with the parent village. In consequence, the "field of possibilities" became smaller, in turn limiting the pool of candidates, especially since the hamlets were under military administration. Villagers had to request permits to move from one area to another, which further reduced contacts among neighboring Arab villages in Israel.

The period following the Sinai Campaign is considered another dividing line between sub-periods. At this time the military administration relaxed movement restrictions which greatly affected life in the villages. The sub-period beginning in 1957 was characterized by easy and frequent contacts among Arabs in all parts of Israel. The fifth sub-period begins in June 1967, with the reestablishment of relations with West Bank residents. The end of this sub-period coincides with the termination of my field work.

Our purpose is the investigation of hamlet marriage patterns as determined by historical events. It is proposed to examine whether any changes occured in the "field of candidates" in or between particularly designated time periods determined by these events. The analytical method explained above will be described and demonstrated in conjunction with the analysis of the field data.

SUB-PERIOD 1918-1930

22 shows that the proportion of FBD and other in-group marriages in the first sub-period (1918-1930) was fairly high (FBD, 21.1 percent and total in-group, 47.7 percent) if compared with the averages from Marx's data or the five-period total from the present study (FBD 14.2 percent and total in-group, 38.9 percent). On the other hand, seven of the two out-group marriages in the first sub-period were among residents of the four hamlets.[61]

The first sub-period may be defined as the experimental phase in the development of the hamlets. It was difficult to find people willing to move into an offshoot in its initial stage. Few fathers were ready to allow their daughters to marry someone who did not possess a permanent home or to expose them to the insecurity

Table 22

Chronological Distribution of Marriage Types: Male Residents

		In-group Marriages (%)			*Out-group Marriages (%)*		
Sub-period	*Total Marriages*	*FBD*	*Other*	*Total*	*Within Hamlets*	*Outside Hamlets*	*Total*
1918-1930	19	4 (21.1)	5 (26.3)	9 (47.4)	7 (36.8)	3 (15.8)	10 (52.6)
1931-1948	57	7 (12.3)	14 (24.5)	21 (36.8)	20 (35.1)	16 (28.1)	36 (63.2)
1949-1956	61	12 (19.7)	31 (50.8)	43 (70.5)	12 (19.7)	6 (9.8)	18 (29.5)
1957-June '67	76	8 (10.5)	13 (17.1)	21 (27.6)	30 (39.5)	25 (32.9)	55 (72.4)
July '67-Sept '74	103	14 (13.6)	15 (14.6)	29 (28.2)	28 (27.2)	46 (44.7)	74 (71.8)
[1957-Sept 1974]	[179]	[22 (12.2)]	[28 (15.7)]	[50 (27.9)]	[58 (32.4)]	[71 (39.7)]	[129 (72.1)]
TOTALS	316 (100)	45 (14.2)	78 (24.7)	123 (38.9)	97 (30.7)	96 (30.4)	193 (61.1)

inevitably accompanying life in a new settlement. In the early days the hamlets residents were not easily included in the "field of eligibles" of marriage partners residing in other villages. Consequently, they resorted to in-group marriages of which FBD is a category. This means, *inter alia*, that marriage patterns were influenced by the circumstances prevailing in the hamlets. Because of the special conditions in which they found themselves, hamlet residents were more likely to turn to co-residents in order to arrange marriages, for this increased social cohesion which a new hamlet aspires to promote. Both their shared past, their present interests and their plans for the future made them favorably inclined to in-village marriages.

Granqvist explains the tendency of intermarriage within the same village by arguing that marriages "tend to even out the differences between the families."[62] In the hamlets, marriages constitute only one of the links that held the residents together. The founders of the offshoots overcame many difficulties together and would not easily have succeeded in surviving without neighborly help. Solidarity was a much needed source of strength. The feeling of shared challenges created a sense of friendship and of mutual reliance. It also created an atmosphere where further ties were gladly established, reinforcing the existing ones and adding to the sense of security and wellbeing of the residents. This feeling of the fate of the community is still perceived in the hamlets though marriages are contracted with "outsiders" as well.

SUB-PERIOD 1931-1948

The second sub-period witnessed a decrease of in-group marriages, including FBD, with a proportionate increase of out-group marriages (36.8 percent in-group versus 63.2 percent out-group). There were a number of reasons for this increase in out-group marriages. Travellers from the mountains would stop in the hamlets on their way to the coast, particularly as long as horses, camels and donkeys dictated slow pace. Under these circumstances the hospitality of an affine or former neighbor was useful and this strengthened ties between the parent villages and the offshoots. Proximity to the fertile plain encouraged the further growth of the hamlets and this increased the "field of consenters" for residents seeking marriage partners (Tables 22 and 23). During the second sub-period, sixteen women from

Table 23

Women Marrying Outside Hamlets

Sub-period	*Number of Women*
1918-1930	8
1931-1948	22
1949-1956	5
1957-June '67	21
[July '67-Sept. '74]	27
TOTAL	83

other villages married into the hamlets, while twenty-two left them after their marriage. During the first sub-period only eight women married non-hamlet residents and no more than three males married women from other villages.

Gluckman stresses that exogamous groups have to marry their potential enemies.[63] This is not just restricted to exogamous groups but refers with equal justification to non-exogamous communities. Gluckman's statement applies to the hamlet complex as well, but I have refrained from defining the four hamlets as either exogamous or endogamous (see later section 'Endogamy Reconsidered'). The following case history is an example of alliance through marriage.

Muḥammad Yazīd was the head of a lineage of his *ḥamūla* dwelling in tents in Ghabāt al-Ṭaybe until 1948, on land owned by Ṭaybe residents. Muḥammad exchanged two women with powerful Ṭaybe families. He gave a fifteen year old girl in exchange for an unmarried woman of about thirty-five, who married Muḥammad's youngest son, 'Alī, then only thirteen. Five years later Muḥammad once more exchanged a daughter with another powerful Ṭaybe family for a second wife for 'Alī, this time of the groom's age. It is significant that the first marriage took place in the late 1920s, in the first sub-period; whereas the second occurred in the early 1930s, in the second sub-period.

Muḥammad's oldest son 'Omar, whose wife was his FBD, arranged that his two sons marry sisters from a small offshoot of Tira village. 'Omar exchanged his daughter for the older of the two sisters. The first son's wedding took place in 1944. Two years later 'Omar's second son married his brother's wife's sister without exchange of daughters, a bride price (*fed*) being paid instead. All four marriages were with members of influential families ensuring the Yazīd lineage access to land in different areas. This promised the Yazīd lineage security which they badly needed since they were a small group of outsiders in the area. Bedouin tribes might easily have attacked their tents had it not been for the connections established with powerful Ṭaybe families through marriage alliances.

The desire for maximum security prompted the Yazīd family to seek alliances with Ṭaybe residents but they also benefited economically. In addition, their status was considerably increased through affinal relations with powerful, prestigious families. Here, a combination of interests were served and the marriage policy apparently dictated by a clear perception of the needs of this group of outsiders. They could count on help in case of aggression and were now much less likely to be attacked after the marriages had been contracted. There are weighty reasons for in-group marriages as there are for alliances with out-groups. External variables may also change the proportions between the two types of marriages.

SUB-PERIOD 1949-1956

A significant change took place in the third sub-period. The percentage of FBD marriages in the hamlets rose sharply, from 12.3 to almost twenty percent, while the total of in-group marriages was 70.5 percent. To some extent, developments in the first and third sub-periods may be seen as parallel but there are differences worthy of consideration. In the first sub-period the primary limiting factor on the "pool of candidates" was the "field of consenters"; while the causes for changes in the third sub-period were linked to all three fields—possibilities, eligibles, and consenters.

A preference for in-group and in-village marriages at this time was the result of closed borders and movement restrictions within the boundaries of the State of Israel. Moving from one area to the other, though not impossible, was difficult. Permits had to be obtained and the contact with bureaucracy was a particular obstacle for a rural population. Every meeting of the usually long, drawn-out marriage negotiations required a whole procedure. It was felt that visiting a married daughter would be an equally time-robbing and complicated process. For this reason marriages within the village were accorded preference. Furthermore, the hamlets were close to the border which constantly reminded them what the outbreak of a war might mean. They would be the first to be affected and were aware of the hazards of their situation. In addition, propaganda from the neighboring Arab countries maintained that sooner or later Jordanian rule would be re-introduced in the area. Given these circumstances, parents were not inclined to marry off their daughters to members of another community. The daughters would have to move to their future husband's residence and if war broke out, contacts would be disrupted. Even worse, a change of borders might mean that a daughter would suddenly be on the other side of the frontier where regular and close contacts would be impossible. This inclination of keeping a daughter in the same community wherever possible characterized other rural settlements as well, so that it was obvious that in-village marriages would be given priority in the hamlets and similar rural communities. In addition to the reduced "field of possibilities," the "field of eligibles" and that of consenters were likewise reduced, being mainly restricted to the inhabitants of one's own village.

The Sinai campaign served as a landmark in the third sub-period. It ended the wait-and-see atmosphere and consolidated attitudes and expectations.[64] This war made the hamlet residents, among others, believe that the existing borders would not easily be removed. They were less uncertain of the future and therefore more inclined to take steps to be integrated in the Israeli economy. They no longer considered the status quo as temporary and feared less that there would be significant changes of frontiers. Inevitably, this influenced marriage patterns and stepped up the rate of marriage with residents of other villages not necessarily within the same region or in close vicinity of the hamlets. Improved public transport also contributed. Distances that had once been considered forbidding now no longer seemed so.

When these "macro" events are analyzed in the context of field data on the "micro" level, the contrast between the second and third sub-periods is evident. In the third sub-period, only six women from other villages (see Table 22, p. 89) married hamlet residents. No more than five women moved away from the hamlets. The corresponding figures for the second sub-period were sixteen and twenty-two, respectively. Also, all five women moving out of the hamlets during the third sub-period, married residents in the village of Jatt, located only three kilometers north of Yamma. They did not take up residence far from their natal family and were within easy visiting distance.

Data on housing changes in the hamlets (see Table 1, p. 36), show that only 8.5 percent of the families moved to new homes during the third sub-period as compared to almost 60.5 percent in the following sub-period. The data on housing also reflects the insecurity of the residents during the period 1949-56. The reluctance to construct new buildings is motivated by the same reasons as the unwillingness to let daughters move away from their parental home. Any community that anticipates sudden upheavals and changes of the general situation, will be unlikely to invest in immovable property. In any outbreak of hostilities the house would be exposed to the hazard of war being close to the border where military operations were likely to take place.

The year 1951 shows a steep increase in the number of in-group marriages in the hamlets, as the circumstances described above amply justify. Early in 1951 the Israeli government conducted a census, the first in the area. This gave rise to a persistent rumor that single Arab males would be drafted for military service, something that has neither been discussed nor attempted at any time since the establishment of the State. The hamlet residents sought to forestall such a mobilization of the unmarried young men by resorting to marriage. As negotiations with inhabitants of other communities were inevitably more prolonged, in-group marriages which could be agreed upon without much delay were given precedence. So great was the desire to become married, that the average age of the couple was lower than in previous years and in those to come. Exchanges of women with close relatives and/or neighbors were simple and easily arranged. It was felt that an emergency existed and that speed was of the essence. This recommended in-group marriages including of course FBD.

Most of the literature dealing with behavioral science is based on the observation of the conduct of modern Western populations. It may be assumed that changes occur at a faster rate in these societies than in simpler ones. In other words past norms are less apparent in the present culture of modern society. This rapid transformation of culture and norms characterizes the urban centers in the Western countries. It may well be that there still exist rural pockets, remote villages and settlements, where culture and norms are less subject to change, or where the process is slower. In recent times however, the impact of the media exercise their influence in small villages no less than in large towns. The author is well aware that not all of the findings of behavioral science literature may be applied without reservation to the hamlets, yet some of the conclusions of the literature are particularly valid.

The findings of Turner and Killian are relevant to any group that finds itself in a crisis situation, such as that experienced by the hamlet residents. They argue that "the more uncertain the situation, the greater the tendency on the whole, towards convergence in group situations."[65] The descriptions, given above, of patterns of marriage conduct in the hamlets confirm this statement and show that reaction to stress is similar even when there are marked geographical and other differences. In other words, human beings, when faced with certain threats, tend to react in a similar manner.

Smelser referred to such situations, saying, "Certain norms, although they do not provide directives as to how to contend with threats, direct behaviour toward some other kind of activity. . ."[66] Here the emphasis is on mutual responsibility. The individual feels that he is a member of a group and cannot simply think of himself only, but must consider the others before taking any steps to safeguard his own security and interest. The emotional reaction to disaster or pending disaster is a readiness for closer contacts with the other members of the group, the willingness to share, to give and take. This is due to a sense of group solidarity, but at the same time, the determination to protect one's own household and those closest, also grows. This, in part, explains the preference for marriage within the group and the hamlet. Members of the household depend much more on protection from close relatives than in less insecure times as the wider frameworks are often paralyzed or rendered ineffective. Duties and functions usually undertaken by official institutions may, in emergency situations, revert to individuals capable of discharging them. In the households, this is as a rule either the pater familias, a son or several sons. The obligation most strongly felt is toward the nuclear family and a married sister or sisters. This may in a large measure be explained by the fact that daughters legally possess a right to inherit from their fathers, but unless there are no sons, rarely claim their share of the inheritance. A brother may have partly compensated his sister through bringing costly presents whenever the occasion called for it, but both sides are aware that the expenditure rarely matches the value of the property not claimed. A sense of indebtedness remains and comes to the fore in stress situations.

Although the percentage of in-group marriages reached a peak of over seventy percent during the third sub-period, this should not be interpreted as a sign of preference for in-group marriage, or for a need to strengthen the descent group, but as a desire to choose marriage partners living in close proximity.

SUB-PERIOD 1957-JUNE 1967

The fourth sub-period started with the end of the Sinai Campaign, the first military clash between Israel and an Arab country since the 1948 War. There was a considerable decrease in FBD marriages as well as in the entire category of in-group marriages. The figures (FBD, 10.5 percent and total in-group, 27.6 percent) are the lowest recorded for the hamlets in any sub-period (Table 22, p. 89).

Several factors contributed to this change of rate of in-group and out-group marriages. After the Sinai Campaign, the Arab propaganda to which Israeli Arabs were exposed from the neighboring states no longer prevented a realistic assessment of the situation. Informants have told the author that at this time they expected the existing Israeli borders to remain unchanged for many years. It is not surprising that building activity was stepped up, 60.5 percent of the hamlet families constructing new homes during the fourth sub-period. Although the military administration was abolished only in 1966, permits to travel within the area were no longer required from 1956 on and it became possible to travel almost anywhere within the country during daytime, including Jewish towns. In April 1962, regulations changed again and transit permits were granted, good for any time of the day or night and valid for a period of one year. During the fourth sub-period, seventy-three percent of the male inhabitants above the age of eighteen began working outside their hamlets, holding either full or part-time jobs.[67] Many worked in the Jewish sector. There, residents of different villages met at work and established social relations. Mutual visits to the homes of Arab villagers living in other communities and sometimes even in other areas ensued and these new acquaintances were often candidates for marriages.

Table 22 (p. 89) shows that fifty-five men (72.4 percent) married outside their in-group during the 1957-67 sub-period. The distribution of sub-categories was as follows: there were thirty marriages within the hamlets, as against a total of twenty-five with women from other rural communities. Eleven of these twenty-five unions were with residents from Jatt and Bāqa al-Gharbīyya, two neighboring villages. The others included eight with residents of three villages south of the hamlets (four from one, three from another, and one from a third); while three were with women from two villages north of Bāqa al-Gharbīyya. All the marriages were contracted within the Triangle which came under Israeli rule in 1949. The three remaining out-group marriages in the fourth sub-period were with women outside that area. In one case the wife came from a village in the Haifa region while the other two women came from a settlement in the Galilee.

Table 23 (p. 91) indicates that a total of twenty-one hamlet women married husbands from outside their community. All of these marriages, with the exception of two, were within the Triangle area. Changes in the pool of candidates evidently influenced the range of marriages. Applying the marriage pattern data (representing the 'micro' level of events) to the 'macro' level, the dividing line between the sub-periods 1949-56 and 1957-67, seems to be appropriate. There were a number of other general changes that took place within the fourth sub-period, modifying partner selection. One of these was a decrease in the number of Arab cooperative associations of varying types which Yaqir has noted,[68] while Cohen refers to the growing opportunity for paid employment for Arab villagers, many of whom chose to work in the Jewish sector.[69] The changes in the fourth sub-period were caused mainly by external factors influencing the three fields and in turn, the pool of candidates. The above analysis explains why the high rate of in-group marriages (over seventy percent) in the 1949-56 sub-period dropped to a low (less than twenty-eight percent) in the succeeding 1957-67 sub-period, while out-group marriages increased (from 29.5 to 72.4 percent).

SUB-PERIOD JULY 1967-SEPTEMBER 1974

Most factors of the previous sub-period remained unchanged although the distinctions between any two previous successive sub-periods were very conspicuous. For this reason the data in Table 22 (p. 89) has been arranged to illustrate the fourth and fifth sub-period individually and together. The beginning of the fifth sub-period, however, was marked by one entirely new dimension. The pool of candidates for marriage was enlarged by border changes. Table 22 shows that there was a slight decrease in the number of out-group marriages (71.8 percent), with a correspondingly insignificant increase of in-group marriages (0.6

percent). According to the analysis of the fourth sub-period the very opposite might have been expected. The fifth sub-period, however, was characterized by a disproportional change in the number of FBD marriages as compared to the entire in-group category.

The 10.5 percent FBD marriages in the fourth sub-period was the lowest recorded while in the fifth sub-period there was an increase of 3.1 percent. The shift was the result of the Six Day War in June 1967 which led to the renewal of contacts between the parent village and the hamlets. Marriage unions with relatives in the parent village were one means of reviving earlier kinship ties. It would also help overcome any differences that might have developed between the parent village and the four offshoots in the interim period. The marriage partners though usually blood relations, were actually strangers to each other. Many of them had not previously met, as is usual when brothers or cousins live in one village or neighborhood. The desire for close ties with Deir al-Ghusūn was due to the fact that, with the exception of one single family (that of 'Attīli whose parent village was 'Attīl) all hamlet residents still had close relatives in Deir al-Ghusūn.

The choice of marriage partners took a number of directions, including, of course, FBD marriage among the in-group category. Some of the residents of the parent village, who had lived there before 1949, chose to move elsewhere during the Jordanian rule, usually to urban centers. Their new residence led, in the fifth sub-period, to several marriages between men from the hamlets and women relatives from West Bank towns and villages other than the parent village. Two hamlet residents working in the vicinity of Jerusalem, married women from this area. This was not extraordinary since, as one relative remarked, "after all, it takes no more than three hours to get to the hamlets from the bride's villages." Not long ago this distance would have been prohibitive. The couple would probably not have met since the groom would have lived in his village and would not have taken on work so far away, so that he would not have been able to make the social contacts with a girl's male relatives which precede marriage negotiations in Arab rural society.

Another direction taken in marriage choices was the building up of new alliances through marriage arrangements with non-relatives of villages on the West Bank. The geographical location of the hamlets was important for the villages in the mountains of the West Bank for the mountain dwellers needed links with families close to employment opportunities, while the hamlets were interested in gaining access to the social and political centers of the West Bank. The renewal of contacts with the West Bank resulted in a much higher rate of women marrying into the hamlets and other villages in the "Triangle," than of hamlet women who moved to the West Bank upon their marriage. Since it was important for both West Bank residents and Israeli Arabs to increase their contact with each other, marriage negotiations were usually smooth and concluded quickly. The bride-price for West Bank women was no more than one third or one quarter of that customarily demanded by Israeli Arab villagers. However, in the course of time, the sums requested by West Bank families equalled or almost equalled those customarily asked for by Israeli Arabs. Furthermore, West Bank women unlike those in the hamlets, did not insist that the groom build a house before the wedding.

Table 22 (p. 89) shows that fourteen FBD marriages were contracted in the fifth sub-period, three of them with women from the parent village. Five of the fifteen in-group (but not FBD marriages), were with residents of Deir al-Ghusūn. The distribution of the forty-six out-group marriages where the wife came from another village, is as follows: fourteen women came from villages within the pre-1967 boundaries; while thirty were from the West Bank, eight of whom were from the parent village. Thus a total of sixteen women moved to the hamlets from the parent village during the fifth sub-period. Eight of them were related to their husbands and the other eight were non-relatives. The remaining thirty included two Jewish women.[70]

Table 23 (p. 91) shows that only twenty-seven hamlet women were married to inhabitants of other villages (as contrasted with the total of forty-six who moved to the hamlets) in the fifth sub-period. Seventeen of these women married Israeli Arab villagers and nine women married West Bank residents. The other woman moved to a village east of the Jordan River. Five of the West Bank weddings fell within the in-group category—three women marrying their father's brother's sister (FBS); while the other two were of the broader in-group range. The trend demonstrated in the fifth sub-period may be summarized very simply: whereas thirty-eight women from West Bank communities married hamlet residents (eight of these representing in-group weddings), only ten women from the hamlets were married to West Bank males.

EXCHANGE MARRIAGES—BADAL

The disproportionately large number of West Bank women who married hamlet residents in the fifth sub-period meant that some of the hamlet women had little chance of marrying, a fact which worried their families. One means of securing a husband for a daughter is by a *badal*. A *badal* is an exchange marriage where siblings marry siblings, the two unions being linked—if one union breaks up the other union automatically breaks up. Brothers frequently agree to such an exchange under paternal pressure. Goldberg quotes informants as repeatedly explaining their *badal* marriages as undertaken for their sister's sake,[71] usually in response to their father's urging. The *badal* which secures two husbands for two females is definitely considered a last resort by many. Its disadvantages are especially recognized by the educated younger generation. Other marriage patterns are usually preferred and only when there is no possibility of a daughter being married off will a son be offered as a partner for another girl.

Eighteen cases of *badal* are recorded for the fifth sub-period. In a few cases, the wife was older than her husband. In an emergency a father will try to marry his daughter to his closest relatives or neighbors and will exert pressure on them to achieve this. Occasionally the right of a cousin to marry his FBD may actually turn into an obligation.[72] The fact that cousins were forced to marry their FBD explains the 3.1 percent increase in first patrilateral parallel cousin marriages during the fifth sub-period.[73]

As background for the case studies which follow, Table 24 illustrates the age group distribution of unmarried males and females (aged eighteen or over) as found in the hamlets at the time of the field work, that is the final phase of the artificially terminated fifth sub-period. Between 1967 and 1973 the median age of female hamlet residents at the time of their wedding was 20.7 years. In 1965 the corresponding figure for all Muslim females in Israel was 19.9 years and 23.8 for males.[74] Table 24 indicates that there were several single female residents in the hamlets. This situation was, inevitably, a cause for concern on the part of fathers, especially if there were several daughters of marriageable age (or older) in one family. The fact that the unmarried male residents of the hamlets could find wives on the West Bank whose bride price was lower and who made fewer demands on the marriage partner and his family than could be

Table 24
Distribution of Unmarried Residents

Age Group	*Male*	*Female*
18-20	25	24
21-22	25	25
23-24	21	23
25-26	14	7
27-28	3	8
29-30	8	6
31-32	2	1
33-34	1	3
35 and over	0	3
TOTAL	99	100

expected with girls from the hamlets, only served to increase the possibility of spinsterhood. These issues will be elaborated in the following case histories.

Ibrāhīm 'Attīli was offered an exchange for his twenty-four year old daughter by a family in the neighboring village of Jatt. Ibrāhīm refused, answering that he was looking for a triple exchange. He had two other daughters, both unmarried, and both older than the girl requested in the *badal* proposal. Ibrāhīm's refusal was widely discussed in the hamlet *diwāns*. Many of his neighbors thought that he should have agreed to the exchange. The head of one section of the Yazīd group said that Ibrāhīm should at least have 'saved' his second daughter, though this would still have left him with two, no longer young, unmarried daughters. So far none of Ibrāhīm's daughters has found a husband, so that the criticism voiced of his marriage policy for his daughters seems justified. Next is an example of a *badal* whose cancellation led to FBD marriage as a last resort, although a *badal* was originally preferred to an FBD.

In 1972 Khalīl Jabali was looking for a *badal* for his daughter, aged twenty-six. Two of his sons were already married. The oldest, Hatām, had married his FBD in 1964, while Khalīl Jabali's second son, Sabri, had married a non-relative from the parent village, Deir al-Ghusūn. This wedding was the first to be contracted between a resident of the hamlets and a woman from the parent village after the reopening of the border following the June 1967 war. Khalīl's nephew's daughter (by his eldest brother) was married to a resident of Jatt. As noted earlier, Jatt was the village closest to the hamlets and has been the source in the past of numerous marriage contracts with the hamlets. Khalīl found a resident of Jatt to act as middleman (*wasita*) between himself and a family living in Jatt in arranging the desired *badal*. Once agreement had been reached, the two betrothal ceremonies, one in each bridal home as is customary in cases of *badal*, were celebrated. Two months later a rumor spread through the village that Ḥalīma, Khalīl's daughter, had some time before undergone an operation that rendered her incapable of bearing children. The family of the betrothed girl immediately asked for a cancellation of the wedding plans leading automatically to the cancellation of the betrothal of the second girl as well. The source of the rumour had been Khalīl's nephew's wife, after her mother had incited her.

In 1973 another family from Jatt, this time from a different *ḥamūla*, proposed another *badal* for Khalīl's daughter, offering a suitable bride for his son. Unlike the first time the betrothal ceremony was on a modest scale but Khalīl showed physical signs of extreme nervousness. One of the dignitaries present consoled him saying that things looked much better this time. About a week later Khalīl told me how pleased he was that the exchange had been arranged with a *ḥamūla* enjoying high status and possessing political power.

However, the joy was of short duration. Ḥalīma's prospective husband was taunted by members of his peer group who sarcastically congratulated him on being about to marry a woman who would soon be eligible for a National Insurance old age pension. Ḥalīma was no more than twenty-six, but the young man was sensitive to these contemptuous remarks, being younger than his fiance by three years. A similar situation existed with respect to the other couple in the *badal*; the Jatt woman was older by four years than Khalīl's son Ḥilmi. The young man from Jatt, influenced by his friends' talk, turned to his sister for advice; she spoke to her sister-in-law, who originating from Marja, knew the Jabali family well. Not much later the bridegroom's sister and her husband paid an unannounced visit to Khalīl's home though both families were on the phone. There was the inevitable bustle while the refreshments were hastily prepared. Ḥalīma climbed up a ladder to take down some provisions, fell and lost consciousness for some seconds. The guests promptly cut short their visit and spread the rumor that the girl suffered from epilepsy. Once again the wedding arrangements were cancelled.

This time however, the annulment of the betrothal involved legal proceedings, since according to Islam it is considered a binding registration for marriage. Khalīl appealed to the religious court in Ṭaybe for alimony on behalf of his daughter, so as to bring about the renewal of the betrothal. At the same time he refused to cancel his son's wedding arrangements. Subsequently, friends of the young man in Jatt attacked Ḥilmi at his work place, threatening to kill him if the court proceedings were not suspended and the wedding arrangements cancelled. Khalīl gave up his fight in despair.

Not much later, one of Khalīl's brothers, who had moved from Deir al-Ghusūn to Tul Karem, suggested another marriage deal. He not only offered a *badal*, but in addition, another daughter for Khalīl's younger son Salīm without asking a bride price for her. The three weddings were celebrated together, all of them between first parallel patrilateral cousins. But the story was not to end there. Ḥalīma's marriage lasted for only four months. One day her husband told her that their oldest father's brother (*'amm*), their mutual uncle, had died in the hamlet and that she should go there immediately. He would join her later since he had an important appointment to keep. After his wife's departure the man crossed the border into Jordan taking with him all of Ḥalīma's jewelry. It had all been a carefully conceived plan, since a new bride would never leave her valuables behind except to pay a visit of condolence to a house of mourning. Although no one knew the reasons for the husband's action, it was known that he agreed to the marriage only because of his father's urging. He returned in 1976 after prolonged negotiations between the two families.

The reasons prompting Khalīl's brother to suggest the marriages were not hard to guess. He was fairly new in Tul Karem and in need of political support. Close contacts with Israeli Arabs familiar with officials would be useful to him. He had earlier unsuccessfully proposed a *badal* to three other hamlet families and saw his chance after the cancellation of Ḥalīma's second betrothal.

This case of *badal* may be explained by Barth's theory that this form of marriage usually serves political interests above all. Khalīl's first intention was to negotiate an out-group marriage for his children, but since his daughter was in danger of remaining single, he accepted his brother's suggestion and let her marry her FBS. This case illustrates that final marriage statistics may not always reflect actual marriage preferences.

Statistics do not register the critical fact that Ḥalīma's father tried to find her a husband who was not her FBS (father's brother's son) and that he was reluctant to resort to an FBD. When Khalīl's nephew agreed to marry Ḥalīma he did not make use of a "right," but obeyed an order. The element of preference is entirely absent in this FBD marriage.

FBS may at times be resorted to so as to avoid "shame." In two cases parents intended to arrange out-group marriages for their daughters, but had to agree to FBS instead. When the girls learned of their father's arrangements, they confessed to having had intercourse with their first patrilateral parallel cousins. If they married others, they said, "a great stain of shame would replace the good name of the family." The parents who had not until then considered in-group marriage agreed to FBS.

In the above cases, none of the previously discussed "explanations" for the FBD phenomena is applicable since preference is not involved. Statistical data must be accompanied by other facts in order to be fully understood. Circumstances similar to those in the cases cited above may have influenced marriage patterns in earlier sub-periods, and FBD marriages may have been contracted under compulsion rather than due to ideological preference. Not all recorded FBD marriages may be considered preferred. The data indicates that brothers often put heavy pressure on each other when it comes to the marriage of their children.

No satisfactory interpretation of marriage patterns can be found without considering the background and the complexity of human nature which is fully brought into play in a decision relating to the future of one's children. The social and cultural anthropologist may not be sure of many things but he has learned one basic truth: in the context of highly personal decisions, no one convincing explanation will do. It seems that those who put forward one cause only for the arrangement of marriage by a father err by the vary nature of the case. The element they stress plays its role, but in conjunction with others.

These case histories show one conspicuous fact—the fathers' wish to provide for his daughter by marrying her off. This often seems stronger than the desire for political benefits, for social advancement or for economic status. This does not mean that other objectives are not in evidence, but that a father is prepared to sacrifice certain other interests to make sure that his daughter or daughters are not condemned to spinsterhood. Lévi-Strauss maintains that the exchange of women is analogous with that of gifts.[75] This does not do justice to the infinite variety of human nature. Women are not, as a rule, simply property in the eyes of their fathers who seek profitable alliances for them. Other motives play their part as well. These other motives cannot be reflected in the statistics. While statistics show the relationships of preference marriages, it cannot be known, except by participant observation, whether a particular marriage took place because it was 'in family', or because of other reasons.

FBD marriage is sometimes seen as a means of accumulating power through in-group unions. There is, however, no reason to choose FBD in preference over other in-group marriages. Barth suggests that a man marries his daughter to his nephew in order to secure the latter's support as well as that of his father. But the close relationship already existing between the men should be sufficient guarantee without an additional inter-family marriage. Where a brother's loyalty is wavering, it may not be depended on to be strengthened after he has become a father-in-law. On the other hand, out-group marriages may result in valuable new alliances where men may enlarge their sphere of influence and win new allies. Against this, FBD marriages at best reinforce existing loyalties, but do not add new ones.

The cases of Khalīl and Ibrāhīm 'Attīllī show that the characteristics required of a marriage partner may change when a *badal* is considered desirable or inevitable. What makes this marriage pattern acceptable is the fact that it may help a girl whose chances of marriage are very small to find a husband. If she has a brother who can become one partner of the exchange arrangement, the father may often persuade his son to consent.

The disadvantages of *badal* are obvious. Layish points out that "it is difficult in everyday life to maintain strict equality between the exchanged women." Envy and jealousy are more easily aroused than in other marriage patterns, and may "spoil relations between spouses."[76] Above all, the women's status is negatively affected by a deal where "women were pawns in the game between their families: their moves were usually determined against their will."[77] However, the males are no less dependent on what happens to the other couple and their life is similarly determined by this. Resistance to such unions is especially great among the more educated young men who wish to choose wives by themselves.

Opposition to a *badal* arrangement is illustrated by the following case.

Aḥmed Amin asked the author to help him convince his son to agree to such a marriage. His twenty-six year old daughter had little chance of finding a husband unless her brother agreed to an exchange of brides. Aḥmed was prepared to compromise in other respects, as long as his son Tawfīq did "what was required" to help his sister. He said that his son could choose any girl whose brother was eligible for *badal*. For two full years Tawfīq was adamant in his refusal. In the end he threatened to move to Tel Aviv to escape his father's importunities. Tawfīq's behavior may be understood against the background of his economic independence. He holds a well-paid job outside the hamlet and can afford if necessary, to forego his heritage. Furthermore, Aḥmed possesses no more than two *dūnams* of land, to be divided between his four sons, so Tawfīq had little to lose economically. Employment conditions partly accounted for Tawfīq's conduct, but more probably the reaction of his peer group contributed to make him reject a deal in which he may have felt to be no more than a pawn.

The case of Muḥammad Yazīd (B_2, chart I, appendix C) is different. He has three sons, Maḥmūd (C_1), Ḥamed (C_3) and Aḥmad (C_5) and in the past owned large flocks. He was among the first to leave Deir al-Ghusūn to pitch his tent in the plain west of Yamma at the beginning of the establishment of the offshoots, where former 'Attīl residents were already living. Muḥammad wished to create marriage alliances with his new neighbors. Another segment of the Yazīd lineage (the case has been described and analyzed earlier) had done so through marriage with powerful landowners of Ghabāt al-Ṭaybe. In Muḥammad's case, however, the alliances were between equals with the exception of the fact that the herders from 'Attīl rightly claimed a kind of 'seniority' as the result of having been the first to settle there. The alliance needed by Muḥammad was formed when two of his sons, Maḥmūd and Aḥmad, married women from 'Attīl – Karīma (C_3) and Luṭfīyya (C_6), respectively.[78]

Another relevant case, in the same family, was that of Rafīq ($D_1$8) and Ṭareq ($D_1$9). Their wives Sharīfa ($D_1$1) and Zakīyya ($D_1$2) were Maḥmūd's daughters. After their father's death, Aḥmad, acting as guardian for the two girls, registered his deceased brother's property under the girl's name. He then decided to marry them to his two eldest sons and arranged for his brother's widow Karīma (C_2) to marry Ḥusnī ($D_1$4), the son of his eldest brother. Karīma gave birth to four children and died soon afterwards. Her daughter later married 'Omar ($D_1$10), the youngest of Aḥmad's four sons. Thus the wives of Aḥmad's two elder sons had the same mother and were half-sisters of his fourth son's wife. Forty-three days after Karīma's death,[79] much earlier than is customary, Ḥusnī married Amna (D13), a resident of the parent village, who bore him nine children. The result of all this activity was that there were three groups of siblings, all members of the middle group, having half-siblings in each of the other two groups.

Aḥmad had divided his property while he was still alive. His sons Rafīq and Ṭareq managed their shares jointly while Salīm (D112) and 'Omar (D110) cultivated their fields separately. The transfer of property to sons before the father's demise is a new practice in the region, the reasons for which are not relevant to the present case.[80] The two brothers not only owned their land jointly but also pooled their financial resources, Rafīq acting as treasurer. In the four years preceding my field work, the brothers repeatedly spoke of splitting up and even set definite dates for the transaction, but put it off again and again. Each of them had a twenty-two year old son and a twenty-five year old daughter. In 1968 the brothers decided upon *badal* marriages among their children. Jamīla (E20), Rafīq's daughter, was supposed to marry her FBS 'Alī (E22); and Laṭīfa (E21), Ṭareq's daughter, was to become the bride of her first cousin Ṣabrī (E19).

Meanwhile, Lea (E8), Ḥusnī's daughter (D14), was discovered to be pregnant. She admitted having intercourse with Ṣabrī who denied the charge. Ṭareq found himself in a very difficult situation: Lea was not only his cousin's daughter, but also the cousin of Ṣabrī's father. Ṭareq knew that if Ṣabrī did not marry Laṭīfa, she would probably remain a spinster. Accordingly, he convinced Ḥusnī and Dāūd (D22) (Ḥusnī's oldest son), that Lea should have an abortion. Ṭareq explained that the decision regarding Ṣabrī's marriage to Laṭīfa had been planned years before. He suggested that the two originally planned weddings take place simultaneously. He further arranged that Lea be married to Mansūr (E17), another of Rafīq's sons. Ṣweliḥ (E18), Mansūr's older brother, was not considered because it was known that he would never agree to such an arrangement. The negotiations for Lea's betrothal were completed by Ṭareq, Ḥusnī and Dāūd. Rafīq refused to participate, pleading ill health as his excuse knowing that nothing would come of these negotiations.

Lea's pregnancy was not the only obstacle to the original *badal* plan. 'Alī did not want to marry his FBD and after a child had been born to them, he complained: "I grew up together with

Jamīla; we have known each other for as long as I can remember. I wanted a wife from outside the village, not one who is like a sister to me. Our fathers are brothers, our mothers are sisters, and our fathers and mothers are cousins." What has been described by many Middle Eastern scholars as a compelling reason for FBD, was a deterrent to 'Alī.

The attitude of 'Alī is reminiscent of that observed by Shepher in the Kibbutz community he studied. The girls and boys who lived together in one children's house and community were reluctant to have sexual relations with members of this in-group.[81] What deterred 'Alī was not so much consanguinity as reluctance to have intercourse with someone so familiar who could not easily be romanticized. Another reason why 'Alī felt ill at ease when he thought of being married to a close relative was that he wished to avoid too rigid a control by his kin over his family life. He himself gave the clue when he mentioned the family ties between him and his wife. If 'Alī's reluctance is more than just a personal trait, and there is a lot in favor of this interpretation, then FBD marriages are often shunned. Both interpretations have been given and both may be valid though in varying degrees.

Hamlet residents have not been questioned about this, though the author has overheard random remarks testifying to similar attitudes. On the other hand, in-group marriages are numerous in the hamlets, including FBD marriages, and no reluctance is displayed. 'Alī's attitude may perhaps be traced to the influence of his Jewish fellow-students at the agricultural high school. Though the Jewish religion does not prohibit cousin marriage, and instances are found in families of Middle Eastern origin, Israeli born Jews especially of European or American parentage, tend to avoid them.[82]

Some marriage partners in FBD-FBS admitted that they did not feel attracted to each other though, while as already mentioned, clandestine relations among cousins raised together took place. Khuri points out that family relations between relatives continue unchanged if marriage occurs between them,[83] and that this does not intensify the emotional bonds between paternal cousins.[84] At the same time, he argues that FBD marriage harmonizes family relations.[85]

When illicit relations between cousins occur, this is to no small extent due to the fact that formal meetings between members of different sex are almost impossible in Arab Muslim rural society. When cousins grow up in neighboring houses, some encounters inevitably take place and for lack of other opportunities they may lead to intercourse. This, in turn, is usually followed by marriage which prevents loss of face and averts the pressure on the agnates to murder the offending girl. Loss of virginity, once it becomes known, compels them to "save the honor of the family." In Lea's case, immediate intra-family marriage was planned because the very fact that she had had an abortion would have guaranteed her spinsterhood. A girl who is known not to be a virgin could never expect to receive a voluntary proposal of marriage. This is another instance where FBS-FBD marriage is a last resort and definitely not a preferred pattern of marriage.

It seems that there are two main reasons why unions of this type are planned. First, there is the desire of a father to prevent shame and second, the wish to provide a husband for a no longer young daughter. Neither motive is conducive to harmonious family relations. On the contrary, such marriages are decided under strain. Harmony depends on the absence of tension. In one of the few cases of marriage following premarital sexual relations between first patrilateral parallel cousins, encountered during my fieldwork, the young man involved knew that his father had already initiated negotiations for marriage with a girl from another village and had even engaged a go-between. In the end he married his FBD. But neither he nor his nuclear family, and perhaps not even the girl's parents, preferred this solution because all thought that the two partners were too closely related.

Returning to the case history under discussion, 'Alī Yazīd only consented once he had extracted two concessions from his father and uncle. The first was that he be built a new house even though 'Alīs' cousin Ṣabrī and wife (the second half of the *badal* exchange) lived in the home of Ṣabrī's parents and his ('Alī's) parental home was far from overcrowded. (It is usual in *badal* marriages for the conditions in respect of initial residence to be the same). The second concession was that his younger cousin Ṣweliḥ (E18), Ṣabrī's brother, pledge himself to marry 'Alī's younger sister Bahīyya (E23). The first condition was met; the second was agreed to but never fulfilled. Ṣweliḥ claimed that the promise had been given by his father but not by himself.

In the summer of 1972 Ṣweliḥ became acquainted with a West Bank girl through a friend, the girl's brother, and decided he would like to marry her. He obtained the support of his mother and sister in attempting to convince his father that the girl's family should be approached with a marriage proposal. It is customary that a young man who wishes to marry reveal his desire to his mother, with whom he has a less formal relationship. It then becomes the mother's duty to pass the request on to the father.

When Ṭareq found out about his nephew's intentions, he asked his brother Rafīq to divide the jointly held property. Meanwhile, the girl Ṣweliḥ had wanted to marry accepted a proposal from someone else. At this point Ṣweliḥ declared that under no circumstances would he marry his FBD Bahīyya. He was able to do this being economically independent, working for wages outside the hamlet and not contributing to the joint "money box" of his father and uncle.

After Ṣabrī (Ṣweliḥ's oldest brother) had married Laṭīfa, Rafīq told Ḥusnī that none of his sons had agreed to marry Ḥusnī's daughter Lea (the girl with whom Ṣabrī had had sexual relations). Until that time only members of Muḥammad Yazīd's lineage (see chart 1, appendix C) had known of Ṣabrī and Lea's affair and its consequences. Soon after, the story spread in the hamlets. 'Omar (D1 10), Ṣabrī's father's brother and the husband of Ḥusnī's daughter Mariam (D2 6), tried to kill Ṣabrī. 'Omar's wife was a half-sister to both Ṣabrī's mother and Lea. 'Omar sympathized with the plight of his father-in-law and took after Ṣabrī with a stick. When other relatives came to Ṣabrī's rescue, 'Omar rushed home and returned with a pistol. If Ṭareq had not stopped the quarrel, it might have ended in bloodshed.

The problem of finding a husband for Lea was abruptly ended when her father Ḥusnī killed her by striking her over the head with a hoe while she was asleep. With this turn of events, Ṣabrī and his father Rafīq felt even more insecure and even more in need of Ṭareq's support. Under such circumstances murder is no uncommon occurrence in Arab rural society. Antoun mentions a case where a girl's father stabbed her to death;[86] Abou Zeid, who studied the Bedouin of Egypt, reports a similar instance.[87] In the hamlets there was consensus as to the right of a father to restore the family honor by killing a daughter who had brought shame on her family. Ḥusnī's deed was not condemned most people believing that he had done right.

Other factors contributed, though they were not decisive. Rafīq and Ṭareq were closer than most brothers as a result of intermarriage in two generations, in addition to holding property jointly. The author's interpretation of their marriage policies is not in keeping with the views of other researchers.[88] It is argued here that economic considerations were not decisive, the overriding motive was to prevent daughters from remaining single. It is, of course, impossible to state one single reason for the priority accorded to marriage for daughters. One informant, a man enjoying considerable status and in touch with many hamlet residents, explained this by saying that emotional reasons combine with considerations for status. A father fears that his daughter's life may be very hard unless she is married. Once he himself dies, responsibility for her usually reverts to her brother whose wife may or may not welcome a sister-in-law in the house. She may be looked upon as a kind of servant and lead a lonely and unhappy existence. Where marriage is considered the norm, remaining single is a deviation with all its accompanying features.

Whenever a norm is not observed, suspicions are ripe. Gossip seizes upon the subject and insinuates various causes most of them far from complimentary toward the father whose acknowledged duty it is to arrange for his daughter's marriage. Furthermore, he may be accused of preferring her to stay at home so as to benefit by her work in the fields and about the house. A no less important reason is the fear that a girl may find illegally what has been denied her in the accepted way. Her father may even be said to be responsible for her illicit sexual intercourse by not having properly provided for her (in the sense of finding a husband for a daughter).

Returning once again to the case history, Ṭareq is a man with more than usual foresight and education. He may have been influenced by the consideration that inter-family marriage often leads to backward or handicapped offspring but he did not allow himself to be deterred. The only possibility for his daughters to find husbands was among close kin, because out-group marriage was difficult to arrange. One of the girls was close to the age where she would no longer be considered eligible for marriage so he did not want to lose time. Negotiations with kinsmen could be conducted quickly, as no go-between was needed and a close relative might more easily overlook her age. Both Rafīq and Ṭareq faced similar situations. Had it not been for changes in the "field of possibilities" resulting from the Six Day War, both might have solved the marriage problems of their daughters by means other than FBD exchange. Under the existing circumstances, however, it was much simpler to apply the ideology of preference for FBD.

If Ṣabrī had married Lea (with whom he had sexual relations), Jamīla would have remained single. The issue was no less important for Rafīq than for Ṭareq, Jamīla's father (Rafī) felt compelled to find a husband for his own, now no longer young, daughter. The threatened division of property between Ṭareq and Rafīq did not take place after the *badal* had been arranged. But there were additional difficulties to be overcome. Ṭareq wanted his nephew Ṣweliḥ (Rafīq's son) to marry his second daughter Bahīyya, and whenever Ṣweliḥ showed an interest in girls outside the hamlets, Ṭareq threatened to divide the joint property. There was tension between the families over the property. Ṭareq's sons and daughters resented the fact that they worked harder in the fields than did their cousins (Rafīq's children. They were perturbed that Ṣweliḥ never helped in the fields after work. 'Alī, a school teacher, assisted with the farm work every day. Moreover, as mentioned previously, Ṣweliḥ never contributed his salary to the joint income of the two families; instead, he opened a bank account of his own. Tareq made light of these grievances for Bahīyya's marriage was of primary concern to him.

Rafīq and Ṣabrī had good reason to feel insecure, particularly after the incident of Lea's pregnancy. They needed Ṭareq's support in every respect. Some informants in the hamlets hinted that the joint ownership of the brothers' land was Ṣabrī's best "insurance policy." Their relationship as kinsmen existed on other levels and was of less significance. In this case the economic factor took precedence and the joint ownership of property proved the strongest link between them. This close economic tie, faltering because of inter-family tensions, was maintained because of the need to exchange sons, as husbands for their daughters—a consideration accorded priority. Subsequent developments confirm this interpretation. In 1976 Ṣweliḥ began building a house, making it clear that he did not intend to marry Bahīyya. Rafīq told his brother that his son had not consulted him before beginning to build. Ṣweliḥ did not ask for any financial help and presumably had no need of his father's assistance. This meant that Ṭareq could no longer hope that Ṣweliḥ might marry his daughter. He now had no reason to continue the joint ownership with his brother and it was subsequently dissolved.

What I assumed at the time of my field work was later proved correct. Ṣweliḥ married a West Bank girl in early January 1978. His uncle Ṭareq failed to show up at Ṣweliḥ's betrothal ceremony. He apparently hoped to prevail upon his brother to exert his influence on the young man making him retract his promise to another woman in order to marry his (Ṭareq's) daughter. Though the betrothal ceremony is a binding, official act, practice seems to indicate that it is nevertheless not considered final. Ṭareq did show up at the wedding, when his hopes of persuading his brother and the prospective groom could no longer be upheld. When he saw that Rafīq's position was much more difficult after the liquidation of the joint ownership of land, because of difficulties encountered in securing the required manpower for the cultivation of his field, he acquiesced. Perhaps he wished to avoid any public display of resentment and not perpetuate the split within the family. There is no doubt that Ṭareq tried his utmost to bring about the union between his daughter and Ṣweliḥ. Only when he realized that further efforts would be fruitless, did he renounce pressure. He could not very well disregard a wedding in his family, the invitations for which were in the name of his own father, the groom's grandfather.

Another case history showing that joint ownership by brothers may be determined by factors other than economic, is that of Muḥammad Yazīd and his brother Fares. They did not divide their land until 1976 when Muḥammad's second son became engaged to a woman from a different lineage of the Yazīd descent group. This destroyed Fares' and his wife's hopes that the young man would marry their daughter. In their disappointment they did not attend the betrothal ceremony and demanded an immediate division of the joint property. This was especially important because Muḥammad was Yamma's representative in the Regional Council and depended on political support including that of his brother. His son's marriage also antagonized Ibrāhīm, a Marja resident who had wanted his son to marry Muḥammad's sons's bride.

This man was of the Naser lineage while Muḥammad and Fares belonged to that of Hasān lineage (see chart I). Ibrāhīm's wife and the bride's mother were sisters and they had plans for their children's marriage. However, Dāūd (D_22, chart I) needed Muḥammad to help his father (D_14) and his brother (E_2) who had both been sentenced for life after the murder of their unmarried daughter and sister Lea (E_8), to save the family honor. Dāūd considered winning the political support of his agnates an overriding consideration. Ibrāhīm joined Ṭareq's faction and when the betrothal of Ibrāhīm's son to a woman from Jatt took place in 1976, Ṭareq appeared at the head of all Muḥammad's opponents, publicly demonstrating the strained relations, as did Fares and his wife. Gossip concentrated on the split between the two brothers. It was stressed that Fares had always displayed great loyalty to his brother Muḥammad, who now found himself rather isolated in his descent group after Fares had decided to join Ṭareq's faction. The causes for the division of the joint properties in both case histories were not identical. In the first economic reasons were subordinated to social ones, while in the second they were social, though of a different nature and on a different plane.

Fares' case history indicates that joint ownership may also have political implications. Two brothers will not easily attach themselves to different political camps, even if they do not share the same opinions. In this case the joint ownership was dissolved once a non-economic objective, that of marriage of a daughter, had not been achieved. Marx argues that in the Negev, FBD is often arranged by brothers who wish to ensure continued joint management of property during their lifetime.[89] My data indicates that in most cases the joint management of property is economically motivated, but that neither economy nor kinship predominates. Sometimes there is preference for the one and sometimes for the other, and at other times both reasons operate in conjunction.

This complex relationship between two brothers may be described in Goffmann's terms as a team, "a set of individuals whose intimate cooperation is required if a given projected definition of the situation is to be maintained. A team is a grouping not in relation to a social structure or social organization but rather in relation to an interaction or series of interactions in which the relevant definition of the situation is maintained."[90] In other words, economic factors are not active all the time. They must be seen in the wider context of social interaction in any relationship between partners, which may of course include brothers.

FBD MARRIAGES: FACT VERSUS IDEOLOGY

Rosenfeld's view that FBD marriage prevents property from being taken out of the extended family is not convincing.[91] He himself says elsewhere that "the woman who takes her share of inheritance, loses her rights in her father's house"[92] and thus concedes that many women, if not all, choose not to claim their rightful heritage.[93]

In the hamlets there was not a single case in which a woman, who had a brother (or brothers) and was married, had claimed any share of her legal inheritance. The situation was the same in all categories of marriage, FBD, other in-group, as well as outside the family or the village. In the combined sub-periods covered by the study, a total of fifteen brotherless women had married. (These cases represent the female offsprings of only ten men, since some involved two or more sisters). Eight of the fifteen women were married to their FBS. A total of six of the fifteen women received their share of the inheritance. Three of these married their FBS, two others within the village, and the sixth, outside the village. Two of the latter six women were the sisters married to their cousins, Rafīq and Ṭareq. Immediately after their father's death, their uncle Aḥmad (Rafīq and Ṭareq's father) had the land in question registered in the girls' names in order to forestall the possibility of the property being claimed by the girls' mother and her second husband. At the time the land was transferred, it had already been decided that the girls would marry Aḥmad's sons.

This case is unusual in that it supports the contention that FBD marriage is economically motivated. Such cases occur only under the following circumstances: where there is no male to inherit and where (at the same time) the father dies before the mother. In rural Arab society it is unusual for a male not to take a second wife if his first wife dies. If this event occurs and if a male heir results from the second marriage, the issue of daughters claiming their share of the inheritance will not arise. In two cases the grandfather of the married women survived his son, so that according to Islamic Law, they were not entitled to any inheritance. In another case, the father was alive and had six unmarried daughters beside one married.[94] Peters is correct in stating that "the reduction of marriage to property relationships is not merely an over-simplification, but a fundamental error."[95]

The following case history is another example of the disregard of the supposed right to marry one's FBD. Muḥammad 'Alī was the only son of Musa. Several years earlier Muḥammad's father had wanted him to marry his second cousin. With the help of her mother, the girl refused and married her mother's brother's son instead. Muḥammad himself was indifferent to the negotiations and their outcome. In the spring of 1972, Musa died. Three months later Muḥammad's mother Fahīma (referred to in the hamlet as the "female father" because of her strong personality) started looking for a prospective bride for her only son. Fahīma and her daughter Khaḍra approached Walīda 'Attīlī who had a daughter named Sihām. Sihām had three first parallel cousins, two of whom lived in Israel, while the other, whose brother was married to Sihām's sister (Khaḍra), was a resident of the West Bank. Walīda, Sihām's mother, was in favor of Sihām marrying Muḥammad. She considered an only son a desirable candidate as he was his father's sole heir, and thought that her daughter was likely to be indulged by her mother-in-law (Fahīma) who would depend on her if she wished to remain close to her son. Usually it is the mother-in-law who tries to rule over the daughter-in-law. Such a relationship can lead to tension between the two. In a case where a mother has an only son, she tends to be more careful in her relationship with her daughter-in-law.

While secret negotiations for the marriage were still in progress, of which even the *ḥamūla* was unaware. Muḥammad's uncle was killed in a traffic accident. However, this did not prevent the weddding ceremony from taking place only four months later, before the year of mourning for the bridegroom's father was over. Muḥammad's uncles and their families did not attend the wedding, saying that the ceremony should have been postponed out of respect for the deceased member of the family. There were, however, even more compelling causes. One of Muḥammad's uncles complained that he had only been invited to the wedding one week before it took place. He felt that he and other members of the family should have been consulted, as it was customary not to open marriage negotiations before speaking to the members of one's *ḥamūla* and listening to their advice. Muḥammad's youngest uncle mentioned another grievance. Two of Muḥammad's father's brothers had daughters who should have been preferred and there were six other female relatives who had precedence over the chosen bride.

The excuse given for not attending the wedding was only that—an excuse. It was the choice of marriage partner for Muḥammad rather than the date of the wedding that perturbed them. The grievance about the other relatives who should have been preferred indicated that in-group marriage is the preferred pattern, though not necessarily FBD. The eligible FBDs mentioned were only two of the eight candidates available. It is important to note that the category of candidates included all eligible in-group women. The uncles were simply protesting that Muḥammad's new bride was not a member of the *ḥamūla*. The fact that they had not been consulted about the wedding arrangements meant that they had had no opportunity to try to prevent an out-group marriage. FBD marriage is again shown to be no more than a sub-category of in-group marriage.

The total of possible FBD marriages for every man and woman for each of the five sub-periods have been tabulated and can be compared with the number of actual FBD marriages. In order to determine the number of possible FBD marriages, the qualifying criteria put forward by Marx has been taken into account: "neither of the cousins .... should be mentally or physically incapacitated, nor should their parents have quarelled .... The women should not be more than ten years younger or over five years older than her male cousin." [96] A more restricted age differential has been used, the tabulation presented only including women who were not more than five years younger or not more than three years older than their male cousins.

The results are presented in Table 25. In only forty-five of a total of ninety-nine possible cases was the presumed "right" of FBD marriage exercised, which does not confirm Goldberg's explanation for the limited number of FBD marriages contracted. He argues that "in a given population not everyone will have an FBD or an FBS of marriageable age."[97] Goldberg's statement is true, in and of itself, but it does not account for the disproportionately larger number of non-FBD marriages in the hamlets, since fewer than forty-five percent of all possible FBD marriages were actually contracted. This figure would have been even smaller if it were taken into consideration that four of the ninety-nine males concerned had more than one eligible FBD (three had two, while the fourth had three).

From the opposite point of view there were cases in which FBD marriage was both possible and desired, and yet not contracted. For example, in twelve of the fifty-four cases in which FBD marriage did not occur, the marriage proposals were rejected. There were thus two distinct reasons why possible FBD

Table 25

Possible Versus Actual FBD Marriages (%)

Sub-period	*Total Marriages*	*FBD Marriages Possible*	*Actual*	*Non-FBD Marriages*
1918-1930	19	5 (31.5)	4 (26.3)	1 (5.2)
1931-1948	57	14 (24.6)	7 (12.3)	7 (12.3)
1949-1956	61	17 (28.9)	12 (19.7)	5 (8.2)
1957-June 1967	76	27 (35.5)	8 (10.5)	19 (25.0)
July 1967-Sept. 1974	103	36 (35.2)	14 (13.6)	22 (21.6)
TOTAL	316 (100)	99 (31.3)	45 (14.2)	54 (17.1)

marriages were not contracted—either the male chose not to marry his FBD, or he wished to and was refused. Whatever the reason, the discrepancy between ideology and fact is considerable. If FBD marriage were genuinely preferred, this would be reflected in the proportionally large number of proposals. Only fifty-five out of a possible ninety-nine proposals were made to first patrilateral parallel cousins.

This gap between ideology and actual fact is the more remarkable in view of the fact that the eligibility criteria had already eliminated the most obvious grounds for either non-preference or rejection. The wrong conclusions of some researchers can be ascribed to an erroneous use of the term *bint 'amm*. Here are some of the definitions: Ayoub explains that the "term /ibn 'amm/ in its cousin meaning, had also the classificatory extension to all age peers in the kin group. . ."[98] Marx finds that in the Negev the term applies "not only to the age mates of one's own group, but also to matrilateral cousins in an allied group." He adds that *bint 'amm* was used in a more limited sense, but might "also be employed by men and women, for a woman of approximately their own age born in the co-liable group."[99] By using the term 'close cousins', Antoun avoids controversy, specifying that "marriage between close cousins [is] up to the fifth patrilateral cousin."[100] Sweet goes as far as to apply *ibn 'amm* to related tribes.[101] However, the terms are also used in reference to husband and wife respectively. Jaussen reports that Arabs referred to their wives as *bint 'amm*,[102] which Granqvist confirms.[103] Marx maintains that in the Negev wives are only addressed as *bint 'amm* when "they were true kin," though he realizes that in other areas custom is different.[104]

In the hamlets, the term *bint 'amm* is used only with reference to in-group marriage. When male residents were asked how they are related to their wives, many answered that the woman was "*bint 'ammi*,"—the daughter of my father's brother. The next question was more specific, "Is she your father's brother's daughter?" The reply was often, "No, she is the daughter of 'so and so' who is the cousin of my father." It should be noted that "*bint 'ammi*" was given in answer to the first question only when the wife was a member of the in-group as defined here. The different responses to the two separate questions makes it clear that in the hamlets the term *bint 'amm* is considered the appropriate designation for any female member of the in-group, not only one who is specifically the individual's FBD.

Table 25 shows that the fluctuations in the proportions of possible versus actual FBD marriages, from one sub-period to the next, correlate with the entire in-group category of marriages (see Table 22, p. 89). In the 1949-56 sub-period, seventy percent of all marriages were of the in-group type (twenty-nine percent within the "possible FBD marriage" category), and 19.7 percent were actually FBD marriages. By contrast, only 27.6 percent of all marriages were contracted within the group during the 1956-67 period, and FBD marriages amounted to only 10.5 percent (out of the 35.5 percent possible).

A slight increase in the relative proportion of FBD marriages occurred in the fifth sub-period (13.6 percent out of the possible 35.2 percent). Changes in the "field of possibilities" enlarged the pool of candidates and the result was an increase of exchange of women on various levels, within and outside the village, and within the group. The rate of actual FBD marriages was affected by new possibilities of marriage due to Israeli occupation of the West Bank. These changes in the "field of possibilities" were significant in the hamlets. In the 1949-56 sub-period, when the border between Israel and Jordan and the military administration restricted the "field of possibilities," the incidence of FBD marriage was high. When obstacles to inter-village contact were removed, there was a decrease in the relative proportion of FBD marriage.

Finally, one additional factor affects the rate of FBD marriage. In some cases, including one example given above, FBD marriages may take place between the children of sisters. Often it is the mothers who plan the marriages. Other instances of marriage between matrilineal cousins involve no patrilineal relationship. Table 26 (overleaf) shows the data regarding marriages of matrilateral affines. Out of the eleven *awlād khālāt*, mother's sister's daughter (MZD), unions recorded, five are also FBD marriages. Informants state that all marriages during the second and third sub-periods, and four out of the six in the fifth sub-period were due to maternal influence. Particular attention should be given to the third and fifth sub-periods. In these periods there occurred the only examples of *awlād* khālāt which were at the same time FBD.

Two of the four MZD/FBD cases in the fifth sub-period represent marriage arrangements initiated by the maternal parents of the couples. (The other two are discussed above in the case history of Rafīq and Ṭareq Yazīd). Three out of five cases of FBD/MZD marriage represent unions contracted on the strength

Table 26
Marriages Between Matrilineal Kin

Sub-period	Total No. Marriages	Number of Matrilineal Kin Marriages: *Bint Khāl* (*MBD*)	*Awlād Khālāt* (*MZD*)
1918-1930	19	1	0
1931-1948	57	4(3*+1)	0
1949-1956	61	2(2*0)	2(1**+1*)
1957-June '67	76	1	3(2*+1)
July '67-Sept '74	103	4(1*+3)	6(4**+2)
TOTAL	316	12(6*+6)	11(5**+3*+3)

* Mother's brother or mother's sister is member of the patrilineage (a member of the in-group category).
** Mother's sister's daughter also father's brother's daughter.

of the MZD relationship involved, rather than the FBD, one case from the third, and two in the fifth sub-periods. The six cases of MZD marriage which are not also FBD, plus the twelve cases of MBD (mother's brother's daughter, *bint khāl*) marriage, indicate the powerful influence that the mother has in certain marriage arrangements. None of the twelve MBD marriages were FBD.

Although the data in Table 26 is based only on a 'micro' level investigation referring to the hamlets only, it would seem reasonable to expect that similar patterns are to be found in other Arab peasant communities. It should be remembered that all FBD marriages, including those contracted on the basis of maternal relationships, are still recorded statistically as FBD marriages. Again, the reality behind the statistics may be obscured.

DESCENT AND HAMULA MEMBERSHIP

It is far from easy to classify marriages as either in-group or out-group, though classification is especially important in view of the proposition that FBD marriages be considered a sub-category of in-group marriages. Some persons who seem to belong to a certain *ḥamūla*, defining themselves as members and considered as such by others in the *ḥamūla*, do not originate from that group. An in-group is usually assumed to consist of all members who trace their descent to one and the same man. Thus, as Chart

1 shows, Ibrāhīm Yazīd was the joint ancestor of the Yazīd descent group, and all marriages contracted between any of his descendants should be defined as in-group unions. Each segment or lineage of the Yazīd descent group claims descent from one of Ibrāhīm's sons, either from Muḥammad or from his brothers. Such a lineage usually has a depth of up to five generations. However, not all members of the Yazīd *ḥamūla* are included in this genealogical scheme. Rather, the Yazīd descent group constitutes the core of the Yazīd *ḥamūla*. They attached themselves to the *ḥamūla* for a variety of reasons but were not absorbed in the genealogy. The term *ḥamūla* can only be defined as a patronymic group, that is a group of persons sharing the same surname. One may bear the same surname without relationship by descent.

The Yazīd *ḥamūla* consists of the four lineages of Muḥammad and his brothers (the descendants of Ibrāhīm Yazīd), plus other individuals who joined the descent group. In many instances it is hard to decide how strong and lasting these affiliations are. The following case history illustrates some of the difficulties in attempting to identify the true lineage affiliation of the residents. The author did not, by the way, discover the facts presented here all at one time. They were discovered almost accidentally, one by one, in the course of the field work. As a result three major reclassifications of the statistical data had to be made and my conception of the *ḥamūla* revised, in order to show that it is not a clearly bounded descent group.

Jabār Ibn Labād ($C_1$11, chart 2) was born in the Mt. Carmel region. He married Waṭfa, ($C_1$12), offspring of a semi-nomadic Bedouin tribe that camped on the coastal strip northwest of the hamlets. After leaving his village, Ibn Labād bought land from a resident of the parent village and settled in one of its offshoots in the early 1920s. Later, he married Jalīla ($C_1$10), a member of the Amin *ḥamūla* and took their name. In 1933, 'Oda Ṣaqer ($C_2$1), a Bedouin from the Samarian mountains, came to the hamlets as a *harāth* (ploughman), a tenant farmer in the employ of Jabār Ibn Labād. He later married Faḍa (D 27), Jabār's daughter by his Bedouin wife, he too adopting the name Amīn. Jabār's two sons by Jalīla married members of the Amīn descent group, but from two lineages other than their mother's. 'Oda's sons married members of the fourth lineage of the Amīn group, his eldest son Hamād (E 30) marrying in exchange for his sister (E 27).

In this case members of two entirely unrelated descent groups, one from a peasant farming village and the other from a Bedouin tribe, became fully integrated into the Amīn patronymic group. When the author first met them, all members of the three different descent groups of the Amīn *ḥamūla* identified themselves as of the "Amīn *ḥamūla*." Only later did the author learn that 'Oda was of Bedouin origin, and it took even longer to find out that Slīmān and Dāūd (D 21 and D 20) Jabār's sons, were not descendants of the Amīn group either.

Another descent group, this time from Egypt, arrived during the campaign of Ibrāhīm Pasha as part of the "Masarwa wave" (Masarwa means Egyptians) and settled in the parent village. They lived in the residential concentration of the 'Ali descent group and had already changed their name to 'Ali before they moved into the hamlet village Marja. Cohen notes that new groups, originally of low status, are gradually accepted as equals though it may take several decades before they begin to intermarry with other villagers.[105] The Qarūm family was so fully accepted in the hamlets that the members of the original 'Ali lineage did not even think it worth while to mention that they had changed their family name. Two further examples of voluntary name change indicate the problems of collecting and categorizing data.

Three descent groups, those of 'Ali, Ibn Hajar and Assad, were neighbors in Kharita, a neighborhood of the parent village. When the area came under Israeli rule in 1949, some members of each of the three descent groups registered under their original surnames while others gave Kharita as their family name. In collecting and categorizing data, members of each of the three descent groups bearing the name Kharita had to be identified and regrouped with their actual lineages. In the second example a member of the Yazīd family was a leading terrorist during the Arab rebellion of 1936-39. When Israel took over the area some of his close relatives left for the parent village in Jordan while two lineages of the Yazīd descent group changed their name to Amīn. In 1952, a member of the Amīn *ḥamūla* was convicted of murder, aided and abetted by the victim's wife who was his mistress. Several families of the Yazīd descent group wanted to dissociate themselves from their adopted *ḥamūla* and officially changed their names back to Yazīd, while three of the Yazīd families remained registered as Amīn.

Table 22 (p. 89) shows that 38.9 percent of all marriages within the hamlets were of the in-group category. It is worth noting that the figure obtained at first was fifty percent. After rechecking the data and rearranging for changes in the family name, the new figure was obtained. It can be assumed that similar complications in lineage-descent group identity are to be found in other Arab communities. Peters gives examples of individuals adopted by, or grafted on to, other tribes.[106] As long as the newcomers are not recognized as equals they are distinguished from members of the core group. This is especially marked in times of emergency. Peters mentioned that when water resources dwindle, "it may be necessary to detach a grafted group."[107] A joint patrynomic is often only a partial recognition of acceptance.

This shifting membership may cause inaccuracies in classification, especially when historical data are not available. The composition of the hamlet *ḥamūlas* have not been analyzed but only dealt with in the context of marriage patterns. There are two major reasons for leaving a *ḥamūla* and adopting the name of another: to gain status, or to escape 'shame'. In the latter case, the connection with those responsible for the loss of honor may be permanently severed after some time and no blame will attach to the bearer of the new name.

PLANNED MARRIAGES

As already established, the out-group category of marriage is composed of two sub-categories: marriages contracted within the hamlets as a group and those involving one partner from outside. Marriages in each sub-category may be further subdivided into two groups, unions planned in advance and others best defined as "exigency weddings." Planned marriages often have various economic or political motivating factors. The third sub-period was representative of a time during which many marriages were contracted on an exigency basis. The particular demarcation of the pool of candidates during that period influenced not only the proportion of in-group marriages but that of in-hamlet marriages as well. Sixty-six percent of all out-group marriages were within the hamlets.

The figures reported by other researchers for in-village marriages vary. Granqvist cites 23.5 percent,[108] Cohen 31.7 percent,[109] and Rosenfeld 40.5 percent. Rosenfeld explains the difference between his figures and those of Granqvist by the fact that the village she (Granqvist) studied was very small and there were fewer possibilities of finding a suitable partner than in the larger settlement he investigated.[110] Layish points out that "despite the disintegration of the extended family, endogamous marriages in

Israeli Muslim society were on the increase compared with earlier periods, mainly as a result of the numerical growth of families and clan."[111] He adds that "marriages . . . within the clan and exchange marriages . . . may create strong family pressures to circumvent the legal age of marriage. In one case, the couple explicitly admitted that the reason for the wife's marrying below the legal age was their common family background."[112] Since it is easier to circumvent the law within one's own family, in-group marriage becomes desirable where the intention is to marry off a daughter who is still a minor.

In the hamlets, the percentage of in-village marriages was 30.7 percent, and the distribution of in-village and out-village marriages within the total out-group category was approximately equal. From a total of 193 out-group marriages, ninety-seven were contracted with women from the hamlets, and ninety-six from outside them.

How is one to interpret marriage between villagers of different patronymic groups? According to Granqvist, marriages between *ḥamūlas* in a village "created a feeling of solidarity."[113] Merton uses the term "group solidarity."[114] Rosenfeld speaks of intermarriage as "a mechanism for tipping the balance of power" and argues that "clan intermarriage over generations makes for a feeling of true paternal relationships."[115] Cohen also stresses the political function of inter-*ḥamūla* marriages, calling intermarriage between three specific families an "alliance."[116] He adds that representatives of *ḥamūlas* friendly with each other, especially if they intermarried, "stood together on one side," unlike those with strained relationships who are "divided into opposing factions."[117]

Solidarity appears to have been a significant factor in the hamlets particularly in the first and third sub-periods. Concerning the first sub-period, Granqvist's statement, "that they who together form the village will intermarry in order to knit themselves more closely together."[118] In the third sub-period, a time marked by great uncertainty, village solidarity, in the form of drawing all four hamlets together, was most important. During this time, inter-hamlet marriages were no less important than inter-*ḥamūla* ones.

Many cases of intermarriage between descent groups were intended to create alliances, though economic considerations were by no means unimportant. One type of marriage was that of children of owners of adjoining fields. Physical closeness of children and parents at work, in other words, family loyalty,

Table 27

Marriages within Hamlets

% in brackets

Sub-period	Total Marriages	Total Out-group Marriages	Total Marriages within Hamlets	Marriages between Neighbors*
1918-1930	19	10 (52.6)	7 (36.8)	2 (10.5)
1931-1948	57	36 (63.2)	30 (35.1)	4 (7.0)
1949-1956	61	18 (29.5)	12 (19.7)	5 (8.2)
1957-June 1967	76	55 (72.4)	30 (39.5)	1.8)
July '67-Sept '74	103	74 (71.8)	28 (27.9)	3 (2.9)
TOTALS	316	193 (61.1)	97 (30.7)	23 (7.3)

* Who own adjoining fields.

played no less a part than economic considerations. Table 27 shows the chronological distribution of this form of marriage. Granqvist, too, stresses the function of marriages in joint agricultural operations together with the solidarity factor.[119] Several informants emphasized the satisfaction of seeing their daughter work in a neighboring field, a feeling shared by the daughters.

In the third sub-period, the fact that some of the former residents of Manshīyya, Zelefe and Jeleme ('Attīl offshoots) resettled in Yamma, exerted some influence. These new residents received their share of land within the boundaries of the hamlets in most cases taking possession of absentee property, finding themselves with new neighbors in the fields and orchards. This should be taken into consideration, along with the other causes previously discused, when formulating an explanation of the documented increase of in-group marriages in the hamlets.

In the fourth sub-period, new methods of cultivation demanded greater cooperation among villagers. Sharing one water-line was a way of reducing expenses. Joint usage intensified social contacts between neighbors. As a result marriages between neighboring families (neighbors with respect to the location of agricultural fields, as opposed to places of residence) became more frequent and certainly more desirable. The following two cases illustrate this type of marriage.

Ḥasan Khaḍer had water rights but neither of the cooperatives whose fields adjoined his would permit him to use their supply lines. In the spring of 1965, two significant events took place, a sprinkler system was installed in Khaḍer's fields, and Ḥabib

Jabali, treasurer of the Jabali Water Cooperation, married Khaḍer's daughter. Whether Khaḍer's daughter was the price of the sprinkler system or the reward for it is not known. But there is little doubt that the marriage was connected with the permission to draw water for the sprinkler system from the cooperative's line. Sometimes marriage is both politically and economically motivated. Rushdi, the secretary of a water cooperative, wanted to accumulate power. He convinced his uncle, who needed more water than he had been officially allocated, to let Yūsuf Asad marry his daughter. In return, Rushdi promised his uncle an increased allocation of water, knowing he could count on Yūsuf Asad's vote in the cooperative as a result.

Table 27 indicates that the highest proportion of marriages between hamlet families with adjoining fields was found in the fourth subperiod when traditional agricultural methods were being replaced by modern systems of intensive cultivation. Almost forty percent of all such marriages were contracted within the fourth sub-period. In addition, 30.7 percent of all in-village marriages were contracted between residents who owned adjacent fields.

When the children of owners of neighboring fields marry, such alliances reinforce mutually beneficial economic cooperation, and there is reason to expect that the arrangement will continue for at least another generation. In-group marriages and their sub-category, FBD marriages, sometimes seem to have been arranged for the same reasons as unions between unrelated families owning adjacent fields. In other words, some marriages motivated by agricultural economics may be with FBDs so that once again caution is indicated in explaining FBD marriage by ideological preference alone.

FURTHER DISCUSSION OF BADAL

The *badal*, planned marriage involving an exchange of women, is a distinct category of marriage patterns. Table 28 shows that forty-six marriages, 14.6 percent of the total, were *badal*. Granqvist reports a percentage of 26.5 percent;[120] Rosenfeld 27.3 percent;[121] while Cohen gives figures closer to those in the hamlets.[122]

Badal is frowned upon by religious leaders but nevertheless is often resorted to. Rosenfeld emphasizes the economic motivation of *badal*. Expenses were "immediately matched by the other person" and "feasts are . . . shared by the participants in the

Table 28
Distribution of Badal Marriages
(percentages in brackets)

Sub-periods	*All Marriages* Total	Badal	*In-group Marriages* Total	Badal	*Out-group Marriages* Total	Badal
1918-1930	19	3 (15.8)	9 (47.4)	2 (10.5)	10 (52.6)	1 (5.7)
1931-1948	57	8 (14.0)	21 (36.8)	3 (5.3)	36 (63.2)	5 (8.7)
1949-1956	61	11 (18.0)	43 (70.5)	7 (11.5)	18 (29.5)	4 (6.5)
1957-June 1967	76	3 (3.9)	21 (27.6)	1 (1.3)	55 (72.4)	2 (2.6)
July '67-Sept '74	103	20 (20.4)	29 (28.2)	6 (5.8)	74 (71.7)	15 (14.6)
TOTAL	316	46 (14.6)	123 (38.9)	19 (6.1)	193 (61.1)	27 (8.5)

marriage . . . no tremendous sum of money need be raised in terms of immediate cash outlay for the bride price,"[123] a view shared by Marx.[124]

Keyser rejects this argument and claims that "every marriage involves some sort of exchange and the woman, if she were not exchanged for another woman, would be exchanged for goods, services, or money."[125] Rosenfeld's argument would only be applicable in cases where both brides are from the same village, since only then as Granqvist notes, can "common feasts" be celebrated.[126] Layish gives many reasons against *badal*, quoting a Sheikh as having said that it was "a malignant disease."[127] He also maintains that "exchange marriage is a striking example of a clash between social custom and religious norm."[128] Several scholars mention the political advantage of *badal*, for example, Rosenfeld and Antoun,[129] while Granqvist stresses that it has both advantages and disadvantages.[130]

One resident married to his FBD pointed out the disadvantages. Whenever his sister's marriage was threatened and she returned to her natal family, his own wife went back to hers, automatically. Cohen explains that a woman must follow the example of her "substitute woman, that is the woman given in exchange for her . . . Relationships are thus strained for the whole duration of the dispute."[131] Antoun points out that "violation of norms by one of the pairs is followed by violation of the same norms by the other pair."[132]

Sometimes *badal* marriages are contracted as a last resort due to a family's bad reputation. The following case illustrates this. Nimmer Zamīl married a resident from a village northeast of the parent village in exchange for a husband for his sister. He was far from pleased with the arrangement but finally agreed in obedience to his father's wishes who wanted Nimmer's elder sister to marry. The family knew that there were serious obstacles in the way of marriage for the girl, for Nimmer's eldest unmarried sister had become pregnant, a fact that was not a secret in the hamlets. Also, in the early 1950s, Nimmer's father's sister (*'amma*) had committed adultery with her FBS and worse still, had been accomplice to her husband's murder. Although she was not convicted for lack of evidence, she was generally considered guilty. Under these circumstances, Nimmer's refusal of the *badal* would have condemned his sister to spinsterhood.

When *badal* is concluded among families not living in the same village, the bride is accompanied by members of her family and friends on part of the way to her future home. Some very close female relatives, usually her mother and sister, go all the way with her. Usually, the two parties meet halfway between the villages. However, Nimmer's father Shāmmel arranged for a meeting place considerably closer to his own domicile than to that of the other family living on the West Bank. He boasted that they had to travel twice as far as his party, interpreting this as a sign of his superior status. According to tradition, the couple has dinner in the late afternoon and then moves into the bedroom. The bridegroom's mother takes her place outside until her son signals that the bride's hymen has been pierced. She then makes the sound of the traditional *zagharīt* (singing a shrill, warbling tone to express joy).

However, Nimmer's mother had no occasion for rejoicing on the wedding night, since her son proved impotent. His father lost no time in taking him to a doctor in neighboring Tul Karem but the groom continued to be impotent. When professional medical help failed to produce the desired results Nimmer and his father turned to witchcraft. Unless the bridegroom managed to prove his virility he would be pronounced *marbūt* (literally, tied,—made impotent by either sorcery or other causes).[133] Worse still, the bride's parents would take their daughter home, which would amount to a public announcement of Nimmer's impotence and his bride's virginity. Though Nimmer had not consumed his marriage, his sister had already become a *mara* (literally, woman). Yet, according to the rules of *badal*, if Nimmer's marriage were dissolved she too would have to return to her natal family. As she was no longer a virgin, her chances of contracting a second marriage would be greatly reduced. Shāmmel, Nimmer's father, was greatly upset and grew even more desperate as the date of the ceremonious visit of the bride's family grew near, for it had already been put off as long as custom allowed. He remembered a similar case where the groom's father had used a stick to break the bride's hymen. The bride, however, had reported the event to her parents and they had insisted on her returning home. As a result both *badal* marriages had been annulled. Fortunately, Nimmer managed to consummate the marriage on the ninth night, thus saving both marriages.

Had Nimmer been successful on the night of his wedding, he would have had the required blood-stained *badlet-eṣ-ṣimmad* (wedding lingerie) to display as proof to his mother. She, in turn, would have shown it to the bride's family at the time of their visit the following week. Congratulations would then be in order for everyone concerned. Such is the custom in the hamlets, though traditions regarding the wedding night and the breaking of the hymen vary throughout the Arab world. Luṭfiyya describes the wedding night ritual where the groom "rushes outside and fires a couple of shots in the air . . . He then strolls out to where the men are gathered and receives congratulations. If the groom is unsuccessful . . . he is ridiculed. . ."[134] Randolph notes that the custom of displaying a bloody bed cloth as proof of virginity is not practiced among Negev Bedouin.[135] In Peters' description of the Bedouin of Cyrenica, the hymen is broken "through piercing it which is done by the groom using his finger."[136] It would seem that the Bedouin are alert to the possibility of the groom's failure and want to avoid the problem. Patai describes a similar practice among Egyptian peasants who are occasionally helped by midwives. He states that "the first cohabitation often takes place only the next day."[137] Luṭfiyya depicts how the groom's peers try to "listen and peek through windows and keyholes," and do not leave before they have watched intercourse.[138]

A wedding is an event in which many residents participate. It is of special relevance to the members of the bridegroom's peer group, for now their relationship with him will change. He will have different obligations and objectives, and there will no longer be that easy-going relationship that characterizes persons belonging to the same generation and being in a similar position. The responsibility that marriage implies, especially when patrilocal residence is not practised, distinguishes the young man from his contemporaries and brings him closer to other married men even older ones. The bridegroom is in some way considered a "traitor" who opts out of the peer group and prefers a different way of life. The "peering in" is an expression of disapproval as well as curiosity, the joking and ribald remarks that result express protest. "In the morning," Luṭfiyya adds, "such spectators will amuse themselves by telling others what they had witnessed the night before."[139] It is not only the moment when the young men peer into the bedroom to watch what goes on that provides entertainment. What has been witnessed may be discussed again in days to come. When the members of his former peer group meet the married man, they can embarrass him by hinting at what they have seen. Teasing him and reminding him of their earlier relations is a way of maintaining contact. Luṭfiyya's description adds a new aspect to the ceremony—that of gossip among the groom's peer group. Observation of the sexual act is considered part of the wedding ritual, entertaining and providing a subject for talk.

Nimmer's mishap was the subject of a great deal of gossip in every guestroom until he finally proved his virility and settled down to married life. There are still residents who will even tell a stranger the tale of Nimmer's bad start to married life. Most of the men in the guestroom expressed contempt for Nimmer and showed no compassion. They boasted of their own virility, making no attempt to hide feelings of superiority. The older men take an active interest in the sexual prowess of bridegrooms and if a much younger man is shown up as a failure, they have an opportunity to hint that their age is not necessarily a disadvantage. Such comparison, in sexual matters and others, is characteristic of Arab rural society. A man's ability is shown up against another's defect. Even when all was over, there was no sympathy for Nimmer's dilemma, but rather disappointment that an exciting situation was no longer topical. There remained smugness and the hint that "it can't happen to me." Incidentally, Nimmer attributed his failure to excitement!

In one guestroom, the author tentatively mentioned the possibility of eliminating the show of proof of a man's virility on his wedding night, without any reference to Nimmer. One guest remarked that it might indeed prevent a lot of trouble. Another mentioned two similar incidents in the hamlets, one of them in a *badal* marriage. In this case, the groom's parents had tried to protect their son by simply declaring that the bride had not passed the virginity test and forcing her to return to her natal family. At the same time, the groom's parents demanded their daughter's return and claimed compensation. A medical examination later proved her virginity.[140]

Nimmer's *badal* marriage was contracted not only for economic and political reasons. It also was a double alliance with a Samarian mountain ridge village family close to the West Bank hinterland. The political aspect was less decisive than the urgent need to provide a husband for Nimmer's sister. It was an "exigency" marriage, one made necessary by compelling personal circumstances. The bride's father attempted to find a groom from a West Bank village, hoping perhaps, that the bad repute of his family had not spread so far. The West Bank bride's parents consented to the proposed *badal* mainly for economic reasons, Nimmer's father found work for his son-in-law, also helping to obtain jobs for his son-in-law's brother and nephew. Thus both families had sufficient reasons for the *badal*.

Table 28 (p. 127) illustrates the distribution of *badal* marriages. Fewer than fifteen percent were exchanges of women, the total number of exchange marriages in each sub-period also being small. Closer scrutiny reveals some interesting patterns. Differences in category distribution become evident when the first and third sub-period are compared with the second and fourth. In the former, in-group marriages were more numerous than out-group ones, while in the latter the situation is reversed. The differences between the fourth and fifth sub-periods are of special interest. In the fourth there were no more than three *badal* marriages (3.9 percent of all marriages). The corresponding figure in the fifth was twenty-one *badal* marriages (20.4 percent).[141]

This is doubtless due to changes in the "fieid of possibilities" which occurred in the wake of the Six Day War. The young men in the hamlets were no longer prevented from choosing a bride from those villages that were in the past on the other side of a closed border. This meant sharper competition for female residents of the hamlets. While the brides from the West Bank did not object to living near the parents and natal family of the young men from the hamlets; the parents of the girls from the hamlets preferred a marriage partner for their daughter who lived close by. This decreased the chances of finding suitable husbands for the hamlet girls. The preference given to West Bank girls may be explained by the fact that the hamlet men knew that the demands of the bride's parents would be less stringent. As already mentioned, Israeli Arab girls expect a house of their own and are not content with a room in the home of the extended family. The bride price was also lower in the West Bank. Furthermore, parents of the West Bank girls encouraged marriages with Israeli Arabs as they wished to establish contacts in Israel. They often depended on the connection of their new affines both for jobs and for smooth contacts with the authorities. In sum, the girls living in the hamlets had more difficulties in finding husbands than before the war of June 1967.

Most of the *badal* marriages in the fifth sub-period were in the out-group category, as were non-*badal*. Again, if FBD were the preferred marriage pattern, the question arises as to why out-group marriage should have been sought. Yet this is what actually occured. Khalīl Jabali, for example, only consented to FBD *badal* for his daughter when two earlier out-group engagements had been cancelled, leaving him no alternative. The new possibilities of marriage in the fourth sub-period resulted in increased numbers of out-group marriages, while *badal* decreased. If economic or political motives were decisive in the selection of marriage partners, the single-link type of marriage would be given preference, since it is free from the accompanying complications of *badal*. It may be assumed, therefore, that many 'exchange of women marriages' should be classified as "exigency" unions.

Three young single males in the hamlets, all above the age of twenty-five with post-secondary education, expressed their rejection of *badal* in strong terms. All of them had sisters above the age of twenty-four. They refused to leave the choice of their future wife to their father. Two of them had younger brothers who, they thought, should contract *badal* marriages, as they had not completed their high school education: the less educated to be entrusted with unpleasant duties and expected to follow tradition while the qualified break away from the confining framework of custom. Education is an important factor in the selection of a marriage partner. Those who have studied at teachers' colleges or universities, usually prefer literate women. Individuality is used as a criterion for the girls status, rather than the prestige of her family and *ḥamūla*. The same phenomenon is also found where women successfully manage the family farm while their husbands work outside. They acquire status within the family. Achieved status for women is not an entirely new phenomenon in Arab rural society, but in recent years more and more women have come to enjoy it. Achieved rather than ascribed status was especially conspicuous as a factor in marriage partner selection during the fifth sub-period. Achieved status became a required attribute for inclusion in the "field of eligibles."

ENDOGAMY RECONSIDERED

Many studies of marriage patterns in Arab society indicate that there is a preference for endogamy, though few researchers adequately define the term. Some use it in connection with FBD marriages, while others apply it to in-group marriages in general and others still to intra-tribe or intra-village marriages.

For Patai, endogamy stands for preferred marriage with close blood relatives, though he does not define the term 'blood relatives.'[142] Barth associates endogamy "with a strong emphasis on the father's brother's daughter as a preferred spouse, [which] has been assumed to be associated with a desire to maintain family property."[143] Ayoub holds that endogamy be considered in the wider context of preferential marriage.[144] Rosenfeld, on the other hand, relates endogamy to the lineage,[145] which he defines as the *ḥamūla*, as does Cohen.[146] Barth explains that in the Kurdish community he studied, the term endogamy is used with reference to the whole village; he speaks of 'village endogamy' rather than of endogamy within a descent group.[147] In the same article, Barth applies the term in two senses. First, with regard to FBD marriage (blood relatives), and second, with regard to a communal in-group (the village), based on physical and social proximity. Chelhood terms all marriages within the tribe as endogamous.[148] Bromlei supplies examples of ethnic endogamy (ethos endogamy) from the Caucasus though Patai defines the same groups as exogamous.[149] If endogamy refers to unions with FBD or with close blood relations, a marriage contracted with unrelated partners is *ipso facto* exogamous. It will be seen that there can be no clear-cut definition of the term. Barth's statement that anthropology has not yet succeeded in evolving a "generally acceptable theory of exogamy" indicates the problem.[150]

It might be expedient to consider the definition of the *Encyclopaedia of Social Sciences* that "the rule of endogamy exists where the field of possible spouses is limited to persons within an individual's territory and/or social group."[151] The scope is enlarged by researchers such as Bromlei who claims that endogamy "is the custom forbidding marriage outside a given group"[152] and adds that it should be understood as "preferential marriage with one's own community."[153] Marx rejects the term endogamy as inapplicable to Bedouin society.[154] Since there is no explicit rule forbidding marriage outside the group in Bedouin or other Arab communities, Marx is right. Yet if behavioral norms are applied, endogamy cannot be denied.

Arab communities are best not classified as either 'endogamous' or 'exogamous'[155] since there would then be value terms applied to behavioral norms. It is argued here that endogamy is not a preferred marriage pattern. Some scholars correlate preference for FBD marriage or other in-group marriage patterns such as those within the clan, *ḥamūla*, village and tribe, with endogamy. In terms of behavioral norms there is endogamy in Arab rural and nomad society, yet the terms in-group and out-group marriage seem preferable.

SUMMING UP OF METHOD, MODEL AND MARRIAGE PATTERNS

This study presents a new approach to the analysis of marriage patterns in Arab rural society, which, it would appear, is equally applicable to Arab nomad society. A descriptive model of a variable pool of candidates for marriage has been combined with a methodology for the diachronic study of marriage patterns, together with a detailed examination of the factors determining marital choice. This approach may be applied to any field study in which the researcher can define appropriate dividing lines between sub-periods significant to his specific 'micro' field. This does not mean that a similar approach may not be applied on the 'macro' level. For example, modern means of transportation, by diminishing travelling time, has enlarged the "field of possibilities". Shortened distances makes it possible for people to accept employment in places once considered very far away. This greatly enlarges the scope for meeting possible marriage partners. Also, fathers are now much more willing to allow their newlywed daughters to move to other villages previously considered forbiddingly distant. On the 'micro' level, the pool of candidates for hamlet residents was enlarged in the fifth sub-period. Marriage to Jewish women should also be taken into account. The cases of three such marriages in the hamlets have already been mentioned, representing a change in the "field of eligibles".

Both of the above modifications in the pool of candidates (better transport conditions and marriage to Jewish women), affected not only the hamlets, but Israeli-Arab village society in general. Changes on the 'micro' level are thus paralleled on the 'macro' level. Cohen ascribes the effects of greater mobility partly to better road transport and partly to the integration of the Arabs in Israel's economic and educational systems which, in turn, provides opportunities for Arab males to meet Jewish girls.[156] During the fourth and fifth sub-periods there were changes in the "field of consenters" since Arab males were now included in the "fields of eligibles" of Jewish girls. Moreover, Jewish girls were even preferred by some Arab males because of their higher level of education.[157]

The Arab male is in a very different situation from that of the Arab female. He often takes employment outside the village and has many opportunities to make contact with Jewish women. Arab girls and women work and travel in groups. They have almost no opportunity to make contact with Jewish men. When away from his residence the Arab male often adopts a Hebrew name so as to appear a member of the dominant national group. Only after he has become well acquainted with the Jewish girl will he reveal his origin. By this time a close relationship, that sometimes leads to marriage, may have developed in spite of different backgrounds. Frequently this is in the face of parental opposition. Such an occurence is not possible between an Arab girl and a Jewish male, and is the reason why mixed marriages are usually contracted between Arab males and Jewish girls.

Muslim law does not require Jewesses and Christian females to convert in order to legalize their marriage. Children of such a union are considered Muslim at birth. If a Jew marries a non-Jewish woman, her children are not considered Jews, for according to Judaism, it is the mother's faith that determines the religion of the children. The legal situation in respect of intermarriage is different for males and females. The marriage of a Muslim male and a Jewess is less bound up with complications than if the male is Jewish. The children of a Muslim mother either have to convert or are considered non-Jews as well as non-Muslims. In matters of personal status, the Rabbinical or Islamic law rules supreme. No legally binding civil marriage can be concluded in the state of Israel (see note 70).

As the number of female university students increases, so opportunities for meetings between Arab Muslim girls and Jewish males have become more frequent. This newly emerging situation will surely lead to an increasing number of marriages between Jewish males and Muslim females. Against this, the legal position explained above will continue to impose some restraint. It is not easy for a girl to defy her natal family and perhaps be subject to the visible disapproval of her community.

The data and interpretation presented in this chapter serve to demonstrate the general effectiveness of the analytical approach.

The descriptive model is a convenient framework for conceptualizing the marriage partner selection process in the hamlets, while the sub-period divisions help to find a meaningful interpretation of statistically recorded marriage pattern distributions. Many important shifts would have been totally obscured if the entire time period, 1918-74, were treated as a single statistical unit. The sub-divisions permit a more sensitive analysis of the factors effecting marriage.

To test the wider applicability of the methodology, additional studies were undertaken outside the hamlets. Three communities, distinctly different from the hamlets and from one another were chosen. Marriage pattern data was collected according to chronological sub-periods. Discernible trends with viable explanations emerged in the diachronic analysis of each community. Although the techniques used in defining the sub-periods of each of the communities are the same as applied to the hamlets, the resulting sub-divisions are not identical. In each case locally significant events and changes in circumstances affecting marriage arrangements had to be acknowledged in order to provide an appropriate framework for understanding the recorded marriage bonds. The results of the supplementary studies are summarized in appendix D.

Significant dividing lines between sub-periods are evident in several studies of Arab societies, yet the authors do not show how the changes may effect marriage patterns. Cohen describes a situation closely resembling that prevailing in the hamlets. The events determining his division of sub-periods were the 1948 War of Independence and the 1956 Sinai campaign with the subsequent relaxation of military government. In Luṭfīyya's study, the dividing line would be approximately 1949, when refugees from Deir Hasīn settled in the village he studied, and the period when many young males left to make money in the United States. On returning from abroad they built what Luṭfīyya calls the 'American Quarter', a series of modern houses. Both developments marked changes in the pool of candidates by enlarging the "field of possibilities".

In Marx's study, the Bedouin in question started working in the North in 1959-60 when employment opportunities became available. At the same time there was a drought in the Negev which compelled them and their small flocks to move to the central part of the country where some of them stayed for several years.[158] The "field of possibilities" for the Bedouin youth was enlarged because working opportunities and satisfactory grazing land were available in a location other than their home area which of course led to new contacts and relationships.

Antoun notes that residents of Kafr al-Ma, the community he studied in Jordan, started working outside the village after World War II. Later, the 1948 War marked a reversal in the "field of possibilities," as it closed the border between Israel and Jordan, cutting the villagers off from Haifa, Jaffa, Tel Aviv and Acre where many of them had been working. Another subperiod began in the early 1950s when many villagers entered the Jordanian army or worked for it. Friendships formed which added a new dimension to the "field of possibilities."

In each of the communities described above, external events call for a division into sub-periods. Marriage patterns may be expected to differ from one sub-period to another. Although most of the sub-periods were marked by wars, the above studies illustrate a variety of external events determining such divisions.

Again and again, fieldwork provides an added dimension to statistics. People's declarations as to what is desirable may be colored by the prevailing ideology but this may not guide their decisions and actions. In a small rural community the acknowledged norms are not easily made light of. Even when they are not observed, they are at least paid lip-service. The attempt to find one single explanation for a marriage can rarely succeed. Such an attempt disregards the complex nature of human action. Similarly, marriage patterns are varied and complex in nature. A marriage can not always be unambiguously classified as belonging to one pattern or another. At times, it may justifiably be identified as falling into two categories, as for example, when children of owners of adjacent fields marry. They may be the children of brothers, yet the motivation for the marriage may be economic, FBD preference having nothing to do with the union.

There are two main marriage pattern categories, in-group and out-group. Each category is further sub-divided as previously described. Even where figures indicate a relatively high evidence of FBD marriage this does not mean that this is a preferred pattern. Various reasons may exist that make such a marriage desirable in certain circumstances. However, the same may be said of other patterns as well. FBD is best defined as a variation of in-group marriage. A study undertaken by Bates comes to similar though not identical conclusions. In the Turkish community investigated by him, he reports preference for close cousin marriage including FBD. He admits, however, a preference for in-group marriages in general, as not all close cousin marriages are of necessity FBD. He is also aware of the dangers of relating to ideology as if it were reality and warns that "if one were to do simply an analysis . . . statistically confirmed by kin type to the ideology of marriage, one would derive a very limited picture of the actual system."[159] Data presented here indicates that FBD should be included in the in-group marriage category. In Arab nomad and peasant society, in-group marriage is ideologically preferred but again, this does not mean that there is *de facto* preference. Even when an FBD marriage is contracted, it may be prompted by social needs, an aspect still awaiting investigation.

If ideology justifies and explains reality, as claimed by Talcott Parsons,[160] a considerable gap exists between ideology and reality as far as FBD marriages are concerned.

NOTES

1. James M.B. Keyser, "The Middle Eastern Case: Is There a Marriage Rule?" *Ethnology* 13 (1974): 293.

2. The Arabic word *'amm* means "father's brother," whereas"mother's brother" is called *khal*; *Bint* means "daughter." In Arabic, unlike in many other languages (including Hebrew), there is a clear distinction between paternal and maternal uncles.

3. Philip J. Baldensperger, "Women in the East," *Palestine Exploration Fund Quarterly Statements* 32 (1900): 181.

4. Hilma Granqvist, *Marriage Conditions in a Palestinian Village, Vol. I* Commentationes Humanarum Litterarum Vol. 3, No. 8. (Helsingfors, Finland: Soceitas Scintiarum Fennica, 1955), pp. 71-2.

5. Taufik Canaan, "Unwritten Laws Affecting the Arab Woman of Palestine," *Journal of the Palestine Oriental Society* 11 (1931): p. 178. See also Alios Musil, *The Manners and Customs of the Rwala Bedouins*, Oriental Exploration and Studies, (American Geographic Society, Oriental Explorations and Studies, No. 6, 1928), p. 137.

6. Fredrik Barth, "Fathers' Brothers' Daughter Marriage in Kurdistan," *South-Western Journal of Anthropology* 10 (1954): 167; Raphael Patai, "Cousin-Right in Middle Eastern Marriage," *South-Western Journal of Anthropology* 11 (1955): 376-78.

7. Abdulla Luṭfiyya, *Baytin, A Jordanian Village* (The Hague, Netherlands: Mouton, 1966), p. 129; Fuad I. Khuri, "Parallel Cousin Marriage Reconsidered: A Middle Eastern Practice that Nullifies the Effect of Marriage on the Intensity of Family Relationships," *Man* 5 (1970): 568, 606; Gideon M. Kressel, "The Dynamics of Israeli Arab Community in a Process of Urbanization." Ph.D. dissertation, (Tel Aviv University, 1972), pp. 168-9 (Hebrew); Robert F. Murphy and Leonard Kasdan, "The

Structure of Parallel Counsin Marriage," *American Anthropologist* 61 (1959): 24; Henry Rosenfeld, "An Analysis of Marriage and Marriage Statistics for a Moslem and Christian Arab Village," *International Archives of Ethnography* 48 (1957): 35; Emrys L. Peters, "Aspects of the Family among the Bedouin of Cyrenica." In *Comparative Family Systems*, ed. by M.F. Nimkoff (Boston: Houghton Mifflin, 1975); Ahmed M. Abou Zeid, "Honor and Shame among the Bedouins of Egypt." In *Honor and Shame*, ed. J.G. Peristiany (London: Weidenfeld and Nicolson, 1965), pp. 256-57; Abner Cohen, Arab Border Villages in Israel: *A Study of Community and Change in a Social Organization* (Manchester, England: Manchester University Press, 1965), pp. 71-2; Emanuel Marx, *Bedouin of the Negev* (Manchester, England: Manchester University Press, 1967), p. 228; Barth calls it "Preferred rule." See also Fredrik Barth, "Descent and Marriage Reconsidered." In *The Character of Kinship*, ed. Jack Goody (Cambridge: Cambridge University Press, 1973), p. 7.

8. Cohen, p. 74.

9. Jacob Black-Michaud, *Cohesive Force: Feud in the Mediterranean and the Middle East* (Oxford: Basil Blackwell, 1975), p. 46.

10. Ibid., p. 63.

11. Granqvist, *Marriage Conditions, Vol. I,* pp. 77-78; Henry Rosenfeld, "An Analysis of Marriage and Marriage Statistics for a Muslim and Christian Arab Village," *International Archives of Ethnography* 48 (Summer 1957): 37.

12. Barth, *Marriage in Kurdistan*, p. 171. In a more recent paper, Barth is ". . . concerned with the frequency of the event and its implications, not its causes." See Barth, *Descent and Marriage Reconsidered*, p. 11.

13. Barbara C. Aswad, "Property Control and Social Strategies: Settlers on Middle Eastern Plain," *Anthropological Papers, No. 44* (Ann Arbor: University of Michigan, 1971): 82.

14. Murphy and Kasdan, *Cousin Marriage*, p. 21.

15. Emrys L. Peters, "The Proliferation of Segments in the Lineage of the Bedouin of Cyrenaica (Libya)." In *Peoples and Cultures of the Middle East: An Anthropological Reader, Vol. I: Cultural Depth and Diversity*, ed. by Louise E. Sweet (Garden City: The Natural History Press, 1970), p. 388.

16. Peters, *Aspects of Family*, p. 133.

17. Richard R. Randolph, "The Social Structure of the Qdiirat Bedouin." Ph.D. dissertation (University of California, 1963), p. 170.

18. Richard T. Antoun, *Arab Village: A Social Structural Study of a Trans-Jordanian Peasant Community* (Bloomington, Indiana: Indiana Univeristy Press, 1972), p. 141.

19. Harvey Goldberg, "FBD Marriages and Demography Among Tripolitanian Jews in Israel," *South-Western Journal of Anthropology* 23 (1967): pp. 176-77. Gilbert and Hammel proposed mathematical models and simulation studies in a theoretical study not based on empirical

observations. See John P. Gilbert and E.A. Hammel, "Complete Simulation and Analysis of Problems in Kinship and Social Strucutre," *American Anthropologist* 68 (1966): 71-93.

20. Khuri, *Cousin Marriage*, p. 616.

21. Khalil A. Nakhleh, "Shifting Patterns of Conflict in Selected Arab Villages in Israel." Ph.D. dissertation (Indiana University, 1973), pp. 217-8.

22. Khuri, *Cousin Marriage*, p. 597.

23. Edward Westermarck, *The History of Human Marriage* (London: Macmillan, 1921), pp. 452-53.

24. Keyser, p. 306. See also ibid., p. 304.

25. Raphael Patai, *Golden River to Golden Road: Society, Culture and Change in the Middle East* (Philadelphia: University of Pennsylvania Press, 1969), pp. 175-76. For the entire analysis of the phenomenon in the different countries and ethnic groups of the Middle East, see Ibid., pp. 135-176.

26. Goldberg, p. 189.

27. Kressel, *Dynamics of Israeli Arab Community*, p. 279.

28. Ibid., p. 234.

29. Ibid., p. 13.

30. Ibid., p. 20, For Kressel's cultural approach see also Gideon M. Kressel, *Individuality Against Tribality: The Dynamics of a Bedouin Community in a Process of Urbanization* (Tel Aviv, Israel: Hakibbutz Hameuchad, 1976), pp. 205-14 (Hebrew).

31. Peters, *Bedouin of Cyrenaica*, p. 387.

32. Marx, *Bedouin*, p. 229.

33. Ibid., p. 228-29.

34. Luṭfiyya, pp. 129-30.

35. Patai, *Cousin Right*, pp. 28-31.

36. Antoun, *Arab Village*, p. 139.

37. Nakhleh, pp. 217-19.

38. Claude Levi-Strauss, *The Elementary Structure of Kinship* (London: Eyre and Spottiswoode, 1969),

39. Ibid.

40. Millicent R. Ayoub, "Parallel Cousin Marriage and Endogamy: A Study in Sociometry," *Southwestern Journal of Anthropology* 15 (1959): 274.

41. Gilbert and Hammel, p. 89.

42. E.A. Hammel and Harvey Goldberg, "Parallel Cousin Marriage," *Man* 6 (1971): 489. See a letter to the editor of *Man* in answer to an article by Khuri (1970). They claim that Khuri misinterprets Gilbert and Hammel's paper on Computer Simulation pp. 71-93, as well as Goldberg's article *FBD Marriage and Demography*, pp. 176-91. This is not the first time it is argued that an interpretation of parallel cousin marriage has been misunderstood. Murphy and Kasdan's paper is an answer to Patai's article, who in turn, attacks Murphy and Kasdan, *Cousin Marriage*. See Robert F. Murphy and Leonard Kasdan, "Agnation

and Endogamy," *Southwestern Journal of Anthropology* 23 (1967): 1p14; and Raphael Patai, The Structure of Endogamous Unilineal Descent Groups," *Southwestern Journal of Anthropology 21* (1965): 325-50.

43. Rosenfeld, *Analysis of Marriage*, p. 35.

44. See Robert F. Winch, *Mate Selection* (New York: Harper and Row, 1958); William Joshia Goode, *The Family* (Englewood Cliffs: Prentice-Hall, 1964); Yochanan Peres and Ruth Schrift presented their model in a paper read before the Annual Convention of the Israel Sociological Association, in May 1975. The author would like to thank the researchers for allowing me to use their unpublished study. Ruth Schrift, "Interethnic and Interracial Marriage: A Comparative Study between Israel, the USA and South Africa." M.A. dissertation (Tel Aviv University, 1975), pp. 35-39 (Hebrew). See also: Yochanan Peres, *Ethnic Relations in Israel* (Tel Aviv, Israel: Sifriat Hapoalim and Tel Aviv University, 1976), pp. 137-139 (Hebrew); Yochanan Peres and Ruth Schrift, "Intermarriage and Interethnic Relations: a comparative study," *Ethnic and Racial Studies* 4 (October 1978): 428-51.

45. The term "pool" is used here as in Goode, pp. 33-43.

46. The use of the "field of possibilities" in the context of the model of Peres and Schrift (see note 44), is my addition to their model.

47. The designation "field of eligibles" was first used by Winch, pp. 88-89. Winch implies that each individual, in selecting a mate, searches within his field of possible candidates for someone with the required qualifications. Further usage of the term has been made by Winch. In his chapter on mate selection he says "unlike Americans, most other people do not seem to have regarded love as essential . . . two principles . . . determine whom one may marry . . . incest avoidance and the principle of ethnocentric preference. It is the joint operation of these principles that determines for each marriageable person... his field of Eligibles." Robert F. Winch, *The Modern Family* (New York: Holt, Rinehart and Winston, Revised edition, 1973), p. 315. Freeman discusses mate selection in non-Western societies. He uses the term in connection with preferential mating. See Linton C. Freeman, "Marriage without Love: Mate selection in Non-Western Societies." In *Selected Studies in Marriage and the Family*, ed. by Robert F. Winch, Robert McGinnis and Herbert R. Barringer (New York: Holt, Rinehart and Winston, 1962), p. 44.

48. Concerning the argument that the "field of consenters" determines the pool of candidates, reference may be made to Malinowski's discussion of the consent of the wife's family: "Thus, although her mother's brother is her legal guardian, and her own brothers will in the future occupy the same position with regard to her own household, they must all remain passive until the marriage is an accomplished fact. The father say the natives, acts in this matter as the spokesman of the mother, who is the proper person to deliberate upon her daughter's love intrigues and marriage." Bronislaw Malinowski, "Avenues to the

Trobrianders." In *The Family: The Structure and Function*, ed. by Rose Laub Coser (New York: St. Martin's Press, 1966) pp. 96-97.

49. Peres and Schrift refer to two kinds of changes in the pool, in addition to those mentioned in the present study: the ascribed and achieved attitudes of the population.

50. Marx, *Bedouin*, p. 225.

51. Ibid., p. 113.

52. Khuri, *Cousin Marriage*, p. 598.

53. Antoun, *Arab Village*, p. 125.

54. Jean Cuisenier, "Endogamie et Exogamie dans Le Marriage Arabe," *L'Homme* 3 (1962): 84-85.

55. Joseph Chelhod, "Le Marriage Avec La Cousine Parallelle Dans Le Systeme Arabe," *L'Homme* 5 (1965): 156-161.

56. Aswad, p. 77. Aswad's findings, concerning the correlation of polygyny with parallel cousin marriage are irrelevant to the situation in the hamlets—the 'micro' level of the present study—but apply to many other Middle Eastern rural communities on the 'macro' level. In Israel, polygyny has been illegal since the 1950s, though it was rarely practised in Palestinian rural communities before this time. In the West Bank, a man would sometimes take a second wife only when his first had failed to bear a son. Even then divorce rather than polygyny was chosen. See Luṭfiyya, p. 146.

Referring to polygamy, Luṭfiyya stresses that, "although Islam . . . allows a man to marry as many as four wives at a time, only very few practice plurality in marriage. Polygamy is the exception, not the rule, in the village." Ibid., p. 161.

Antoun, who conducted field work in a village east of the Jordan river where some of the rural communities are of Bedouin origin, writes: "Here, in a traditional rural Arab Muslim community in an area of the world that social scientists classify as 'polygynous' . . . a census revealed an extremely high incidence of legal monogamy (ninety percent) and an overwhelming preponderance of de facto monogamy (97.5 percent)." Antoun, *Arab Village*, p. 155. According to Kressel there has been a steep increase in polygyny since 1967. Kressel, *Individuality Against Tribality*, pp. 135,39.

57. Aswad, p. 77.

58. Henry Rosenfeld, "Patrilineal Endogamy in the Arab Village in Israel," *Social Research Review* 1 (1973): 45-46.

59. Kressel, *Dynamics of Israeli Arab Community*

60. The methodology used in this approach was presented by the author in an unpublished paper, "Marriage Patterns and Political Structure in an Arab Village," at a graduate seminar in April 1970, Department of Sociology and Anthropology, Tel Aviv University.

Field work lasted only until March 1974. Data concerning all marriages up to September 1974 have been classified and included. The marriages that took place in the period between September 1974 and September 1976 show the following distribution:

Total Marriages (males): thirty-one (100 percent)
FBD: four (12.0 percent)
Others within the in-group: six (19.4 percent)
Total of in-group marriages: ten (32.3 percent)
Marriages within the hamlets: nine (29 percent)
Outside the hamlets: twelve (38.7 percent)

Thus the total of out-group marriages is twenty-one: (67.7 percent)

The above data show almost the same percentage of FBD as those referring to the July 1967-September 1974 period. However, there is an increase of almost five percent in in-group marriages and about two percent within the hamlets. On the other hand, there is a six percent decrease in marriages with girls from other villages. These slight differences are not significant, especially as the data only covers a two-year period.

61. The total number of marriages for the first sub-period must be viewed with reservation. In some cases, both the husband and wife (or wives) had died, and in others the people had returned to the parent village (or moved elsewhere). They were not included in the study. Nevertheless, despite the small number of cases recorded, the sample is representative.

62. Granqvist, *Marriage Conditions, Vol. I*, p. 88.

63. Max Gluckman, "Political Institutions." In *The Institutions of Primitive Society*, edited by Edward Evan Evans-Pritchard (Oxford: Blackwell, 1956), p. 69.

64. Joseph Ginat, "Cooperation in the Arab Sector in Israel," in *The Cooperation in the Arab Sector in Israel*, ed. by Yehuda Dan (Tel Aviv: International Research Center on Rural Cooperative Communities, 1974), p. 47 (Hebrew).

65. Ralph H. Turner and Lewis M. Killian, *Collective Behaviour* (Englewood Cliffs: Prentice Hall, 1957), p. 56.

66. Neil J. Smelser, *Theory of Collective Behaviour* (New York: Free Press of Glencoe, 1963), p. 165.

67. The figure of seventy-three percent is calculated from data used in preparation of Table 10 (see Chapter 3).

68. Yair Yaqir, "Problems in Management and Supervision on Arab Cooperatives." In *Cooperation in the Arab Sector in Israel*.

69. Cohen, p. 24; although there is a growth of employment outside the village, the example of the hamlets does not confirm the claim that residents have become proletariats living in villages. See Henry Rosenfeld, "From Peasantry to Wage Labour and Resident Peasantry in the Transformation of an Arab Village," in *Process and Patterns in Culture: Essay in Honor of Julian Steward*, ed. Robert A. Mannen (Chicago: Aldine, 1964), p. 229.

70. One of the two husbands moved to Tel Aviv with his Jewish wife and children. The other husband, after continued pressure from his parents, married again, this time to a resident from a neighboring Arab village. The three daughters of his first marriage were educated in

Jewish institutions with financial help from the Regional Council. In both cases the marriages were not registered since, as long as the husband did not convert to Judaism, no legally binding marriage could be contracted in Israel. In other cases, either the woman embraced Islam or her future husband Judaism. Few Jews married Muslim women, knowing that in the absence of the mother's conversion, her children would not be recognized as Jewish. Thus in several cases, individuals included a wider range of candidates in their "field of eligibles." Rosenfeld, *Patrilineal Endogamy*, p. 51 estimates that in the 1960s and early 1970s, about 1,500 Arab villagers married Jewish girls. No official statistics on the number of such intermarriages are available. An unpublished survey in 1974-5, under the supervision of Dr. Isaac Halbrecht and the author, revealed not more than 500 official and common law marriages of this type.

71. Arlette Goldberg, "Le Changement Social dans un Village Musulman d'Israel." Ph.D. dissertation, Sorbonne University, 1974.

72. Rosenfeld, *Patrilineal Endogamy*, p. 50.

73. Five out of the thirty-one marriages, in the period between September 1974 and September 1976, were *badal*.

74. See Israel, Central Bureau of Statistics, Statistical Abstract of Israel (Jerusalem, 1967), p. 59. According to Mills, the average marrying age for women in 1931 was 20.2 years, and for males 25.8. A survey conducted in five Arab villages near the town of Ramle found that twelve percent of the females married between the ages of thirteen and seventeen, and eighty-eight percent between the ages of eighteen and twenty-two. Eric Mills, *Census of Palestine: Population of Villages, Towns and Administration Areas* (Jerusalem: Greek Convent and Goldberg Presses, 1932).

75. Claude Levi-Strauss, *Elementary Structure of Kinship*, p. 86.

76. Aharon Layish, *Women and Islamic Law in a Non-Muslim State: A Study Based on Decisions of the Shari'a Courts in Israel* (New York and Tel Aviv: John Wiley and Israel Universities Press, 1975), p. 100.

77. Ibid.

78. The women were Karīma (C_2) and Luṭfiyya (C_6) respectively. Since both Mahmūd and Karīma died prior to the field study, they are not included in the marriage distribution statistics of Table 22. The marriage of Aḥmad and Luṭfiyya are included in the statistics for the first sub-period.

79. The customary period of mourning lasts forty days.

80. This case history is not in keeping with custom in Arab rural society. Aswad, p. 98 describes a number of frequently occuring situations such as of a man, close to sixty, who died without receiving his share of the inheritance. In the hamlets, the tendency is increasingly to transfer property to the male children during a man's lifetime. There are several reasons for this. Some residents know that the rightful heirs to the property lived outside the borders of Israel (at the time when the parent village and the West Bank were under Jordanian rule). In such

cases the Custodian of Absentees' Property take over the land in question on the death of the father, but this can be prevented through its distribution before death. Also, when the land is registered under the father's name, he is liable for all the tax on the property, but if the property has been distributed, the tax liability is shared between the sons. Small plots of land are proportionately less liable for taxes.

81. Joseph Shepher, "Mate Selection Among Second Generation Kibbutz Adolescents and Adults: Incest Avoidance and Negative Imprinting," *Archives of Sexual Behavior* 4 (1971): 292-96.

82. According to Jewish religion, forbidden in Moslem religion, a man can marry not only his first cousin but even his niece. This does not often occur but is found more among Middle Eastern than European Jews. In most of the cases a man married his sister's daughter rather than his brother's daughter. In Moslem religion such a marriage is not possible, the relationship being considered incest taboo.

83. Khuri, *Cousin Marriage*, p. 616.

84. Ibid., p. 597.

85. Ibid., p. 616.

86. Antoun, *Arab Village*, p. 42.

87. Abou Zeid, p. 356.

88. Peters, *Aspects of Family*, p. 133, describes such marriages in a corporate group: "the marriage of two brothers to two sisters is followed, in the succeeding generation, by the son of one union marrying the daughter of the other, making this latter a double first parallel-cousin marriage, both a father's brother's daughter and a mother's sister's daughter's marriage"; Rosenfeld, *Analysis of Marriage*, p. 39, points out the links between FBD marriage and property: parallel cousins live together in their father's households, because they depend on their heritage, which is often cultivated together and whose fields are joint property; Antoun, *Arab Village*, p. 140, points out that FBD marriage may blur economic differences between close relatives. In addition it may "confine ownership of land within a small group of close kinsmen." Leach adds another aspect when he claims that economic and political factors should be considered "as well as the kinship structure in isolation." Edmond Ronald Leach, "Rethinking Anthropology" *Monographs on Social Anthropology*, No. 22 (London: London School of Economics, 1966): 123. Dumont and Pocock, together with other scholars refer to economic and political interests as a unifying factor as "the core of social life." Louis Dumont and D. Pocock, "For a Sociology of India," *Contributions to Indian Sociology* 4 (1960): 89.

89. Marx, *Bedouin*, pp. 220-22.

90. Erwing Goffman, *The Presentation of Self in Everyday Life*, (New York: Doubleday, 1959), p. 104.

91. Rosenfeld, *Analysis of Marriage*, p. 37.

92. Henry Rosenfeld, "On Determination of the Status of Arab Village Women," *Man* 40 (1960): 68.

93. Smith disregards this reluctance of a woman to give up her legal rights and speaks of "a tendency to reduce her right of property and inheritance because everything she gets is carried out of the tribe or out of the family." William Robertson Smith, *Kinship and Marriage in Early Arabia*, ed. by Stanley A. Cook, 2nd ed. 1907. Reprint (Oasterhout the Netherlands: Offsetned Rijf H. Zopfi, 1966), p. 115; Granqvist, *Marriage Conditions, Vol. II*, p. 256, reports one of her informants as saying that a women who claims her share of the heritage, "would have no more rights to her father's house." This is confirmed by Aswad, p. 53, and Antoun, *Arab Village*, pp. 139-140. Only Keyser, p. 293, does not mention the tendency of women to renounce their claims but says that "in fact, they often receive nothing."

94. Granqvist, *Marriage Conditions, Vol. I*, pp. 76-79, reported that twenty-five out of a total of eighty-seven married males left no male offspring on their death. In three cases a cousin married the dead man's daughter and appropriated the property. In one case, the daughter actually controlled the inherited property; in all others no inheritance was received at all.

95. Emrys L. Peters, "Aspects of Rank and Status among Muslims in a Lebanese Village." In *Peoples and Cultures of the Middle East, Vol. 2: Life in the Cities and Towns, and Countryside*, ed. by Louise E. Sweet (Garden City, N.Y.: The Natural History Press, 1970), p. 115.

96. Marx, *Bedouin*, p. 227.

97. Harvey Goldberg, p. 176.

98. Ayoub, p. 274.

99. Marx, *Bedouin*, p. 223.

100. Antoun, *Arab Village*, p. 139.

101. Louise E. Sweet, "Camel Raiding of North Arabian Bedouin: A Mechanism of Ecological Adaptation." In *Peoples and Cultures of the Middle East, Volume I: Depth and Diversity*, p. 280.

102. Joseph Antonion Jaussen, *Coutumes des Arabes au pays de Moab* (Paris: Adrien-Maisonneuveau, 1908), p. 45.

103. Granqvist, *Marriage Conditions, Vol. I*, p. 81. For the same usage of the term see Canaan, *Unwritten Laws*, p. 179.

104. Marx, *Bedouin*, p. 223.

105. Cohen, *Arab Villages*, p. 45.

106. Peters, *Bedouin of Cyrenaica*, p. 389. The same process is observed by Keyser. See Keyser, p. 303.

107. Peters, ibid., p. 384.

108. Granqvist, *Marriage Conditions, Vol. I*, p. 92.

109. Cohen, *Arab Villages*, pp. 111, 130.

110. Rosenfeld, *Analysis of Marriage*, p. 40.

111. Layish, *Women*, p. 9.

112. Ibid., p. 21.

113. Granqvist, *Marriage Conditions, Vol. I*, p. 88.

114. Robert K. Merton, "Intermarriage and Social Structure: Facts and

Theory." In *The Family: Its Structure and Function*, edited by Rose L. Coser (New York: St. Martin's Press, 1964), p. 141.

115. Rosenfeld, *Analysis of Marriage*, p. 41.

116. Cohen, *Arab Villages*, p. 44.

117. Ibid., p. 106.

118. Granqvist, *Marriage Conditions, Vol. I*, p. 88.

119. Ibid., p. 85.

120. Ibid., p. 111.

121. Rosenfeld, *Analysis of Marriage*, p. 50.

122. Cohen, *Arab Villages*, pp. 113-13 tells us that "in Bint al-Hudud, a Triangle village a few miles south of the hamlets, eighty-four out of a total of 524 marriages [sixteen percent] are by direct exchange."

123. Rosenfeld, *Analysis of Marriage*, p. 51.

124. Marx, *Bedouin*, p. 121. See also Antoun, *Arab Village*, p. 139.

125. Keyser, p. 302.

126. Granqvist, *Marriage Conditions, Vol. I*, p. 118.

127. Layish, *Women*, p. 109.

128. Ibid., p. 110.

129. Rosenfeld, *Analysis of Marriage*, p. 52. See also Antoun, Arab Village, p. 138.

130. Granqvist, *Marriage Conditions, Vol. I*, p. 115.

131. Cohen, *Arab Villages*, p. 124.

132. Antoun, *Arab Villages*, p. 138.

133. A man is said to become impotent (*marbūt*) if he is cursed during the writing of the marriage agreement. According to popular belief only a witch doctor can lift the curse and restore the man's virility.

134. Luṭfiyya, p. 141. See also, Hani Fakhouri, *Kafr El-Elow: An Egyptian Village in Transition* (New York: Holt, Rinehart and Winston, 1972), p. 70.

135. Randolph, p. 152. The author has been told by Bedouin of the Negev that ritual "signals" and "displays" are used to publicize (within the tribe) the bride's virginity. Red and white flags are hung on the nuptial tent (*birza*). The white color stands for peace and purity, the red symbolizes blood. (The colored flags are also used at circumcisions). A scarecrow, called *'omariyya*, again dressed in red and white, with red predominating, is set up. If the bride is not a virgin, the Bedouin take the *'omariyya* and the flags down. Bedouin claim that only the members of the tribe understand the significance of the signs.

136. Peters, *Aspects of Family*, p. 122.

137. Raphael Patai, *Sex and Family in the Bible and the Middle East* (New York: Doubleday, 1959), p. 69.

138. Luṭfiyya, p. 14.

139. Ibid.

140. There are cases in which the hymen is broken only at the time of the first childbirth. It is not impossible for a case to arise where a girl

may be suspected of having previous sexual relations even though she is really a virgin. The consequences of such a mistake could lead the bridegroom to return his wife to her natal family, who might impose a drastic sanction. Personal communication from Dr. I. Halbrecht, Professor of Gynecology at Tel Aviv University. According to Dr. Halbrecht, it is far from unusual, among cases observed in his practice, for a woman's hymen to remain unbroken after first intercourse.

141. Five marriages out of the thirty-one that took place between September 1974 and September 1976 were *badal*. Two were in-group, one FBD and one within the descent group. The other three were out-group, two within the hamlets and the third with a resident of a neighboring village.

142. Patai, *Sex and Family*, p. 19.

143. Barth, *Marriage in Kurdistan*, p. 167.

144. Ayoub, *Parallel Cousin Marriage*, p. 266.

145. Henry Rosenfeld, "Change and Contradictions in the Arab Village Family," *American Anthropologist* 70 (1968): 740. See also Rosenfeld, *Patrilineal Endogamy*, p. 45.

146. *Villagers*, p. 123; see also Rosenfeld, *Patrilineal Endogamy*, p. 42.

147. Barth, *Marriage in Kurdistan*, p. 169.

148. Chelhood, pp. 119, 159.

149. In V. Bromlei, "Ethics and Endogamy," *Soviet Anthropology and Archeology* 13 (1974): 55,69. See also Patai, Cousin-Right, p. 381.

150. Barth, *Descent and Marriage*, p. 6.

151. A Marshall, "Marriage." In *International Encyclopedia of the Social Sciences*, ed. by David L. Silla (New York: Macmillan and the Free Press, 1968), p. 11.

152. Bromlei, p. 65.

153. Ibid., p. 50.

154. Marx, *Bedouin*, p. 223.

155. Tsafrir and Halbrecht use the terms *endopatric* and *exopatric*. See Jenni Tsafir and Isaac Halbrecht, "Consanguinity and Marriage systems in the Jewish Community in Israel," *Annual of Human Genetics* 35 (1972): 344-45.

156. Eric Cohen, "Mixed Marriages in an Israeli Town," *The Jewish Journal of Sociology* 11 (1969): 43.

157. Ibid.

158. For details on the migrations of Bedouin into the central area of the country during drought years, see Joseph Ginat, "The Bedouin of the Negev in Ayalon Basin," in *The Western Ayalon Basin*, ed. Shlomo Marton (Tel Aviv Israel: Hakibutz Hameuchad, 1970), pp. 240-48. The Arab-Jewish towns of Ramla and Lod (Lydda) have become economic and social centers of the Bedouin in the central region.

159. Daniel G. Bates, "Nomads and Farmers: A Study of the Yörük of Southeastern Turkey." *Museum of Anthropology Anthropological*

Papers, No. 52. (Ann Arbor, Mich.: University of Michigan, 1973): 85-86.

160. Talcott Parsons, *The Social System* (Glencoe, I11.: Free Press, 1949), p. 519.

5

Woman's Status and Role

The status and role of woman have been considered in the present analysis of marriage patterns, yet a woman's place should also be viewed in connection with other aspects of social organization.

The Arab village woman plays an important role in both family and community. She is involved in decision making in her own household; she is a conveyor of information important to both her natal family and that of her husband; and she is often an independent owner of property. Socially, she is a key figure in some ceremonies and while not directly involved in village politics, she can influence the course of political events. Accordingly, women have power which enhances their status. When speaking of woman's power in Arab society, it must be realized that two kinds of power are involved. In contrast to the power she accumulates directly from being an active member of her family, or as the result of changing economic situations, she also has the power and status derived, paradoxically, from being a 'powerless' woman. This will be referred to as the "power of the weak."

Turner speaks of the "powers of the weak" in an analysis focusing primarily on ritual reversals of social roles.[1] The same term can be borrowed and applied here in a different context. The term seems appropriate in cases where a woman is disadvantaged vis-a-vis her male relatives and where she may choose to forego even legal rights, as for example, her right to inherit. This may seem to weaken her position in the eyes of a casual observer, but a woman may in this way acquire certain benefits which, in her eyes, outweigh those of ownership.

A Muslim Arab woman acquires power as a property owner precisely because she, being a woman, is deprived of property inheritance. Were she not deprived in this fashion it is logical to assume that her share of the inheritance would simply be absorbed into her husband's holdings, over which she would have no control. Instead, her brothers, in whose hands she leaves her heritage, consider that she has accrued a debt that may be partly and gradually discharged but usually remains for life. She personally receives gifts from her male relatives, as partial "recompense" for the inheritance she has not been given. These gifts she can do with as she likes.

In this way she obtains a valuable privilege: she is a potential member of her father's or brother's households as of right and not due to hospitality or charity. When she is in distress, or feels threatened by her husband or by members of his family, she has a place to go. This is not temporary shelter, for she feels that the house of her natal family is her home too. The existence of this alternative greatly strengthens her position in her family of reproduction.

The rapid growth of modernization and the changes in attitudes and norms such growth brings, must be borne in mind when data presented here and the conclusions drawn, are compared to other studies on Arab villages. The four hamlets have established economic and political links with Jewish society in Israel. Farmers in the kibbutzim and moshavim in the area have developed large industries and enjoy a high standard of living, which has greatly influenced the self-image of their Arab neighbors and brought about a corresponding change in attitudes.

Education has affected the social mobility of the Arab villager. Gubser, in his study of a small Jordanian Arab town, is conscious of the fluidity of the situation. He is aware that "in the traditional, political system [of the towns], socio-economic strata certainly existed. But [they] were of minor importance . . . entrance into one of these strata was mostly ascriptive. However, traditional achieving ability also had a role."[2] This "achieving ability" has been enhanced by easy access to educational facilities now open to women. They too may acquire individual status. Their place in the social order is no longer determined by the prestige of their male relatives. As a result a woman's status is not only a function of that of her natal family, but her status may also change within her family of reproduction according to the tasks she undertakes. Layish states that "the liberation of women from agricultural work has in recent years become a matter of prestige."[3] He continues, "since agricultural work was hard, many women preferred to marry landless men."[4] Most of these women had either elementary or secondary education. Layish believes that reluctance to work in the fields is "probably due to the advanced social position of women."[5]

While it is true that families can now afford to let women members stay at home and not work, such an attitude only demonstrates traditional values. A woman's status in her family of reproduction is usually dependent on her economic contribution. If her husband can depend on her to run the farm well, freeing him to pursue his own occupation outside the village for wages or a salary, this usually adds to her status within her family of reproduction. Increasing modernization means that the status of the family as a whole will no longer entirely depend on wealth and descent, but now also on education. This does not however, prevent men from lending a hand to their wives in farm work once their workday outside the village is over. Neither husband nor wife renounce their role as farmers. They know that he will inherit his share of land either upon his father's death or prior to it if the old man chooses to evade inheritance tax and divides his property during his lifetime. Their readiness to work in the fields is proof of their continued attachment to the rural pattern of life. It contradicts any assumption that these young couples have become urbanites living in a farming community.

WOMAN'S POWER

The power of the Arab rural woman is of two kinds. Some of it is direct, such as her influence on decision making in domestic and communal affairs proves; and some is indirect, through "the power of the weak." Woman's accumulation and use of power, as well as her status in the family and community, are dealt with in a comparison between real situations observed in the hamlets and the ideological role ascribed by members of her community. This approach will demonstrate the two forms of woman's power in their proper perspective.

Power in the context of Arab rual society, is used in two distinct meanings. First, there is formal power which is usually exercised by the males of the family. The power of women is mainly informal, influence on their husbands being brought into play in a private setting, where there are few or no witnesses. Their influence, however, is not restricted to their husbands and not even to their close relatives. A women may take part in the decision making of other male members of the lineage of her family of reproduction. Her voice is not usually heard in large gatherings but she uses various opportunities in private talks to influence things her way. There are women in the hamlets who, as the case histories show, are directly (though not formally) involved in politics. They exert their influence on important decisions such as adherence to this or that faction.

Informal power includes the "power of the weak." A woman may use her brains and charm to achieve an aim or to prevent something she does not want to happen, as for instance the giving of a loan to a relative. She may begin influencing her husband after an especially tasty meal, or she may choose the bedroom with all it implies as a background for her pleadings. Often, she may have 'bought' his resilience by submitting to him in public, allowing him to feel lord of the house and demonstrating this before all. Once desire for acknowledgement of his status is fulfilled, he may not mind so much being graceful and yielding to his wife's urgings. He may even explain this readiness by his being modern and well educated.

A woman also accumulates power through the presents she receives from her father and brothers. If she has renounced her right to her share of the inheritance, such presents can be quite substantial. What she receives is hers alone, she may dispose of it as she sees fit. She may purchase gold but more often acquires land or livestock. In any case, these valuable presents enhance her status in her family of reproduction giving her a sense of security. At the same time, the present giving is symbolic of the 'debt' members of the natal family owe to her. Informal power is derived from the fact that women are links between their natal families and their families of reproduction. They act as a channel for information, visiting their former homes and returning well equipped with details on developments there. In a community where local politics play a major role, the role of informant gives power. A woman has often to be cajoled and made to feel important before disclosing what she has learned. Many husbands humor their wives before they leave on a natal family visit, giving them presents and making them feel a sense of obligation toward them. The preoccupation with local politics in Arab rural communities is unparalleled in western society, but should not be interpreted as interest in politics per se. Everything that occurs in the community is dissected and discussed in the context of local politics.

Women possess sources of information not available to their husbands. Meetings at family ceremonies and during the weekly visit to the cemetery provide occasion for exchanging information. In the closed Arab rural society, one's neighbor is often one's most powerful rival, and may at the same time be one's closest kin, so any information women can supply of kinsmen is of vital interest. Access to this source of information is an asset and consequently a source of power. For instance, a woman may be in a position to report changes in the method of cultivation a neighbor has made, important information of material benefit. It may also be useful to know who originally suggested the idea and who was the first to implement it.

Women also possess formal power. They often work in the fields belonging to the family, in many cases running the farms unaided or almost unaided by their male relatives who are otherwise occupied. By relying on their womenfolk, the men can earn salaries or wages outside the hamlets. If a woman is entrusted with economic responsibility, she must not only be consulted but (in reversal of traditional roles) may also consult the males of her family, reserving the right of decision to herself as manager of the property. Her influence toward the financial standing of the family increases her status and prestige, which she uses to make herself heard in other matters. Another source of formal power is woman's legal status in the religious and civil court. In extremis, she can threaten to turn to a civilian court regarding the guardianship of her children. Possession of assets can help if she has to fight for her right, though up to now, cases where the threat was carried out have been rare. No case occured in the hamlets.

Woman's power is mainly informal, but to the extent to which women have become an important factor in the economy of the household, directly contributing to the budget, their formal power is also on the ascent. As to the rights woman possesses according to the legislation of the country, she will make use of them and they can serve her as a weapon in defending her position if she is conversant with them. The rapid spread of formal education for girls in these rural communities has led some women to claim rights they presumably might not have claimed in earlier times.

IDEOLOGY VERSUS WOMAN'S OWN VIEWS

Several scholars have analyzed woman's status in the light of Islamic law and tradition. Yusuf specifies man's rights over woman and woman's right over man mentioning the "twenty obligations imposed by the 'Holy Lawgiver of Islam' on man, from which woman is exempted . . . on account of her deficiency."[6] Antoun, when discussing the "modesty" of woman in Arab Muslim society also deals with the influence of Islamic tradition on woman's status and role.[7]

Some researchers have stressed the rural ideological view regarding the status of woman. Antoun claims that woman is considered ethically inferior in the spirit of Islam. He states that "there is the firm belief that women are the initiators of any illicit sexual relations."[8] Granqvist maintains that man's superiority is acknowledged in rural Muslim society,[9] as does Canaan who mentions the belief that a girl "tries not to be born since she knows the conditions of life awaiting her."[10]

Significantly, there is a marked discrepancy between statements made in the *diwān*, an all-male environment where man's superiority tends to be emphasized, and statements made in personal conversation. Not only do the circumstances in which statements are made modify them, but a clear distinction between generations is necessary due to the increasing influence of the wider environment. Older men are heard to exclaim "what can you expect from women?". A remark accompanied by a shrug of the shoulder expressing exasperation mingled with forbearance due to the assumed weakness of the female sex. Some of the elders point out that woman's duties consist of obedience to her husband, childbearing and housekeeping. They further add, "She must, of course, work in the fields as much as she can."

This, however, is no longer an attitude assumed by the younger generation. Those who have acquired formal education, and their number is steadily on the increase, do not hold women in low esteem. The western attitudes with which they have become familiar, at least pay lip service to equality between the sexes. Educated young men avoid making derogatory statements about women, so as not to be classified as "old-fashioned," which in their eyes is synonymous with "poorly educated." Many young men are proud of the formal education of their wives and feel it enhances their own status.

AVERAGE SIZE OF FAMILY

Most of the married men (up to the age of thirty) emphasized that they would like to plan their families, preferring to have three or four children. Some mentioned that their wives used contraceptives, while others explained that they refrained from

Table 29

Woman's Age and Length of Time Married

Age	*Length of Time Married in years (percentages of age groups)* Up to 5	6-10	11-20	21-30	31-40	41 +
Up to 20	100	—	—	—	—	—
21-25	84	16	—	—	—	—
26-30	41	32	27	—	—	—
31-40	2	10	59	19	—	—
41-50	—	—	18	61	21	—
51 and over	—	1	—	11	34	53
All Ages %	26	12	23	17	11	11

intercourse during the fertile time of the menstrual cycle or practised *coitus interruptus*.

Table 29 provides background data on the distribution of women's age groups and the duration of existing marriages. Tables 30 and 31 illustrate various factors affecting the numbers and types of births in the hamlets. Table 30 shows that forty-one to fifty year old women married for more than thirty-one years, had the largest number of live births, the average being 10.6. For women aged fifty-one and above, the average number of live births was 6.7. This figure can be attributed to the high rate of infant mortality in earlier times. Table 31 (overleaf) does not show substantial changes in the number of births over the years. In other words, the changed attitude of the younger generation to family planning is not yet reflected in the statistics.

Though many young couples wish to plan their families, they usually refuse to delay the birth of their firstborn, since in the

Table 30

Average Number of Live Births

Woman's Age	*Length of Time Married (in years)* Up to 5	6-11	11-20	21-30	31-40	41 +	Totals
Up to 20	0.3	—	—	—	—	—	0.3
21-25	1.5	3.5	—	—	—	—	1.9
26-30	1.5	3.8	5.0	—	—	—	3.2
31-40	1.0	3.9	7.1	9.6	—	—	7.3
41-50	—	—	7.4	8.0	10.6	—	8.4
51 and over	—	—	6.4	6.7	5.8	6.7	
All Ages	1.3	3.7	6.7	8.3	7.9	5.8	5.2

Table 31
Distribution of Live Births, Stillbirths and Miscarriages

Woman's Age

Total Births	Up to 20				21-25			
	No. of Women	Live Births Number	Average	Still-born	No. of Women	Live Births Number	Average	Still-born
0	11	—	—	—	11	—	—	—
1-2	2	4 (100%)	2.0	—	20	26 (81%)	1.3	6
3-4	—	—	—	—	17	49 (94%)	2.9	3
5-6	—	—	—	—	3	16 (94%)	5.3	1
7-10	—	8	—	—	1	7 (100%)	7.0	—
11-13	—	—	—	—	—	—	—	—
14+	—	—	—	—	—	—	—	—
TOTALS	13	4 (100%)	0.3	—	52	98 (91%)	1.9	10

Average stillbirths per woman: 0   Average stillbirths per woman: 0.19

Average miscarriages per woman: 0.15   Average miscarriages per woman: 0.007

(Total miscarriages: 2)   (Total miscarriages: 7)

	26-30				31-40			
0	4	—	—	—	3	—	—	—
1-2	15	19 (79%)	1.3	5	3	5 (100%)	17.0	—
3-4	14	48 (92%)	3.4	4	2	7 (88%)	3.5	1
5-6	17	86 (95%)	5.1	5	18	97 (96%)	5.4	4
7-10	3	22 (96%)	7.3	1	40	335 (96%)	8.4	14
11-13	—	—	—	—	12	135 (91%)	11.2	14
14+	—	—	—	—	—	—	—	—
TOTALS	53	175 (92%)	3.3	15	78	579 (95%)	7.4	33

Average stillbirths per woman: 1.28   Average stillbirths per woman: 0.42

Average miscarriages per woman: 0.19   Average miscarriages per woman: 0.11

(Total miscarriages: 10)   (Total miscarriages: 9)

	41-50				51 and over			
0	3	—	—	—	1	—	—	—
1-2	3	5 (100%)	1.7	—	3	4 (80%)	1.3	4
3-4	2	6 (100%)	3.0	—	7	25 (100%)	3.6	—
5-6	4	22 (100%)	5.5	—	17	82 (89%)	4.8	10
7-10	17	151 (97%)	8.9	6	17	125 (89%)	7.4	16
11-13	12	106 (89%)	8.8	13	11	112 (91%)	10.0	11
14+	4	59 (94%)	14.7	4	2	25 (86%)	12.5	4
TOTALS	45	349 (94%)	7.8	23	58	373 (90%)	6.4	42

Average stillbirths per woman: 0.51   Average stillbirths per woman: 0.72

Average miscarriages per woman: 0.57   Average miscarriages per woman: 0.41

(Total miscarriages: 26)   (Total miscarriages: 24)

Table 31 (continued)

All Age Groups Combined

Total Births	**No. of Women**	**Live Births Number**	**Live Births Average**	**Stillborn**
0	33	—	—	—
1-2	46	63 (84%)	1.4	12
3-4	42	135 (94%)	3.2	8
5-6	59	303 (94%)	5.1	20
7-10	78	640 (94%)	8.2	37
11-13	35	353 (90%)	10.0	38
14+	6	84 (91%)	5.3	123

Average stillbirths per woman: 0.41

Average miscarriages per woman: 0.26

(Total miscarriages: 78)

words of one resident, "we would become the subject of local gossip for a long time." Her husband confirmed this observation adding that people would think "something is wrong" with either him or her if she did not become pregnant soon after the wedding. Although they might have preferred waiting for some time before having a child, they had to prove that they could successfully fulfil their role as married man and woman. The thirty year old head of another family declared that he would not have any more children. His two daughters and son were born in quick succession, but his reason for this was his wish for male offspring. The younger generation, while practising birth control, take care not to offend the accepted norms of the community. Their explanations perhaps told only part of the story and other considerations were involved. Hamlet residents would no doubt have in mind their future needs with respect to help on the farm—which sons (and daughters) could provide.

Table 31 shows birthrates, including stillbirths and miscarriages. The number of full-term deliveries amounts to approximately 1,700 (ninety-three percent of which were live births) while the number of miscarriages was seventy-eight (0.26 per woman). The number of births is directly related to the woman's age. Women aged between thirty-one and forty gave birth to 7.4 live children on an average; while the corresponding percentage for the age group of forty-one to fifty was 7.8; the low of 6.4 being recorded in the age group of fifty-one and above. However, the percentage of children born alive in the latter age group was slightly lower than with other age groups. This difference may be due to the fact that the older women's recollections were not precise regarding miscarriages and stillborn children.

FREEDOM OF MOVEMENT

Rosenfeld has claimed that woman's movements within the village and certainly outside it were, in the past, restricted and that she was expected to stay within her walls.[11] In fact women could even then (the 1960s) move about a great deal. Good reasons could always be provided for visits to one's natal family, other relatives, and even friends or neighbors. Women were by no means locked up in their houses, they had opportunities to meet others, and often had their own social circles. In addition, festivals, funerals and mournings were always ample justification for social gatherings as they are to this day.

A regular social gathering (that permits the passing on of information and the exchange of gossip) is the Thursday afternoon visit to the local cemetery. This custom is characteristic of the whole region. Anyone who meets such a group on the way to and from the cemetery, accompanied by their young children, all of them chatting and laughing cannot but be struck by their happy mood. The women sit together around their deceased relatives' graves exchanging information.

Freedom of movement has further increased in recent years. Women have begun to move around outside their villages unaccompanied by men. They owe this newly won freedom to the advent of quick and safe transport in buses and taxis. Here, a woman or a girl can travel without male protection since she is not alone as she would be if she had to ride on a donkey, as in the past. The trip is yet another opportunity for meeting people and gossiping. In many ways it is considered a treat. Furthermore, many men work outside the village and not a few punch the clock. A farmer can interrupt his work for a couple of hours to escort his wife to the doctor or go shopping with her but for an employee or worker this means the loss of a whole day's wages and disapproval from his employer. Some of the restrictions that appear to have been an integral part of the pattern of life of the rural Arab woman, have eased due to changed circumstances.

CHANGES IN WOMAN'S STATUS

Tables 32-34 summarize the hamlets residents reactions and comments on changes in woman's status. Table 32 shows that

Table 32

Changes in Woman's Status since 1957: Woman's View (in percentages)

Age Group	*Change Evident*	*No Change*
Up to 30	84	16
31-50	70	30
51 and over	66	34
All Ages	75	25

Table 33

Factors in Status Change: Woman's View (in percentages)

	Significant Changes			
Age Group	*Greater Freedom of Action*	*Increased Status in Family*	*Improved Education*	*Modernized Clothing Styles*
Up to 30	28	27	28	17
31-50	30	27	27	16
51 and over	33	22	22	23
All Ages	30	26	26	18

Table 34

Changes in Woman's Status since 1957: Man's View

Significant Factors	% of Married Men	% of Single Men (aged 18 and over)
Increased education	67	69
Improved household facilities	27	16
Increased freedom of behavior	47	54
"Modernizing" West Bank influence	38	53
Increased status in family and community	37	40
Less traditional clothing	27	39
Enhanced legal status in marriage and divorce	13	—
Increased political rights (voting privileges)	8	7
Increased decision making power	9	11

seventy-five percent of the women responded that they were aware of a change in woman's status. Inevitably, younger women are most sensitive to their changed status (eighty-four percent), perhaps because they and their male contemporaries usually welcome them. The corresponding figure for the oldest age group is sixty-one percent. Table 33 lists the causes and consequences of these changes.[12] Here there is little disagreement between the younger and the older generation. The consensus among women is that they have not only secured a greater measure of freedom than they formerly enjoyed (thirty percent); but have also improved their status (twenty-six percent); and are given much better opportunities of studying (twenty-six percent). (See also Tables 4, 5 and 7, chapter 2). However, no more than eighteen percent mentioned changes in the style of clothing. It may well be that they do not wish to dwell on this subject since, to all appearances, they camouflage deviations from the traditional clothes to as not to antagonize the older generation.

Freedom is defined in terms of greater possibilities of moving about without a male escort and the fact that they no longer hesitate to make their voices heard in significant matters, not only within the restricted family circle but sometimes in public as well. As a result, the "power of the weak" is less in evidence than before and a woman can openly bring her influence to bear. They are also more involved in decision making than before. The women's comments are confirmed by the men who attribute the changes to better education for girls.

Table 34 indicates man's view of changes in woman's status since 1957. Thirty-seven percent of married men and forty percent of single men confirm that a change has taken place in woman's status within the family; while nine percent of the married and eleven percent of the unmarried men, feel that women now contribute to decision making. The low percentage indicated in this item may be explained by the reluctance of the male to admit the influence of the female on his decisions. The men are aware of the modifications in clothing, especially of the tendency to discard distinctive costumes. This trend was explained by villagers as being due to the example of West Bank women.

WOMAN'S INVOLVEMENT IN DECISION MAKING

Women evaluate their participation in decision making more highly than do the men (Table 35). More than two-thirds of the women thought that their share of the decision making responsibility in the family was considerable. They felt that their initiative regarding the construction of a new house for sons about to be married was especially significant. Those women who manage the family farm expect, as a matter of course, to be

Table 35

Women's View of their Role in Family Decision Making

Decision Making Rule	*% of Women*
Takes Principle Initiative in Decisions Regarding:	
1. Enlarging of own home	42
2. Building house(s) for son(s)	82
3. Purchase of domestic appliances	54
4. Purchase of land	60
5. Purchase of agricultural equipment and/or vehicles	13
Participates in general decision making	68

consulted on all major issues. It is interesting to note that in the above categories, a greater percentage of the men saw changes in woman's status than did the women themselves. The men also consistently listed greater numbers of kinds of changes. For example, sixty-eight percent of the men noted increases in formal education as a factor while the corresponding figure for the women was only twenty-six percent. At the same time, such items as legal and voting rights listed by the men, did not appear as significant factors in the women's responses. This can be explained in one of two ways. Either the men, observing woman's role from a more objective point of view, were aware of changes that the women had long since grown accustomed to (and therefore would forget to mention), or alternatively, the male informants were exaggerating the extent of changes about which they were somewhat uneasy.

The following case history supports woman's contention that their initiative regarding the construction of a new house for a son is especially significant. Hamlet resident Mariam 'Ali recalled an incident from a time she was convinced that the price of building materials was about to rise. Mariam's husband is a day laborer in the orchard of a neighboring Jewish settlement, while she together with her children, cultivate the family fields. A relative of her husband asked for a loan, but knowing the man in question she was sure that any money loaned to him would not be returned quickly. Mariam approached a contractor in a neighboring Arab village asking him to build a three-room house for her son. She made an advance payment of I.L. 1,600 (Israeli Lirot)—the amount of money readily available, on condition that the contractor purchase the materials needed within the next week. When her husband came home, she first served him supper and only then did she tell him that she thought he was in no position to lend money to his relative, since they needed the funds to build the new house for their son. Mariam emphasized, in recounting the story, that she had made the contract without consulting her husband. Her decision was justified when prices went up two weeks later.

In other hamlet incidents the woman's influence on house building decisions was neither disguised nor as decisive. In most cases it was the wife who mentioned the project first or persuaded her husband into building. Ḥadīja 'Attīlī (who arranged for her son to marry her sister's daughter), chose a plot of land belonging to the Land Authority. She then sent her husband to handle the required legal procedures for the transaction. In fact, sixty percent of all land purchases were initiated by women. In most cases agricultural land was bought but there were several instances in which residents had to buy lots for their sons who did not own suitable sites. The purchase of additional agricultural land is considered a good investment in the hamlets now that irrigation water is available. Some residents bought land from neighbors who had more than they were able to cultivate and who were also in need of money. Others bought land adjoining their property from the Israeli Government (see chapter 3).

A case history which throws light on the role of woman in her nuclear family and her relationship with her husband is that of Ḥalīma Yazīd. One day the author and his wife paid a visit to the Yazīd family to see Ḥalīma who had just returned from hospital after a miscarriage. While we were waiting for her to join us, we commented on the tasteful, evidently brand-new furniture in the guest room. Fares, Ḥalīma's husband, was flattered and urged us to express our appreciation in his wife's presence. He explained that Ḥalīma did not like the color, adding that he had already ordered a truck to take the sofa and chairs back for exchange. Fares was clearly put out by the expense this involved but did not even consider opposing Ḥalīma. "What can I do if she does not like it?" he concluded with a sigh of resignation.

In this case it was the husband who initiated the purchase but his wife who had the final say on the selection. She could insist on what she wanted because she ran the farm and the household. She felt entitled to a chief decision making role in household matters such as the choice of furniture. Fares knew that the neighbors would see the truck and know that his wife had made him return the furniture, for the owner of the vehicle was a neighbor. But even if Fares had chosen a driver who was not a hamlet resident, he could not have concealed the transaction from his neighbors. In giving in to his wife, Fares certainly did not conform to the ideology of woman's inferior status in the family. It may well be, of course, that socioeconomic changes in Arab rural society in Israel affect behavior, perhaps modifying if not changing some norms, without however influencing ideology. In the past where a woman was a powerful enough personality, she used the "power of the weak," allowing the male to appear strong, but at the same ensuring that her decisions were implemented.

Modern household conveniences play a role in woman's changing status. The hamlets have not yet been connected to the national electricity supply so there are fewer home appliances to be found than in other Arab Israeli rural households. Yet the benefits of electricity are not entirely dispensed with. Many families use generators and various electric appliances as Table 36 shows. The frequency of solar heaters is most probably due to

Table 36

Distribution of Modern Domestic Appliances

Appliance	**% of Homes**
Refrigerator	6
Solar water heater	70
Gas stove (two-burner)	73
Kitchen oven (gas or electric)	15
Automatic washing machine	2
None of the above	7

the absence of electric supply. The characteristic conductor and tank are visible on about seventy percent of all roofs. A two burner gas stove is used for cooking in seventy-three percent of the kitchens, operated in Israeli fashion with balloons of fluid gas. The rest of the households still cook outside on an open fire or in the *tabūn*. There are relatively few refrigerators or washing machines due to the lack of commercially supplied electricity.

Only seven percent of the hamlet women indicated that they did not have any of the appliances specified.

When men referred to woman's changed status, they frequently pointed to the modern facilities at her disposal which has made housekeeping easier. Stress is usually laid on today's well-equipped kitchens as against the former custom of preparing food outside. This is not only much more convenient, both in the heat of the summer and in the winter, but also frees women from the tiresome task of collecting the kindling, dung and firewood. The time saved through the aid of modern appliances benefits the farm, as women can provide more help with the work in the fields. Husbands express recognition of their wives contribution by accepting the change of status it implies.

The changed role and status of women is illustrated by the following case history. Jamīl Yazīd was entertaining guests in his *diwān* when a woman neighbor, Umm Jalīl,[13] asked his wife for a sack of cement. He jumped from his seat, rushed outside and chased the woman away, shouting to his wife that he did not run a shop. On returning to his guests he apologized, knowing that the author (who was present) and his guests had overheard every word. One guest remarked that it was obvious that he was not a dealer in cement. The others laughed as a sign of approval and the interrupted conversation resumed. Jamīl told me the following day, "That night, my wife said that I should have treated Umm Jalāl better. She was a neighbor from whom one day we might need something. I told her she was right and in the morning I myself brought Umm Jalāl two sacks of cement." Jamīl's example of woman's increased status in the family was followed by one of even greater decision making by his wife. Jamīl's son was about to marry his FBD, who was also his MZD. The decision, however, had not been Jamīl's. His wife, together with her sister had talked the matter over and an arrangement concluded by the mothers of the future couple. Furthermore, his wife had been the one to approach the housing contractor, negotiating for the buidling of the house.

The first story shows that Jamīl's wife behaved differently in public and in private. She did not contradict her husband in the presence of guests, on the contrary, she let him boast and behave according to the ideology of male superiority. She had both the insight and the patience to wait for the proper moment to influence him. The subsequent private interaction showed the actual situation, revealing the true status of the woman.

Jamīl, by taking not only one but two sacks to the neighbor, showed that he did not really fear for his prestige. He had asserted his power in front of a number of persons, now he could afford to accede to his wife's wishes, and admit and correct an error. Whatever Jamīl's motives may have been, his wife's economic role must have influenced his conduct. He stressed that, unlike others, he was not old-fashioned. He thought it important for his wife to have her say. The author could not find out to whom he referred when he used the word 'others'. He may have meant his guests who had witnessed the fracas over the cement, of whom many presumably adhere to the traditional definition of a woman's role or he may have meant his community in which, so he hinted, he was the exception. What is significant is the declared belief that being progressive is an asset, perhaps because it usually goes hand in hand with formal education, which in turn has become a factor in the determination of personal status.

The ideology of male superiority is, however, not completely rejected. The very fact that Jamīl constantly referred to it, shows that it was very much in his mind. The divergence between the ideal (or ideological) status of woman and her actual status leads, as Antoun says, to "the working out of an accommodation between beliefs and between ideal and practical norms."[14] Though, of course, a society may remold its norms and may act them out before they are formulated as wise maxims. As the Murphys explain "there are awesome gaps between our images of life and life as it is lived, between the rules of society and the course of daily events."[15] Recent work is very much concerned with observing behavior and does not put its trust on the normative statements of informants. The three case histories demonstrate three different levels of influence in the wife-husband relationship. Mariam 'Ali, whose husband was absent most of the week due to his work outside the hamlet, possessed great power. She made decisions concerning both the farm and the household. Mariam felt under no obligation to inform, let alone consult, her husband before deciding on important financial transactions. She was capable of planning and controlling situations, her obvious powerful personality allowed her to shoulder responsibilities successfully. In addition she was well informed regarding economic developments in the country, correctly anticipating that building materials would become more expensive. In the case of Fares and his wife, the situation was different. Though he too was employed outside the hamlet, he spent every afternoon helping his wife in the fields. Her control over the family farm was less complete than Mariam 'Ali's, yet she exerted a decisive influence on domestic matters. In the third case Jamīl ran the family farm, his wife only assisting him. She perhaps felt she had to rely on the "power of the weak," and waited for the night to make her point in the bedroom.

Another case history showing the nature of relations between husband and wife, concerns Ṭareq Yazīd. Here the ideological attitude toward woman is still fact. The first domestic scene in twenty-seven years of married life occured when Ṭareq's wife mistook an official of the Ministry of Trade and Industry, who came to examine proposed business premises in her husband's absence, for an income tax assessor. She did not know the difference between the functions of the two ministries and believing that a shop should be concealed from the eyes of the authorities, denied her husband's intention of going into business. This caused him considerable inconvenience, irritating him to the point of reprimanding her. It was evident from Ṭareq's own words that he respected his wife and treated her with kindness. Yet the story points out the fact that he did not share his business plans with her as a partner in the economic decision making within the family. If he had related to her as an equal she would have been better informed and could have helped him by showing the official the premises.

A woman's contribution to the family income gives her self-confidence and promotes her status in the eyes of the other members of the household. But it is only recently that women have been able to make a significant economic contribution. Bossen says that ". . . differences in physical strength made women unequal in the underdeveloped world."[16] In subsistence agriculture women were unable to play a dominant role. Now that modern farming technology has relieved the farmer of much of his physical labor, women have become a valuable labor force. Even although women now make a significant economic contribution, the ideology of female inferiority cannot easily be modified, for as Mason says, it is "plainly acknowledged in an Arab Bedouin folk saying 'the men make the tribe but the women make the net'".[17] The influence of woman in the incidents reported above may be explained by her changing role in a social life less sharply dichotomized by sex, where exchange of opinion on economic matters has made possible change of opinions in other areas of family interaction.

It is interesting to compare the different levels of woman's participation in decision making and other activities in the hamlets with those observed in Bedouin societies in Israel. Bedouin in the North as well as those living in Southern Sinai will be compared with those of the Negev and Northern Sinai. In the north, in the Galilee, and in Southern Sinai, many men leave the camp for work entrusting the management of family affairs to their wives. In Galilee this may be explained by the fact that the Bedouin neither own large tracts of lands, nor numerous flocks or herds. In Southern Sinai, some males worked in Egypt until the change of border after the Six Day War, while smuggling also led to frequent absence from the camp. Where the male is not often at home the conduct of his wife (or wives), as well as her (or their) relationship to the outer world changes. Women become accustomed to interaction with strangers and to reponsibility. They have to settle matters, sometimes without the possibility of consulting with the pater familias. A similar situation prevails in the Bedouin community of Awlad 'Ali, on the Egyptian-Libyan border. According to Safia Mohsen, these women actively participate in family decision making.[18]

The Negev and Northern Sinai are geographically situated between the Galilee and Southern Sinai respectively. Here woman leads a much more withdrawn existence with little contact with the outside world. Agriculture is more predominant and flocks are larger. The males are much less able to leave frequently, having to cultivate their fields and to mind their flocks. This in turn influences the status and role of woman. In the Negev many males have become wage earners necessitating their frequent absence from camp. Before the military administration in 1948, a certain number of Bedouin used to work away from their camps, but until movement restrictions were lifted they were forced to remain in the Negev. When the military administration was finally abolished in 1966 and the movement restriction lifted, there was an increase in the number of Bedouin seeking outside employment. Woman's status is thus positively influenced by the responsibilities and duties she undertakes. Usually the more she is involved in the production process, the higher her status.

It is evident that the process of change in the station of the Arab rural Muslim woman is reflected in the selection of marriage partners (the choice of her own marriage partner and of her children). If a woman makes her husband change the color of the furniture he has chosen her request may cause expense and inconvenience; furthermore, where the ideology of the inferiority of woman is still adhered to, perhaps some loss of face. But if personal considerations enter into the choice of a marriage partner, one of the avenues to the acquisition of power through alliances may be closed. Furthermore, once the pater familias is ostensibly no longer the one to decide on major matters, the myth of male dominance is destroyed. He not only consults his wife but prefers to listen to her opinion. This is an admission that he does not consider it his right to act high-handedly, that he cannot or will not impose his will. Nor do the neighbors apparently gossip about a man who does not lay down the law in his house in all matters. On the contrary, he may be considered as "moving with the times," as progressive. There might have been a possibility of making an arrangement which would have prevented the neighbors from seeing the furniture taken away to be exchanged if the act were likely to be interpreted as weakness on behalf of the husband. But where a favorable interpretation can be given, there is no reason to hide the fact that a woman has the final word. Not all males, of course, will view the situation in this light. There may be husbands who will point-blank refuse to give in to a request of this kind, making sure that their dominant role is emphasized and the myth of male superiority lived up to. Rogers claims that "the perpetuation of this 'myth' is in the interests of both peasant women and men because it gives the latter the appearance of power. . ."[19] since a "non-hierarchical power relationship between the categories 'male' and 'female' is maintained in peasant society by the acting out of a 'myth' of male dominance."[20]

SELECTION OF MARRIAGE PARTNERS

The growing possibility of woman to influence the choice of her future husband, or even to decide by herself, affects the social order of her society. In the past marriages were arranged to serve the interests of the head of the family and certainly not the mother or the young couple. Table 37 shows that in seventy-seven percent of the cases the woman did not participate at all in decision making concerning her own marriage. One third of all unions were contracted without any consultation with other members of the family, the decision being that of the pater familias alone, while the mother participated in fifty-three percent of all decisions, though only in one percent of all marriages was the bride's mother the one to decide all by herself. In only

Table 37

Decision Making: Selection of Woman's own Marriage Partner

Person(s) Who Made Decision	*% of Married Women*
Both parents	34
Father, alone	32
Mother, alone	1
Woman and parents jointly	18
Woman herself	5
Other relatives*	10
TOTAL (313 Women)	100

* The 10% indicating "other relatives" refers to brothers, uncles, or guardians in cases in which the father died prior to the selection of a marriage partner.

five percent of the cases was the single woman the sole decision maker regarding her own future and in only eighteen percent did her parents consult her before making their decision.

Table 38 shows the influence of women on their children's marriages. That eleven percent of the mothers alone were the sole decision makers regarding their children's marriage indicates the change that has occured in woman's status (compare to table 37). That twenty percent of the young people chose their marriage partners themselves, indicates the change in Arab peasant family structure. It shows a decrease of paternal dominance—a function of woman's status. The percentage given for children's own decisions includes both males and females. Apparently, no more than ten percent of the daughters chose their husbands. This includes some who had selected their husbands themselves and are therefore included in Table 37.

Table 38

Decision Making: Selection of Children's Marriage Partners

Person(s) Making Decisionn	*% of Married Children*
Both parents	24
Father, alone	30
Mother, alone	11
Parents and child jointly	15
Child him/herself	20
TOTAL*	100

* Responses of all 95 hamlet women with married children.

The influence of female members of the family on marriage arrangements is demonstrated in the following case history. The marriage between Mariam (E1, chart 2) and Qāsem (E16) was planned by two women, her paternal aunt (D1) and his father's half-sister (D24). Her father Aḥmed (D3) enjoyed considerable prestige in Ibthān during the 1940s and 1950s, with Qāsem's father as his main rival. Jabār, Qāsem's paternal grandfather (C1, 11), also lived in one of the hamlets. He had married Jalīla (C1, 10) and due to this alliance, his influence had steadily increased. During the four years preceding my field work, Ahmed Abū Bader had begun to feel politically isolated,[21] a fact realized both by his unmarried sister (D1) and by Dāūd's widowed sister, who together engineered the union between Mariam and Qāsem. AḥmedAbū Bader's greatest rival was As'ad Amīn, a young man appointed representative of Ibthān in the Regional Council, who had managed to accumulate power through his position. The two women decided that a faction be set up by Aḥmed and Dāūd that could effectively oppose that of As'ad Amīn. When the news of the forthcoming marriage spread, it was greeted with disbelief, since no one expected Aḥmed and Dāūd to consent to such a union. Nevertheless, the two women succeeded in setting up a new alliance which later led to a new faction, a development which was of benefit to both men.

This case history shows how well some women understand that political moves can be achieved through new kinship links created by marriage. When they possess political acumen and act in the interest of their male relatives, they are often given a free hand.

WOMAN AS PROPERTY OWNER

Several researchers explain woman's inferiority by the fact that they do not usually own land. Accordingly, women are expected to submit tu their father's decisions while unmarried and to their husbands' authority afterwards. According to Islamic law the daughter inherits, *de jure*, one-half as much as each of her brothers. *De facto*, however, women do not as a rule claim their inheritance; they give up their right in favor of their brothers (see chapter 4). There are some exceptions where, at the husband's insistence, a woman does claim her share. Cohen explains that a woman may wish to bolster her husband's economic status by claiming property from her brothers and can turn to a *Shari'a* court to claim her heritage.[22] Peters argues that she usually refrains from doing so due to the fact that she feels free to use her male relatives' home as shelter in case of a quarrel with her husband, and can best negotiate with her husband from this position. This state is known as *za'alane* "She refuses to return until she is placated with a 'gift'. Sometimes this 'gift' is a valuable pair of silver armlets, or one or more sheep. It always represents a redirection of property in favor of a wife."[23]

Not all researchers evaluate the complex relationships between a woman, her agnates and her husband, and the economic benefits she can derive from them in the same way. Rosenfeld claims that "neither the mother-in-law nor the daughter-in-law have property,"[24] while Canaan says that a woman "can acquire property and be protected in her ownership by law." Canaan also stresses that the objects "the bride brings with her from her father's house, her portion of the dowry, her wedding presents (*nuqūt*), remain her own property. No one, not even her husband, may touch them."[25] The occasion when a married Arab woman receives gifts from her natal family are determined by tradition. She is given presents by her male relatives on the two Muslim holidays when they visit her after morning service in the mosque. This custom is observed even if she has moved to another village after her wedding. The male members of the family bless her before they bless members of their own household. Also, a father or a brother may visit a woman (his daughter or sister) at any time and on these occasions presents are also offered to her. During circumcision ceremonies it is the mother who receives the *nuqūt* intended for her son, usually money or gold coins. It is up to her to decide what to buy with the money. The advantages of foregoing inheritance are clearly perceived by women, as are the obligations this decision places on her agnates.

In the hamlets, forty-six women (about fifteen percent of all women) have property of their own. Table 39 (overleaf) indicates which types of land. The average area of land owned by a woman for building purposes is one *dūnam*; while the average plot of arable land in the plain is 3.75 *dūnam*; and for mountainous terrain almost eight *dūnams*. Six women inherited land from their fathers (see chapter 4), four from their deceased husbands, while thirteen women obtained property from their husbands as part of the bride price given to the womans' father by the husband as part of the marriage agreement. In some cases the woman's father settles property on his daughter in this way. Five women inherited land from their mothers and three other

Table 39
Land Owned by Women

Type of Land	*No. of Women*
Zoned for building (residential)	2
Agricultural: orchard	13
Agricultural: fields (in the plain)	18
Building and fields	6
Building and orchards	2
Fields and orchards	2
All three types	6
TOTAL WOMEN LAND OWNERS	46

women received it as a gift from their sons. Fifteen women had bought the land they owned with their own money. Four of the thirty-one women who inherited or received gifts of money, bought additional fields at a later stage. All together, nineteen women in the hamlets owned land which they had acquired with their own financial resources.

After eighteen years of marriage ʻAziza Yazīd, of the Ibn Hajar descent group had saved enough money to buy two *dūnams* of agricultural land in the plain and three *dūnams* of mountain orchards. Soon after her wedding, she acquired a goat to which she added several kids a few years later so that, together with the offspring of her own goat, she owned a small flock. She paid for new animals with money accumulated from gifts received from members of her natal family. Eighteen years later she decided to sell the animals and buy land. She did so without consulting her husband, explaining that she had spent her own money, "I can do with it as I wish," she said.

This case history shows that renunciation of inherited property does not necessarily prevent accumulation of wealth and acquisition of property at a later date. It must be remembered that her accumulated material wealth derived originally from what is referred to as the "power of the weak." In Peter's words "women are disinherited, both as wives and daughters, contrary to Islamic law, and they are well aware of this. But women do not meekly surrender a prime right of this kind because they are submissive by nature, as some writers on Arabs appear to believe. They renounce rights ". . . and in return they are able to make claims against the males who hold their property rights."[26] It is true that gifts are no equivalent for property not claimed as heritage, but in this way, a woman preserves her rights with her natal family, and if she is astute, she may eventually become a property owner.

In Spring 1973, Ḥasan 'Arishi married a woman from the parent village, a member of the Abū Bader family. When the groom's relatives came to take the bride on her wedding day, her family asked the groom's father to sign a new document which had not been mentioned during the previous negotiations. The bride's family demanded that in case of divorce, the furniture (provided by the groom) should become the sole property of the bride. There was an additional stipulation to the effect that if the bride should become *ḥardane*[27] ("offended and angry") and return to her father's house until differences had been settled, she would have the right to take the furniture with her. The groom's relatives did not, at first, approve this unexpected demand but after a noisy argument, the groom's father agreed to sign the paper but without the *ḥardane* provision—that is she could only take away the furniture in case of actual divorce. The father knew that his son, who had both physical and mental defects, was not an ideal marriage partner. Since the young man's "field of consenters" was limited, his father agreed to sign the document, but not before the bride's *khal* (mother's brother) had declared that it might be better to cancel the wedding altogether.[28]

There are instances then, where a woman may gain control over property through special provisions.[29] In this case, the woman in question is recompensated for her husband's physical and mental shortcomings. The option of a woman to leave her husband is a powerful weapon. When she returns to her natal family in protest, the husband is left to look after the children and fend for himself. Her absence is keenly felt in the running of the household. The renunciation of property inherited is of special importance because a woman feels free to become, at least temporarily, a member of her brother's household because she has not claimed her inheritance. Frequently, the husband sends emissaries to induce his wife to return to her family of reproduction. The fact that he has to plead with her to come back increases her status and is a demonstration of woman's power. The decision to leave usually follows a clash and is an expression of discontent, and of having been offended.

Provisions in case of a divorce seem to be an especially important aspect of the marriage contract. While divorce rates are very low, the legal position allows a Muslim, as Granqvuist says "at any time and for the least cause . . . [to] divorce his wife."[30] Even today, the legal obstacles in the way of such a cursory handling of marriage relations are not really prohibitive. Moreover, it sometimes happens that the husband divorces a woman in her absence, so that she learns about her changed status through a third party.[31] In this situation she needs the moral and if necessary, economic support of her natal family, especially since she herself cannot divorce her husband without his consent.[32]

Theoretically, a woman may initiate divorce proceedings in the Islamic court,[33] but no village woman has resorted to this course of action. The right of becoming a *ḥardane*[34] woman may sometimes serve as an equivalent for the man's repudiation of his wife while not requiring an appeal to the court. If a woman leaves her husband and refuses to rejoin him, he may divorce her. If he does divorce her (because she does not rejoin him, she loses her share in the delayed bride price, which would have to be turned over to her in the case of divorce occuring when the woman has not left her husband.[35] A woman may thus feel compelled to return to her husband, even when she is far from happy with him. Often her group of origin may wish her to preserve her marriage in order to maintain the political or economic alliances that perhaps brought about the marriage in the first place. When she does return she can expect to receive a present from her husband—usually a sum of money or gold coins, a custom which prevails with the Bedouin in the Sinai Desert as well.[36]

Granqvist argues that under these circumstances, a man is more responsible for his sister than for his wife and children. It is the brother and not the husband who is her natural protector. The woman's relations with her husband do not possess the same permanent nature.[37] This may be explained by the fact that a man pays the bride price for his own wife with the money his father or he himself received as bride price for his sister. According to Granqvist, this is a further reason for the close relationship between brother and sister. Custom reinforces the bonds of consanguinity by economic obligations and interdependence. The relationship between a daughter and her father and brother, is a very special one in rural Arab society. In Granqvist's words, ". . . it is always her father or her brother who has to arrange" any serious matter, "while her husband remains unaffected, and this also shows that she continues to belong to her father's house."[38]

FAMILY HONOR AND SHAME

In a peasant community, friction between groups is usually over land or a woman's honor. An Arabic proverb states, that *'arḍ* and *'irḍ* (land and honor), are the main causes for tension. The term honor is not an exact translation of *'irḍ*, for as Abou-Zeid explains, it is "used only in connection with female chastity and continence."[39] Mason says that "the strict code of modesty for women and unequal treatment of the female sex in Arab and Arabized societies are well known phenomena. . . Many of the restrictions placed on Arab Muslim women reflect their sexuality, and the most serious breach of the modesty code is an illicit sexual act regarded as sinful in the Quran. . ."[40] The stress on female sexuality is connected with the ideology of the inferiority of women. Antoun says that a woman's inferiority is attributed to her supposed sexual appetite and moral laxity.[41] A married woman is not only protected and offered shelter by her agnates, but is also supervised and controlled by them. Mason points out that "the inclination of the bride's group is to continue protecting its kinswoman long after her marriage, since their honor is still at stake." Yet, he adds "the bride's new kinship group has the same role to play, only in addition to honor, its judgement in selecting a 'temperate' woman for the groom is being tested."[42] Sexuality may also be used as a weapon in marriage politics. A woman who has engaged in illicit sex may in this way assert her right to choose her partner by herself, since family honor and the fear of shame may induce her male relatives to consent to a marriage union they might otherwise not have agreed to.

Although the concept of *'irḍ* is well defined as are male reactions in case it is violated by 'unseemly' conduct of a female relative, this does not necessarily mean that ideological norms reign supreme. A proclaimed norm is not necessarily translated into fact and sometimes it is 'honored by its breach'. There is always a gap between ideology and reality but its dimensions are subject to variation. If the gap is too wide, acknowledged norms lose their hold on the society as a whole. Its members begin to doubt them and the value system they reflect. In the words of Simmel, it is true that "Lie, illusion and ignorance are essential to society" but within limits, since otherwise the core beliefs are destroyed. Some anthropologists are convinced that whenever an unmarried woman is found to have had sexual intercourse, she is killed by the members of her natal family. This is also supposed to be the family reaction to adultery. Here too, however, a gap exists between ideology and reality.

Cohen described the case of a widow who had an affair with a married man and whose male relatives stoned her to death (a traditional form of public justice in the Middle East).[43] Antoun cites the story of a girl whose father stabbed her to death.[44] Three such incidents were reported in the Israeli press as late as 1975. The explanation given was that "the honor of the family" had to be saved. Although there are many instances of killing after the discovery of illicit sexual relations, there are also cases where girls who had 'sinned', were not harmed. For example, there were the two girls who told their parents that the family would be 'put to shame' if they were made to marry the proposed partners rather than their cousins and clandestine lovers. They were spared the fate of other girls in a similar dilemma, not because it was considered less 'shame' if the 'sin' was committed with members of the family but because the affairs remained a secret and ended in marriage.

Antoun claims that when such a case becomes "public knowledge in the village and the subject of whispered conversation,"[45] the girl involved has to be killed. It is thus not the act that calls for punishment but public knowledge of the act. 'Honor' depends on public opinion, not on respect for ethical standards. Honor should not be viewed as an internalized value, for as long as appearances are preserved, honor is not in jeopardy. It is not moral standards but what others say and know that is important. Only when the incident becomes public knowledge does action have to be taken to protect family honor. The following case histories, studied in depth, reveal that the decision to kill often depends on developments not necessarily connected with the offense.

In the 1940s, an unmarried girl (D23, chart 2, Appendix C) was killed by her sisters (D24, D25 and D27). Jabār, the girl's father ($C_1$11), who on hearing that his daughter had had illicit sexual relations with a ploughman (harāth), ordered her sisters to push her into the village well. The inferior status of the lover no doubt played an important part in Jabār's decision to have his daughter killed. The subsequent developments also throw light on the social norms of the society in which this happened. A man hostile to Jabār told the police that the girl's death had been premeditated murder and the police, subsequently, requested the body for a postmortem. Jabār refused to comply contending that religious customs forbade autopsy. When the reasons for the request were mentioned by the officers, Jabār pretended to be deeply offended by the suspicion expressed against him. He suggested that the virginity of the dead girl be tested in a special way. A female police officer together with a hamlet woman was to insert a hard boiled egg into the dead girl's vagina. If the girl was still a virgin, the father explained, the attempt would fail. An old woman pretended to make great efforts to push the egg in, failed, and this convinced the police of Jabār's innocence. It was assumed *ipso facto* that if the girl was a virgin her father had no reason to murder her. Establishing her 'innocence' was convincing proof that the charge of murder was unfounded.

Although the community knew the true facts, they sided with Jabār, actively helping him hoodwink the police. They justified his act and were ready to help him evade legal punishment. Yet, though his society was on his side, Jabār did not lightheartedly decide his daughter's death. It is possible that Jabār would not have killed his daughter if he had not been a relative newcomer in the community and still unsure of his status. A further reason for his decision may have been that he was not originally from the parent village but from a different region altogether. Jabār was clearly afraid of being the subject of hostile gossip. The murdered girl was the daughter of his first wife, a woman of Bedouin origin. (C112). He later married Jalīla (C110), a woman from the Amin descent group. Jalīla accused Jabār of not doing all he had to do in order to protect family honor. Worse still, she voiced her criticism of her husband's inaction in the presence of witnesses, making a public accusation and claiming that she was the injured party. Only when the girl was dead did Jalīla feel her status and prestige had been sufficiently protected.

In the previous chapter, the case of Ḥusnī (D14, chart I) was reported. He murdered his daughter Lea (E8) because she had had sexual intercourse with Ṣabrī (E19). The fact that considerable time elapsed between the 'sin' committed by Lea and her death, was due to her father's hope that she would be married in spite of all. After it was found out that Lea had become pregnant, her father thought that Ṣabrī, who was responsible for her pregnancy, would marry her. Ṭareq (D9), Ṣabrī's uncle, explained to Ḥusnī that Ṣabrī should marry his daughter Latīfa (E21) according to the badal agreement. However, being aware of Ṣabrī's obligation, Ṭareq proposed one of Ṣabrī's younger brothers as a candidate for marriage with Lea (see chapter 4). The pregnancy became a subject of gossip only after Rafīq (D18) told Ḥusnī that none of his sons would agree to marry Lea. Actually

Lea's and Ṣabrī's relations could have been kept secret, since Lea underwent an abortion. However, 'Omar (D1 10), Ṣabrī's uncle, spread rumors about the affair. Now 'Omar's wife (D2 6) was Lea's paternal half-sister and the maternal half-sister of Ṣabrī's mother Mariam (D1 2). 'Omar was influenced by his wife who disliked Rafīq (who was her half-sister's (D1 5) husband and her father's first cousin). The situation that developed, when no husband could be found for Lea, offered a unique opportunity for 'Omar's wife to vent her resentment. She incited her husband to take action against Rafīq and Ṣabrī. She wanted him to threaten the two men and make their lives miserable. She was not restrained by the consideration that Lea's life might be endangered by her actions. She succeeded so effectively that her husband even attempted to kill his nephew Sabrī.[46]

In summer 1972, Muḥammad Yazīd of 'Ali's (B1, chart 1) lineage, who was held in high respect in the hamlets, mentioned that Lea's half-brother Dāūd (D2 2) was planning, with 'Omar, to kill Lea. Muḥammad reported that they had bought a gas cooking stove with the intention to use it to kill her. They would choke her first, he said, and then place her body in the kitchen to make it appear that she had died accidentally of gas inhalation. Muḥammad agreed the girl should be killed, but explained that the truth of her "accidental" death would be discovered in the autopsy. Muḥammad thought he had succeeded in convincing Lea's brother and 'Omar to delay the murder by advising them to work out a more sophisticated plan of action. The peasants should know that the girl had been murdered as punishment for her misbehavior, but the authorities should not be given any clues to prove premeditated murder.

Muḥammad thought it necessary to kill Lea for two important reasons. First, he himself belonged to the same descent group and thought that the good name of the *ḥamūla* could only be preserved by Lea's murder. Secondly, Lea's death would serve as a deterrent in decreasing the danger of other girls' acting as she had done. "If she is murdered, the others will think twice before losing their virginity," said Muḥammad. There was still another factor that Muḥammad did not mention. The girls of the hamlets were showing clear indications of wanting to choose their own marriage partners and it was this freedom that the men were most concerned about. The men wanted to maintain full control over marriage arrangements. This meant that they had to prevent any and all situations that might let a young woman determine whom she would marry, including sexual relationships that could force a wedding to be contracted.

In the spring of 1973, there were rumors that 'Omar and Lea's half brother were about to murder Lea. Her death in August seemed to confirm that behavior conforms to prescribed norms when illicit sexual relations have become public knowledge. But two days after Lea's death it became evident that the murder could not be explained by one single motive and that the killing was unpremeditated. Additional, new circumstances had forced Ḥusnī to take action. He and his wife Amna (D13) wanted their son Sa'id to marry, deciding to build a house for him as was customary. The only lot available had been owned by Karīma (C2), Ḥusnī's late first wife. She and her two daughters had inherited the land after her first husband Maḥmud's (C1) death. After Maḥmud died, his brother Aḥmad (C5) registered the property in the name of the deceased man's daughters (D11 and D12). These two sisters, as mentioned above, later married Rafīq (D18) and Ṭareq (D19) who were Ahmad's sons.

In order to receive a building permit, Husnī needed the signed agreement of Rafīq and Ṭareq's wives. The area in question was no more than three-quarters of a *dūnam* but was owned jointly by the heirs of Karīma and her first husband, namely Ḥusnī (Karīma's second husband), and the children of Ḥusnī and Karīma (D22, D24, D25 and D26). As soon as Rafīq had told Ḥusnī that none of his sons were ready to marry Lea, Ḥusnī, his son Dāūd, and 'Omar (who was Rafīq's own brother, married to Ḥusnī's daughter) stopped speaking to Rafīq and Ṭareq. So Ḥusnī delegated a maternal relative to visit Rafīq to obtain the necessary signatures. Rafīq replied that he had recently had a lot of expenses, among them hospital bills for Lea's abortion. Then Rafīq asked Ḥusnī, through the "go between," to compensate him for his wife's and her sister's readiness to give up their rights on the land. The "go-between" relative delivered the message but was so concerned about the development that he left Ḥusnī's home without even drinking the traditional visitor's cup of coffee, a very unusual behavior.

Amna, Ḥusnī's wife became very distressed. She cried bitterly, "Nākū bintnā wa bidhum yōklunā" (literally, "They have fucked our daughter and now they want to devour us"). This was, of course, a reference to Ṣabrī's relations with Lea. Ḥusnī's wife wanted to indicate that not only had Ṣabrī ruined the reputation of the family, but that his father wished to hurt them financially as well. The normal procedure would have been to provide the signatures without any demand attached. This would have seemed the most obvious reaction, especially after what had happened between Ṣabrī and Lea. She recognized that her husband's handling of the affair and his inability to find a solution had reduced both his and her prestige so much that the insulting request for payment in return for a signature was made. She now knew that she should have insisted on immediate marriage instead of agreeing to the abortion. The person who had caused the pregnancy should, as custom prescribed, have become her daughter's husband.

Ḥusnī, aware of the fact that his wife's accusation had been overheard, was afraid of additional shame. He reacted immediately by grabbing a hoe, entering the room where Lea was resting and smashing her head, injuring her fatally. Seeing her daughter dead, Amna rushed into the street screaming, "Ḥusnī qaṭalha!" ("Ḥusnī has killed her!"). Then she fled to her brother's home in the parent village. (This is another example of the close contacts between a woman and her natal family which cause her to take shelterr with its members in case of an emergency). Ḥusnī went to the hamlet's representative for the Regional Council and asked him to call the police. Ḥusnī's oldest son Dāūd was not in the hamlet that day, but was staying in one of the villages on the West Bank; he returned home only late in the evening.[47]

Circumstances support the assumption that the murder was not planned, a view taken by local gossip. The murder took place about twenty minutes after the "go between" had told Ḥusnī of Rafīq's demand for money in return for agreeing to permit the construction of a house on the jointly owned site. Ḥusnī himself, in telling a relative what he had done, referred to what he considered as a completely unjustified financial demand. His wife made the same point when relating the incident to her natal family. This demand produced a violent reaction under the pressure of which, Ḥusnī committed the murder.

However, earlier rumors had claimed that Ḥusnī's oldest son and 'Omar were planning to kill Lea. These rumors require analysis. It would appear that Lea's murder had actually never been planned at all—rumors about such a plot had simply been spread deliberately. The information could be traced to Ḥusnī's son who had passed it on to the elders of the *ḥamūla*. The events prove that Ḥusni's family wanted the public, and especially their own *ḥamūla*, to think that they would behave in accordance with existing value norms. When they told Muḥammad Yazīd about their plan involving the gas stove "accident," they expected Muḥammad to dissuade them. If they had really intended to kill Lea they would have planned the murder secretly. It may also be asked why they had been searching for a way to do away with Lea for two full years. When a woman is murdered to preserve family honor, it is usually done soon after the incriminating information has leaked out to the community. When the killing is delayed, everybody learns to put up with the situation. Their conduct may be explained in one of two ways. Either they wished to demonstrate their respect for the prevailing ideology and to make it clear that they followed norms based on it; or they wanted to prevent a killing and set the scene to this end. If their desire had been to restore the family honor by killing Lea, they would most probably have known how to keep their own counsel. What is important is that Lea's 'shame' had become public knowledge (Ḥusnī feared that his wife's accusation had been overheard by neighbors). This must be considered the immediate reason for her death, even though special circumstances contributed and set the date for the action.

The special circumstances were brought about by Rafīq who exploited the girl's 'sin' for his own financial advantage (saying that the bills for her abortion were the reason for his demand of payment in return for the required signature). The act of murder was a spontaneous reaction to Amna's reproaches. Ḥusnī suddenly felt as if everyone was against him. Not only was gossip about his daughter directed against him but his own wife criticized him as well. A feeling of hopelessness must have accumulated in the course of time and Amna's words were the last straw. Without her accusations the murder might never have occurred.

In the 1950s, two instances occurred where a woman was an accomplice to her lover's murder of her husband. In the first case, the woman and her lover belonged to different descent groups. Both of them were sentenced to life imprisonment. After eleven years the woman was pardoned and a few months later, her lover too, was released from prison. She expected him to marry her but he preferred a girl from his own descent group, the Amīn. Some time later his former mistress remarried moving to a village in the north. The woman's only punishment in the hamlet was that her four children, raised by her husband's family in a neighboring village, ignored her existence.

In the second case, the woman's lover was her first patrilateral parallel cousin with whom she had had sexual relations while still single. When her parents decided on her marriage with another man, she did not object or demand that her FBS marry her. Her lover lived in the parent village and crossed the closed border clandestinely to continue their love affair after the marriage. Gossip has it that it was she who opened the door to her lover on the night of her husband's murder. He then crushed the sleeping man's head with a rock. The details of the killing were common knowledge in the community though the lovers were never sentenced. The woman's family arranged a second marriage for her this time with a much older man residing in a neighboring village.

These cases illustrate that illicit sexual relations do not automatically lead to the murder of the woman involved. Anthropological literature claims that offenses against *'irḍ* are only punished when they become public knowledge.[48] However, my data does not bear this out. Not all instances of illicit sexual relations that became the subject of rumor and gossip, result in a killing. Murder occurs only when there is not only gossip or rumor, but public accusation by an injured party. Malinowski reports a case of public accusation by an injured person where "certain expressions intolerable to a native,"[49] brought about the accused person's suicide. Here too, public accusation was the cause of death.

Another case supports this interpretation. A girl belonging to the Zamīli descent group (see chapter 4), became pregnant out of wedlock. She gave birth, but not in the hamlet, and the child was given out for adoption. Later, the girl took up residence again with her natal family. In the course of a dispute between the girl's father and a neighbor (a non-relative), the neighbor accused the father of not acting as he should have done with respect to his daughter. In this case the accusation did not lead to any sanction on the girl because the accusation was not made by an injured party.

Becker puts the case similarly when he argues that "the degree to which an act will be treated as deviant depends also on who commits the act and who feels he has been harmed by it."[50] In the case of Jabār, his wife's accusation that he had not protected the family honor was the first reason for murder. For Ḥusnī, the first step leading to murder was his wife's public accusations of his ineffective handling of the situation. Gossip is idle talk but not accusation. In Malinowski's words, "public opinion will gossip but not demand any harsh treatment."[51] Public knowledge alone is not enough to bring about such an act of violence.

It takes a direct accusation to dramatize the issue and to make the killing inevitable.

RELATIONSHIPS WITHIN THE FAMILY

A number of researchers have investigated father-son relations[52]; those between brother and sister;[53] and parent-in-law/daughter-in-law relations.[54] The special relationship that usually exists between a man and his maternal uncle has been investigated;[55] and various researchers have dealt with collateral and affinal relationships.[56]

The mother-son relationship seems to have received less attention than that between father and son and deserves detailed examination. The father-son relationship in traditional village society has been described by Rosenfeld who maintains that "in the agrarian economy fathers held full status and sons were subordinate."[57] Whether the son inherits his father's property or receives his share during his father's life time has important implications. Nowadays, the son is no longer dependent on his father while waiting for his inheritance. He derives his livelihood from sources over which his father has no control. He is either employed outside his place of residence or works independently, in neither case can the father exercise economic sanctions. If a son expects to inherit land upon his father's demise, there is reason for him to submit to his father's authority; but if he receives his inheritance during his father's lifetime, he is no longer restrained by this economic interest and his situation is similar to that of a young man residing in a rural community whose residents are landless. In the hamlets the residents owned land whereas in other rural settlements this is not the case. Where no land is owned by the village, the authority relationship between father and son is affected.

The mother-son relationship is less complicated by financial interests and of a much less formal character. In early childhood, it is the mother who is closest to the child. It is she who provides emotional security and his physical needs. The bond created between mother and son in the early period of the child's life is usually strong and this closeness is reflected in their relationship later on. There is no rivalry between them, as there often is between father and son, and thus no reason for rebellion and self-assertion. When he grows up he feels free to discuss his problems with her. "When I am in a bad mood or upset, my mother invariably notices this. She always succeeds in making me tell her what troubles me," 'Ali Yazīd said. He added emphatically "and this is true even now that I am married and the father of two children." Many other hamlet residents confirmed what 'Ali explained.

Mothers supply more than just emotional security. They often own independent property and can help their sons financially if the need arises. Furthermore, the mother's relations with her natal family may be turned into a source of power for the son in case of need. The same does not apply to a daughter, for obvious reasons. She does not so much seek independence as economic and emotional security. She does not rebel against the authority of the male members of her natal family but needs their continued sense of obligation towards her as an additional safeguard. There is no rivalry between her and her father as there is between father and son, for there is no struggle for supremacy. A son wishes to secure his inheritance while the daughter foregoes her legal claim as a guarantee of continued protection.

Mothers are deeply concerned with their sons' careers and often succeed in promoting them. Rasmi 'Attīlī wanted to study medicine but was not accepted at medical school in Israel because his grades for the matriculation certificate were too low. He was upset and ready to forego his ambition but his mother persuaded him to apply to universities abroad. The author met the young man when he was in his fourth year of medical school and there was no longer any doubt that he would soon become a qualified physician. Without his mother's encouragement he would not have persisted. It was she who gave him the backing he needed and the faith in the eventual success of his plan. He did not hesitate to admit how much he owed her. "I don't think I would ever have made it, hadn't it been for mother," he said with pride in his voice.

Most studies of intra-family relations restrict themselves to the analysis of interaction between two persons, neglecting the wider family context. The following will include a focus on cases in which mother-son relationships are only a link in a more complex claim of family interaction. Bassām Abū Bader was a good student in high school, but he had no intention of going on to university. His mother, however, persuaded him to continue his studies and he is now a mechanical engineer. Bassām's elder brother hinted that their father did not mind either way and would not have seen anything wrong with Bassām's working on the farm. It is often the father's wish that his son cultivate the soil he is to inherit perhaps feeling that in this way he and his son would remain close. A further obvious consideration is that the father wishes to receive help from his son. The mother may perhaps be more confident of her son's attachment, not fearing that higher education would alienate him from her.

This case reflects the difference of relations between a father and his son, and those between mother and son. The father is not as certain of his bond with his heir as the mother is. The pater familias fears that his authority may be endangered if the son acquires a profession and becomes economically independent. He wishes the son to carry on his work not only because he wants his property to be taken care of but also in order to preserve his status. He can only do this if his son intends to become a farmer and depends on his heritage for his future security. The mother may sometimes provide economic support to her son but her relationship with him is based mainly on other factors. In any case, her financial resources are usually limited compared to those of her husband.

When the young man is thinking of choosing a wife, he usually talks the matter over with his mother. She may show herself more understanding than her husband, often being less interested in alliances through marriage than the males of her family. Luṭfīyya claims that a young man "usually makes a direct request to his father to procure him a bride,"[58] but adds that "he may of course, ask indirectly through his mother or through some other person close to his father."[59] The author found no confirmation of Luṭfīyya's observation in the hamlets. None of the residents turned directly to his father when he wanted to become married. Most of the villagers said that they asked their mother to approach the father. In several cases the mother's brother (*khal*) was requested to "find the appropriate opportunity to tell the father." The fact that a man inherits from his father and not from his maternal uncle, makes the latter the ideal person to act as his sister's representative in matters concerning her son.

The differences in relationship of a young man with his paternal uncle, and with his maternal uncle, reflect the difference in relationship he has with his mother, and with his father. The *'amm* (father's brother) belongs to the agnatic group from which he expects to inherit his share of the family property. In this way a young man's relationship with his *'amm* is parallel to that with his father. In addition to this, the *'amm*, unlike the *khal*, may be connected with the young man's father in other ways. Brothers are often, though not always, members of the same political organization. The different relationship a man has with his paternal and maternal uncles is felt by him in childhood and adolescence. In childhood the maternal uncle is more accessible (because of his obligations to his sister) and as an adult the young man turns to him for help and advice. In both Bedouin and sedentary Arab populations, the *khal* usually intercedes with the father to open marriage negotiations for his sister's son.[60]

However, relations between a man and his *khal* are not always harmonious. Peters cites a case where a man killed his maternal uncle and points out that "they [the Bedouin] have every reason to be disturbed by the killing of a mother's brother, for, whatever personal affections may be involved, a crucial link is threatened."[61] Closeness and affection characterize the relationship between a man and his maternal uncle. It is a significant link and its severance has serious consequences. This applies equally to Bedouin and Arab village society as Peters' description of the relationship between a man and his *khal* shows. They "are characteristically easy, . . . they are not demanding, . . . there is much joking in them, and . . . to kill within this range is, in terms of the general pattern of behaviour, stupid."[62] Some writers analyze joking relations as an expression of suppressed hostility and believe they occur in inter-sex relations.[63] The relationship is not only close but warm and intimate. A man knows for certain that he can rely on his *khal* when he needs help, even if this causes the *khal* great expense or inconvenience. This relationship inevitably brings with it an element of ambivalence.

The influence of the mother and her relatives is shown in the following case history. When Ṣweliḥ Yazīd (E18, chart 1) refused to marry his FBD (see chapter 4), and later wanted to take a woman from the West Bank as his wife, he asked his mother to intercede with his father on his behalf. She not only took up the matter with his father but actively tried to help him marry the girl he wanted. This is all the more remarkable since the FBD whom Ṣweliḥ's father wanted him to marry was also his wife's sister's daughter and shows the closeness of the relationship between mother and son. "My mother understood me when I explained to her that I would never marry my *bint 'amm*" said Ṣweliḥ.

The match Ṣweliḥ hoped for did not come off and when at a later date, Ṣweliḥ wanted to marry another girl, he again asked his mother's support for his father to approach the girl's family with a marriage proposal. The father, however, refused. Soon afterwards the father fell ill. Ṣweliḥ did not visit him in hospital and when he returned home they ignored each other. Ṣweliḥ stressed that his mother and sisters had taken his side in the controversy. During the month of the Ramadan fast, Ṣweliḥ did not join the males at the *fuṭūr* (literally, a "breakfast"), the ceremonious meal taken after sunset following a fast from sunrise to dusk. Instead, at his mother's suggestion, he ate with the women. Ṣweliḥ's mother knew that the festival would have been a good opportunity to restore harmony in family but she chose to disregard the opportunity. The act of eating with the women was a demonstration of Ṣweliḥ's rebellion against his father's authority. Ṣweliḥ's mother publicly acknowledged her dispute with her husband by encouraging her son not attend the customary Ramadan *fuṭūr*.

Another case is that of Faūzi Shāmi, whose marriage in 1968 was planned by his mother Faṭma. She insisted on a 'blessing' ceremony before he entered the bridal chamber for the virginity test. Faṭma stood on two chairs and asking Faūzi to pass between her legs. He was embarrassed and unsuccessfully tried to avoid the ceremony. Later Faūzi's wife gave birth twice but in both cases the baby died within six months. She blamed her mother-in-law for these deaths claiming that they had occured as a direct result of the 'blessing', the symbol of which was clear to all concerned. The mother, whose influence on her sons was strong, wished to emphasize the fact that he had come out of her womb. In this way she asserted that no other woman could completely take her place.

In 1973, Faūzi's younger brother, Fakhrī, married a resident of the same West Bank village to which his mother's natal family belonged. It was again the mother who had asked her relatives to look for an eligible wife for her son. On the wedding day, the bride cried and told the groom that she would not marry him if the ceremony of passing between his mother's legs was to be repeated. Faṭma knew that the only way to prove she was not responsible for the deaths of her grandchildren was to repeat the act with her second son. When Faṭma summoned Fakhrī on his wedding day, he fled from the house. But Faṭma made her husband bring him back to go through the ritual.[64] Faṭma's wish to emphasize the relationship between mother and son is expressed in the proverb *al karsha aqua min al ṣulb* (literally, the belly [womb] is stronger than the backbone).[65] Although

Arab society is patrilineal,[66] in many cases the bonds between children and mother are stronger than those between children and their father.

Cases are recorded where tribes adopted the name of one of their ancestresses rather than that of an ancestor. Peters explains this by saying that "a female name placed at the apex of the Cyrenaican genealogy . . . is a symbol of full brother unity at the highest political level."[67] Kressel mentions a similar case of groups of Libyan origin.[68] Marx, however, disagrees with this interpretation of family or tribal name origins: "Peters rightly links the eponym to the Bedouin's conception of ecological divisions, but he does not explain why the eponyms at the apex of the genealogy are sometimes males and sometimes females. I suggest that the difference refers to specific types of organization at this level. Women stand at the apex of genealogies wherever tribesmen control their area of subsistence, but without a corresponding corporate organization and leadership. The eponym remains female as long as this is the case, but when the tribesmen develop leadership and corporateness the eponym becomes a male. . ."[69] For example, one of the hamlet descent groups was given the name of the mother of the man who had settled in the parent village at the end of the eighteenth century. However, neither Marx nor Peters views "honor to affines" as a symbolic aspect of womens' power. The following case history illustrates that this aspect of power, in this case in the form of status, is recognized and acted upon.

Three full siblings of the Abū Baker descent group wanted to give their mother a present of two *dūnams* of mountainous olive orchard. The siblings had two half brothers (from a different mother) brought up by their father's second wife after the death of their own mother. They objected to the gift and a prolonged dispute between the two groups of brothers resulted in the cancellation of the agreement by which they owned their land jointly. When the division of the property took place in 1969, one of the brothers was absent having left the hamlet when the area came under Israeli Administration. Because of his absence, the Custodian of Absentees' Property claimed one-sixth of the land. This share included valuable lowland fields so that the financial loss was larger than the area of the two *dūnams* that had been the cause of the dispute.[70]

Here the relationships between mother and sons, and mother and stepsons, influenced the entire economic structure of the family. Not only was the small plot not given to the mother, but the joint holdings were broken up and a section of valuable land lost because a stepmother was not thought of in the same regard as a true mother. This case history demonstrates the principle that the bonds among the children of one mother are stronger than those of children of one father. The children of the mother constituted a group bound by a feeling of solidarity and attachment to their mother. That the half-siblings born to another mother but having the same father were much less close, is patently clear in this case. The group of siblings from one and the same mother were prepared to incur considerable financial loss and to sever their relations with their half-siblings, all in the interest of their mother.

WOMEN AS CONVEYORS OF INFORMATION

A woman's close ties with her natal family are often reflected in her readiness to supply its members with information. Opportunities are not usually lacking due to frequent visits to her former home or visits by her father and brothers. Married women are believed to be more loyal to their natal families than to their families of reproduction, but there are cases where a woman is closest to her husband telling him all he wants to know about her natal family. This may lead to conflict in one or both of the families. Generally though, it is the woman's role to serve as a positive link between the two groups. Marx says that, "the woman provides a link between the two groups and carries information in both directions and cares for the continuing relationship."[71] Three elements may be distinguished. Woman serving as a link between groups; as a conveyor of information and as an individual who has a personal interest in continuing relationships.

Antoun adds another factor when he explains that she "remains part of the 'prestige' structure of her father's descent group while in addition becoming incorporated into the 'prestige' structure of her husband's descent group through her children."[72] This 'prestige' factor is actually a consequence of the three elements mentioned above. Belonging to two 'prestige' structures, a woman is interested in linking them through her personal actions. It is she who binds the groups together. Fuller notes that ambivalence and perhaps conflict may characterize the situation of a woman having dual loyalties[73] and Khuri explains preference for marriage with a parallel cousin by the fact that secrets will be kept within the family.[74] Marriage within the family eliminates the danger of having outsiders know what goes on in the most intimate family circle. Here, there is no second 'prestige' structure, for the woman has no dual loyalties and cannot endanger the honor of the family by conveying shameful information.

Relationships between mother-in-law and daughter-in-law are not always smooth. Granqvist notes that many a young wife finds that her mother-in-law considers her an enemy.[75] In Arab villages, as in many other societies, strained relations between the two females closest to a man are far from uncommon. In a way, Faṭma's 'blessing' was an act resorted to in anticipation of her sons' tending to give priority to their wives. Her fear that she may lose their affection dictated her decision to remind them of their link with her.

When a woman is so placed that she can convey information from one group to another, her status is increased. The presents she receives from her agnates, described earlier as a recognition of a debt owed her for renouncing her share of the family property, may also be seen as acknowledgment of the value put on the information she provides. A woman's ties with her natal family may worry her husband. He is often especially demonstrative in his affection for her before a visit to her agnates, wishing to reinforce her loyalty to him and to remind her of it. At the same time, a certain reticence on her husband's part often characterizes the period before a woman's departure for a visit with her natal family. He may try, in the last minute, to keep some of the secrets of his own family from his wife. When she returns she can expect a warm reception as she is now in possession of information about her natal family and its circle. She is made to feel loyal to her husband and to disclose the wanted information. If the family of reproduction and the natal family are closely related, as in the case of FBD marriages, there is less new information to be expected, because the men may also maintain close links. A case history will illustrate the importance of the information relayed in this way.

Rashīd 'Attīlī caused a split in the 'Attīlī descemt group by forming a faction including a section of the Yazīd descent group and several members of the Jabāli. He aimed at becoming the hamlet representative in the Regional Council. His sister had married a member of a lineage of 'Attīlī who had joined his rival's faction. Rashīd admitted that his sister was a great asset to him since her husband's brother was very active in the political faction. Rashīd himself provided false data concerning his own activities for his sister to take back to the other family. "I should give her a high rank as an excellent intelligence officer," said Rashīd.

The case history of Khalīl's attempt to arrange *badal* marriages for his children was described in chapter 4. The cancellation of the first *badal* was due to rumors that his nephew's wife had passed on via her daughter. Khalīl and his nephew's wife had developed a mutual animosity due to a minor misunderstanding between them. Khalīl's nephew, influenced by his wife, stopped visiting his uncle. When the nephew wanted to open an agricultural equipment store, Khalīl tried to prevent him by telling the authorities that his nephew had not paid his income tax dues and that they should not grant him a licence because of this. As Khalīl's nephew's daughter was married to a resident of Jatt, the nephew and his wife were able (through the daughter) to spread rumors to the effect that Khalīl's daughter had undergone an operation which would prevent her from ever bearing children.

Next is an example of woman's role as a fact finder. Musa, whose married sister Safa lived in Bāqa al-Gharbīyya, met a young school teacher in a taxi. He took an immediate liking to her and began corresponding using his sister as an intermediary. When Musa wanted to ascertain whether she was a suitable partner for marriage, he asked Safa to find out all about the girl's family. Difficulties in the marriage negotiations arose because the girl's father would only agree to the marriage on condition that the couple reside in Bāqa al-Gharbīyya. He insisted on uxorilocal residence, a demand contrary to custom.[76] Musa was an only son and did not want to accept this condition, but his sister and mother persuaded him that he should formally agree. They suggested that he buy a plot of land in Bāqa al-Gharbīyya and ask an architect to plan a house for him. The couple would then live with his parents during the first year of marriage and move to their new home later. Musa's sister had learned that the girl's parents were willing to concede to their daughter's living in the hamlet temporarily, since the stipulated condition was contrary to custom in the first place. Musa's mother and sister thought that, after his marriage, Musa would stay in the hamlet for good and sell the plot. The marriage did not take place but it was not a result of faulty planning or lack of necessary information.

Sometimes a woman uses information in her possession to secure economic advantages. Mariam 'Ali controlled the family farm while her husband Sa'id was employed outside the village. Mariam realized that Muḥammad Yazīd was eager to become the representative in the Regional Council. She recognized that to achieve this he needed up-to-date reliable information. Mariam made use of her relations with other women to provide Muḥammad with such information. In this way she put him under an obligation. When Muḥammad later became a representative to the Council his relations with the officials of the different Ministries of the region were very good. He helped Mariam with water allocations for irrigation and persuaded the supervisor of the Ministry of Agriculture not to take Mariam to court for growing two *dūnams* of tomatoes and cucumbers above her production quota, although other villagers were fined for the same offense. Cunnison's remark that "Women operate as arbiters of men's conduct, and can build up a man's career but can also destroy it" applies to Mariam.[77] She was prepared to help the *mukhtār* accumulate political power knowing that he would at a later date reward her in one form or another.

Mariam's advice was sought by many hamlet women who confided their most intimate concerns to her. She used to tell girls who were no longer virgins, that dove's blood would produce stains similar to those made by human blood.[78] She also substituted for a woman's agnates when they were deceased as in the case of a neighbor who had neither father nor brothers. Such a woman is referred to as a *qati'a* (literally, a cut-off woman).[79] The neighbor complained that her husband humiliated her by always demanding she turn away her face during intercourse. Mariam settled the matter with the man to the woman's great relief.

Mariam even placed economic interests above tradition. She invited a distant male relative, employed by the Government, to her daughter's wedding. This relative was a friend of the local *mukhtār*. Mariam suggested that the relative accompany her daughter to the groom's house, an honor traditionally accorded to the father's brother (*'amm*) and the mother's brother (*khal*). Mariam's two brothers objected to this defiance of custom but she was not deterred. The *mukhtār* was helped in his political activities through the opportunity of honoring his friend employed by the Government; and Mariam accrued a debt from the *mukhtār* for his service. As a result her younger brother cut off all relations with her, while her older brother (who had become her in-law) avoided giving her the customary presents on festivals. Mariam sacrificed her right to protection by her male relatives preferring the economic advantages of her alliance with the *mukhtār*. Advantages such as the extra allocation and produce quota cited above.

IMPORTANCE OF GOSSIP

Information and gossip are important to the villagers, they are part of the interaction between individuals within the hamlets and to a certain extent with other communities. Paine claims that gossip is the activity of an individual,[80] but since gossip cannot be indulged in without a recipient, and since it usually leads to an exchange of information, Gluckman is more correct in defining it as a group activity,—or a factor creating "networks of social relationships."[81] Gossip can be seen as forwarding and protecting individual interests.[82] It need not be based on reciprocity in terms of information. Gossip may also be of the kind defined by Cox as having "the particularly salient point of permitting an increase in one's own party's access to power."[83]

For instance, the gossip transmitted by Mariam when she told the *mukhtār* that Rashīd 'Ali had asked the authorities to hold the Regional Council election at an earlier date than planned was both important and necessary. He then succeeded in preventing a change of the election date by exerting his "influence on officials with whom he was on good terms." In this case the *mukhtār* was not a party in Cox's sense but rather a man attempting to set up a faction. Mariam heard about Rashīd's action from women of the 'Arīshi descent group—women whose husbands supported Rashīd 'Attīlī's faction. In other words, the information was first *obtained* through a "social network," (the social relationship between Mariam and the women of the 'Arīshi descent group); and *used* to "increase . . . access to power" (Mariam's support for the *mukhtār*). Gossip may also be directed toward the use of sanctions as in the case of Khalīl's nephew's wife who set gossip afoot in retaliation for what she considered a slight.

The terms "gossip" and "information" have so far been used interchangeably. They need, however, to be defined. Handleman used the terms interchangeably in the title of his article, "*Gossip in Encounters: The Transmission of Information in a Bounded Social Setting.*"[84] Gluckman refers to dictionary definitions, noting that in both the *Shorter Oxford Dictionary* and *Webster's International Dictionary*, gossip is defined as "idle talk," as something not having a clear purpose. The dictionary meaning does not fit Mariam's case. Webster's Dictionary also uses the words "groundless rumor," "chatter," and "news-mongering," which certainly do not apply to the cases cited. The women who engaged in gossip transmitted desired information in return for more or less clearly conceived aims. This information was not obtained through idle talk or chatter.[85]

Men gossip no less than women. Gluckman is right when he says that "every single day, and for a large part of each day, most of us are engaged in gossip."[86] Though there are other avenues for gossip and the transmission of information, the *diwāns* provide a suitable framework for turning gossip into a socially institutionalized leisure-time occupation. Abraham's remarks that "gossip, like joking takes place between individuals who stand in a special relationship to each other,"[87] not only confirms Gluckman's approach to gossip as creating social networks, but supports Baldwin's 'gossip group' theory. Baldwin defines the term "gossip group" as a group distinct from others because, in order to be able to gossip, one has to know those who serve as objects of gossip. It is, therefore, "a device whereby group identification can be tested."[88] In addition, there is a connection between gossip and joking. Both can only be indulged in by the initiated, such activity binding members of the group together.

Local politics play a central role in Arab rural communities and is one of the main topics to be discussed whenever people meet. A great deal is done to obtain political information and gossip is one of the channels through which this information is conveyed. Women, through their double loyalties when they marry non-relatives, are often in a position to give or withhold information. Women have several foci of gossip, such as the weekly visit to the cemetery, visits to neighbors and relatives, and when they go shopping, or encounter one another in buses or taxis. Gossip is not only a means of social control but a source of information vital for local politics.

Sometimes gossip is remembered and used effectively a long time after the event or conduct that caused it, as the following case history shows. When Muḥammad 'Ali married Sihām (see chapter 4), his uncles stressed that it was his mother, Fahīma, who had arranged this marriage with a member of another *ḥamūla*. His uncle Ibrāhīm expressed his feelings: "What can you expect from the son of Abū al-'Anze (literally, "father of the goat"). Ibrāhīm explained that his late brother Musa, Muḥammad's father, was henpecked. Sometimes his wife even refused to sleep with him. Ibrāhīm continued, "Everyone in the hamlets knows that he was caught by Ṣubḥi Arīshi having intercourse with Ṣubḥi's goat."[89] It was the first time that the author had heard this story and when different residents were asked who " Abū al-'Anze" was, the prompt answer given with a contemptuous smile was always "Musa 'Ali." Some even went into great detail describing how Ṣubḥi took the goat to Musa's wife's father and said, "Please, meet ḍurrat bintak ("your daughter's co-wife"). By referring to his late brother Musa as "Abū 'Anze", Ibrāhīm damaged the status of his nephew (Muḥammad), implying that like his father he lacked virility.[90] The young man had evidently refused to listen to his agnates, preferring his mother's advice when choosing a wife. In the case of Khalīl's daughter, the woman who spread the malicious gossip held no grievance against the girl but wished to harm her father by making disparaging remarks about her. The story itself underwent several modifications and was embellished with various details. Thus gossip may also be the telling of a simple tale by artfully filling in missing links and turning the narrative into entertainment, a process which fits Baldwin's contention that gossip may often become art.[91]

ROLES IN CIRCUMCISION CEREMONIES

Circumcisions are part of the prophetic tradition and a most important ceremony for Muslims. In the hamlets, as in other Muslim societies, no age is fixed for the circumcision. The author attended ceremonies where the boys were aged six months and five years.[92] Preparations for the ceremony are simple and do not include a feast.[93] It is usually the mother who decides on the date while the father invites the guests. Sometimes, a mother vows before the birth that if she bears a male child she will have him circumcised at a place hallowed by a saint (*maqām*).[94] Hamlet residents often choose *maqām el khaḍer* (literally, Elijah's holy place), a cave on Mt. Carmel considered sacred by Muslim tradition. When a child is sick the mother often vows to circumcize him in a *maqām* if God cures him. Another vow is that of *qrāyet mōlad*, reciting the story of the Prophet's nativity.[95] To fulfill the *mōlad* vow the boy's mother invites female relatives and friends. A few men are present to recite the *mōlad* with the *imām* (religious leader of the community). A *mōlad* is a more modest ceremony than the regular circumcision ceremony. The religious aspects are more pronounced. No professional singers are invited, leaving the local women to do the singing and dancing.

On the day of the circumcision ceremony, the women gather in one room, rejoicing and singing, dancing and playing a *tambūr* (tambourine). The men sit in the guest room and return there after the ceremony, chatting and enjoying the women's singing. An indication of the dominant role of women in this ceremony is that, unlike in wedding ceremonies, the singing is done by the females and not the males. During the circumcision itself, the grandmother or nearest female relative holds the boy's head, while another woman holds his hands and a male relative his legs.[96] Once the operation has been performed, the mother accepts the congratulations and the gifts (*nuqūt*) which her female guests give to her.[97]

At two of the four circumcision ceremonies the author attended, the father was absent. On one occasion the father went to work as usual in the neighboring Jewish settlement; and on the second occasion, the ceremony included three children. One of the fathers went to town to buy spare parts for his tractor; according to gossip, he did not like his son to be circumcised with the other two boys—but could not change the arrangements made earlier by his wife.

Another ceremony was of the *mōlad* type. The boy's father had been injured in a traffic accident and his wife had vowed that upon his return from the hospital their four year old son would be circumcised. The injured man's brother-in-law, living in a West Bank village, brought along his two year old son to be circumcised on the same occasion. Another brother-in-law, 'Abd al Fatāḥ 'Attīlī, a Yamma resident, told the author that his five year old son would be circumcised with the other two boys. Actually, he was the one to invite some of the guests. On the day of the circumcision, 'Abd al-Fatāḥ attended the ceremony and his wife was the main singer and dancer, but their son was not circumcised, 'Abed later explained that his wife wanted a large feast with a professional female singer and the circumcision of their son was postponed until the agricultural season was over. 'Abd al-Fatāḥ's wife had felt that her sister-in-law had only decided on the *mōlad* because she did not want their son to be circumcised with hers. 'Abed said, "she knew that my wife and our son would receive more attention." 'Abed gave other examples of a father's absence from a circumcision ceremony.

The ceremonies observed in the hamlets differ from those customary in other Muslim societies, especially those of the Bedouin. Among the Bedouin the father is responsible for arranging the circumcision ceremony, not just observing it. As

Peters emphasized: A father, the Bedouin insist, ought to perform three duties for his sons: attend to their circumcision, their education in the Koran, and provide bride-wealth when they marry. All fathers attend to the circumcision of all their sons; few provide for the Koranic education of all of their sons; most bear the burden of marrying off at least one of their sons.[98]

The songs sung by the women before the circumcision open with a praise of the guests and a blessing for the boy and his parents. The boy's colorful dress is the subject of a long description in verse, while many songs are addressed to the person performing the circumcision.

El Shelabi, ya ulād qa'ed 'ala ṣūr
Ṭaher li el walād kirama lilrasūl
Ya mṭaher, ya ulād, qa'ed 'ala elraba
Lamā Shāfu 'aduhū mithel elṣūṣ elmunkafa
[The circumciser, of boys, sits on a high wall,
Circumcise me, the son, in honor of the Messenger,
(Muḥammad)
Oh circumciser, oh boys, he sits on the hill
When his enemy saw him he (the enemy) became like a defeated cock.]

The refrain is

Ya shelabi, khāff idek
[Oh circumciser, be your hand light][99]

Once the ceremony is over, the content and mood of the songs change. Now, the main subject is love and the men are not referred to as fathers but as husbands. A romantic atmosphere is created by a description of a spring evening with the moon rising while a young lover waits for his beloved.

Ṭahat el nakhla tarquṣ ma taqa'
labsu el nakhla thūabat el ud'a
Baddar qamarnā baddar washaraf 'alaynā el dār
Yom qāma ḥabībi asra' min ḥmām waṭār

[The palm tree (the beautiful young woman) came down dancing and will not fall.
Put on the palm tree dresses made of shells,
Our moon rose early and visited our home.
On that day (minute) my beloved one stood up and flew off faster than a dove.]

The song goes on to describe the woman's broken heart and her determination never to love another man. Some songs idealize the days preceding marriage, while others have a different, and surprising content.

> Ufakri ya jārti fataḥna warqa wākul man
> yughani min rāyahā ʻan
> jozek hal nadel ilsʻayi beṭalāq qabel
> ḥtam shbat ʼaw kānūnan.
>
> [Tell, oh my neighbor, we have opened a page (a new page)
> and each one will sing—
> what is on her mind.
> Slight your cowardly husband before the end
> of February or January by divorcing him (before spring comes).]

The open reference to divorce and the attribute "cowardly" given to the husband come as an anticlimax after the earlier lyrical descriptions of everlasting love.

Since the men are in the *diwan* close by, they cannot but overhear the words. Some of the songs are sarcastic, holding the men up to ridicule or even contempt. The song mentioning divorce and the husband's cowardice, a solo, is usually preceded by a noisy discussion as to who is to sing it. The post-circumcision festivities fit Gluckman's analysis of "rituals of rebellion".[100]

A ceremony planned and controlled by women and from which the head of the household can just as well be absent, offers a good opportunity for the woman to perform rituals of rebellion. The free expression of frustration and resentment serves as a safety valve, allowing pent-up feeling to be released. This relief is needed for the preservation of the male myth. Rogers maintains that usually, neither men nor women "will admit publicly that it is only a myth."[101] Nor will either party allow any expression of doubt, "because they assume that the other group believes it to be true. By operating in this manner, they succeed in staving off confrontation."[102] However, this evasive maneuver does not eliminate the need for rituals of rebellion to forestall opposition against authority. If the expression of such feeling were suppressed for any length of time it might lead to a much sharper, more violent reaction. By ritualizing rebellion, the possibility of revolution is reduced. Rebellion, in this form, may be disavowed and shrugged of as a joke, though its message is usually received and properly interpreted. The message is also in a form of words not chosen by those giving vent to rebellion. This makes the rebellion impersonal and eliminates any element of direct, personal attack. Such a ceremony then, is a mechanism for the regulation of relations, and effectively removes the danger of revolutionary change.

Marx and Ammar stress the importance of presents at the circumcision in economic and political terms.[103] The political aspect seems to be most decisive. Women can show their power in this way, since they determine the character of the ceremony and make the arrangements. Husbands are aware too that there is an opportunity to further or initiate political links or weaken existing ones through the choice of the guests. In one case, a man prevailed upon his wife to change the date of the ceremony so that it coincided with the installation of sprinklers in his fields. The man wanted to invite the representative of the Ministry of Agriculture who had helped him obtain the water allocation. His wife was reluctant to comply since she wanted the circumcision to take place together with that of a relative. She suggested that he arrange a separate celebration in the field telling him that serving a ceremonial meal right in the field would most effectively bring out the significance of the event. After the man bought his wife a cooking stove and a new dress, she announced that both mothers had agreed to delay the circumcision, which meant that the "water feast" would take place at the same time. The fact that he felt compelled to buy her costly presents was an admission that she had the right to stipulate the date. He persuaded her to forego this right in return for valuable gifts.

The customs as described above regarding circumcision ceremonies, as they have existed in recent years, can be readily explained by the changing occupational structure of the hamlets. The father's working outside the village and the son's increased education (his being close to his mother while living at home as a student) have broken the traditional continuity of father's and son's occupations. No longer is there an emphasis on that element of the rites of passage whereby a youth makes a decisive transition to the world of men—namely that of his father. The only element of the rite that remains is the religious one. Woman's working in the fields, with her sons helping her, could account for the change in the circumcision ritual,—the woman taking advantage of the situation and assuming the dominant role in the ceremony.

The circumcision ceremony also has another dimension—that of interaction between women. Woman's status is still largely dependent on her fertility. Barrenness is considered a curse and renders her position in the family insecure.[104] After all, the term "family of reproduction" implies her function within it. If she does not fulfil it, she feels insecure. Granqvist observes that some women accept their sterility with equanimity and rarely protest. She also mentions cases where husbands have vented their anger on their barren wives, treating them so harshly that they had no alternative but to become *ḥardane*, leaving the home of their family of reproduction rather than further exposing themselves to hostility and suffering.[105] In these circumstances women will seek for remedies and try out various devices in the hope of becoming fertile. Swallowing the foreskin of the circumcised child is one of the supposed cures for barrenness, together with witchcraft[106] and bathing in springs renowned for their curative powers.[107] In the hamlets there were twelve women,[108] (a large number considering the size of the population) who chose to use the foreskin of the circumcised child in order to relieve barrenness.

Barren women, therefore, take an active interest in circumcision ceremonies and are very much in evidence during them. They not only use the foreskin in the hope of becoming fertile but also believe that it will bring them a male child. Granqvist gives a very different description when she says that the foreskin is buried "lest the dogs eat, it, since if they do, harm will come."[109] Ammar said that Egyptian mothers threw the boy's foreskin—inserted into a loaf of bread—into the River Nile.[110] In both cases, the need to get rid of the foreskin is stressed and the desire to make sure that it cannot reappear to bring harm. Custom in the hamlets is different. The boy's mothers often agree to let the barren women among their guests take their sons' foreskins to cure their sterility. Others prefer to place it in a small bag which they lay under their son's pillow to keep away the "evil eye." Others, so the author is told (though they added it was not the practice in the hamlets) bury the foreskin close to the house of a man possessing high status in the community. They hope in this way to ensure that the son will one day also enjoy prestige and high socioeconomic standing.

Miscarriages, especially repeated ones, frequent stillbirths, or the death of one or more children in infancy are ascribed to the "evil eye." The case of Faṭma, earlier narrated, is relevant here. Her ceremony, symbolizing her sons' dependence on her and the importance given to their links with her, is supposed to have caused the "evil eye" which led to the death of two of her grandchildren. The act, which confirmed the important role she played in her son's life, robbed the young man of his capacity of producing healthy children.

A barren woman is supposed to possess the power to protect a healthy child born to another woman against becoming the victim of the "evil eye", or more precisely, she is the one ready to undertake the ceremony required to keep evil at bay. Any woman who has had several miscarriages or still births, or whose children have died in early childhood, considers herself and is considered as such by others to be under the influence of the "evil eye." The foreskin is considered so good a cure of sterility that it represents an object of value in exchange for which one can ask an equivalent favor. The way to repay the favor is to undertake a ceremony, the so called "re-delivery," which is considered a means of keeping away the much feared "evil eye." When a woman has a live born child she asks a barren woman to "redeliver" him, that is to place the body under her dress and let him slide out between her legs. Then, if the child's own mother is "caught by the evil eye," the infant will not be affected.

The "redelivery ritual" gives the barren woman, who is otherwise considered inferior in Arab rural society, a positive function and value among women. If a childless woman through the symbolic act of "redelivery," makes a young mother believe that she need not fear the "evil eye," this gives power to the woman undertaking the act. It means that she is in some way connected with childbirth and her stigma is consequently reduced.

The circumcision ceremony, arranged and conducted mainly by women, has various aspects not directly connected with the declared purpose of the ceremony. It is an opportunity for woman to appear as decision maker and organizer. It also gives her a chance to express rebellion, helping in this way to reduce tension between the sexes. At the same time, it provides an opportunity for barren women to obtain what they consider a cure against their condition and to become involved in childbirth and childraising through a symbolic act of giving birth.

WOMAN'S PLACE IN THE POLITICAL STRUCTURE

During the time of my field work intra-*ḥamūla* struggles were no longer the main political manifestation in the communities. The pattern was changing and factions came into existence that were not entirely organized on *ḥamūla* lines. A man's place in the political structure is no longer mainly determined by birth. He now has the opportunity to make choices and to switch from one faction to another—individuals have become more important. Women have realized that their husbands are not bound to their *ḥamūla* but can join a different faction and this has provided the scope for them to enter the political arena, though not often openly.

Any analysis should be preceded by a definition of the term 'faction' in the special context of Arab rural society. Shokeid following Firth, defines a faction as ". . . an ephemeral group which emerges in order to operate in the interest of a specific aim or conflict."[111] Here what keeps the group or faction is not a joint *weltanschauung*, or socioeconomic platform, but a well defined and limited objective. This group, Shokeid continues, is "mainly based on personal aspiration . . . and not upon any . . . kinship ties, religious affiliations, common caste membership, etc."[112] Shokeid's definition is appropriate in the context of the hamlets. An additional characteristic should be added, namely that the term 'faction'[113] emphasizes a leader led relationship. This approach in anthropology toward defining factions is not the only one. Nakhleh, in referring to Bailey's theoretical model, "distinguishes between 'core-based' group and 'factions' based on the criterion of the attachment between the leader and the follower. . ."[114] But Nakhleh notes the difficulty of isolating 'core-based' (within the family) group and 'faction', when it comes down to real life situations. The following case history clearly illustrates the difficulty of isolating family ties and faction affiliation.

Members of the 'Attīlī *ḥamūla* were divided into three factions. One faction was led by Rashīd 'Attīlī and included members of other *ḥamūlas*. Other members from the 'Attīlī descent group joined a second faction led by Muḥammad Yazīd; and another group of the 'Attīlī followed a third faction led by 'Abdal-Qader, a member of Ibn Sina *ḥamūla*. 'Abd al-Fataḥ 'Attīlī, who was a member of the faction led by Rashīd 'Attīlī, wished to leave it. He was a member of the hamlet committee within the Regional Council, proud of his political standing and thought that he should have been the faction leader. 'Abed's wife (see section on circumcision) prevented him from dividing the faction in the spring of 1973, for she felt that such an action would help

Muḥammad Yazīd accumulate further power. In the winter of 1973 the hidden power struggle between Muḥammad Yazīd and Ṭareq Yazīd (D19, chart 1) came into the open and reached its climax with Ṭareq's manifested support to Rashīd 'Attīlī. Again 'Abed's wife succeeded in persuading her husband not to divide the faction.

One of the main opponents to the affiliation with the Regional Council was 'Abd al-Karīm Yazīd, a descendant of the Ḥassān lineage (B3, chart 1). He was Muḥammad Yazīd's rival. When tension between Muḥammad and Ṭareq increased, Muḥammad sent a "go between" to Ḥamed (C3), 'Abd al-Karīm's eldest brother who had left the hamlet for the parent village in 1949. Muḥammad wanted to use Ḥamed's influence on his brother in order to reunite the family ties. 'Abd al-Karīm's wife, who learned about the message from Ḥamed's wife, did her best to intensify the struggle by pitting her husband and his followers against Muḥammad and his supporters.

One of the points at issue was the construction of paved roads across the hamlet fields planned by the Regional Council. 'Abd al-Karīm's wife spread rumors that the Council had originally had another plan (according to which the road would have passed through the other end of the plain), but that Muḥammad Yazīd had convinced the Council to change the routing. Some of the residents, though not all, whose land was affected by the new roads, were members of 'Abd al-Karīm's faction. 'Abed's wife contacted everyone through whose fields the road passed, condemning Muḥammad. On the day work was to begin, the farmers built a barrier where the road was intended to run. 'Abed's wife added to the tension by throwing stones at Muḥammad Yazīd, clearly intended as an insult and an attempt to injure his prestige. In this case a woman set in motion a whole chain of action, influencing the membership and activities of political factions.

Sometimes a faction is set up as a result of a marriage. The marriage between Mariam Abū-Bader (E1, chart 2) and Qāsem (E16) is an example. Mariam's father, the *mukhtār*, was released from his duties in favor of Qāsem's father in the 1950s. When the Regional Council was set up, the position of representative went to somebody else. The previous change in authority between the fathers of Miriam and Qāsem had led to rivalry and animosity between these two families. The aunts of the married couple planned the marriage union in order to unite these two families in one faction against the Regional Council representative.

Women not only influenced inter and intra-faction struggles, but also brought their influence to bear on the Knesset (Israel Parliament) elections. In the 1969 general election campaign,[115] Fauzīyya 'Ali convinced her relatives and other residents, especially women, to vote for Raqaḥ, the New Communist Party,[116] of which her nineteen year old son Radī, a high school graduate, was a member. He intended to study medicine and, according to several informants, had been promised by the Regional Secretary of the Party that he would be sent to an Eastern European medical school on condition that a substantial increase in Raqaḥ votes occurred in the hamlets. He was also told that he would be granted a scholarship if he succeeded in strengthening the party.

Fauzīyya considered this an arrangement with no ideology attached. She wanted her son to become a physician. Accordingly she invested all her energy in helping her son gain his objective by recruiting Raqah voters. Fauzīyya had to contend against the well organized election campaign of the Labor Party, then the dominant party in Israel, linked with the left-wing United Workers Party (Mapam) in what was called the Alignment.[117] In elections a woman in an Arab village is usually given the ballot by her husband, and if she is single, by the closest male relative. With the help of other women in her own *ḥamūla*, and some belonging to different *ḥamūlas*, Fauzīyya distributed Raqaḥ ballots among female hamlet residents, asking them to use those instead of the ones supplied by their male relatives. Many women consented out of solidarity for Fauzīyya. They were prepared to disobey their male relatives so as to help another woman.

Table 40

General Election Results in Hamlets
(percentages in brackets)

	Voter Data			*Distribution of Votes*		
Election Year	*Eligible Voters*	*Actual Voters*	*Valid Votes*	*Alignment and 2 allied Arab lists*	*Communist Party*	*Other Parties*
1961	442	403 (91.2)	388 (96.3)	337 (86.9)	39 (10.0)	12 (3.1)
1965	575	470 (81.7)	456 (97.0)	312 (68.4)	33 (7.2)	111 (24.4)
1969	711	517 (72.7)	501 (97.0)	381 (76.0)	94 (18.8)	26 (5.2)
1973	839	537 (64.0)	528 (98.3)	301 (57.0)	89 (16.9)	138 (26.1)

Table 40 indicates the 1969 election results, as compared with those of 1973 and two previous elections.[118] Votes for the Communist Party in the hamlets were not constant over the elections. In 1965 there was a decrease of 2.3 percent as against an increase of 11.6 percent in 1969 and then a decrease of 1.9 percent in the 1973 elections. If the votes for Raqaḥ in the hamlets are compared with those of the entire country and small villages (settlements with a population of less than 2,000), the picture is as follows:[119] In 1965 Raqaḥ received 23.6 percent of the entire Arab vote; 13.1 percent in small villages, and only 7.2 percent in the hamlets. In the 1969 elections Raqaḥ obtained 29.6 percent in the entire country, there was no change in the small villages while a peak of 18.8 percent was reached in the hamlets. In the 1973 elections Raqaḥ received thirty-seven percent of the total Arab vote. In small villages there was an increase of 5.6 percent to 18.7 percent of the vote, while there was a decrease to 16.9 percent in the hamlets. The increases in Raqaḥ votes over the whole country and in small villages is in sharp contrast to the decrease in the hamlets. These figures indicate that the increase in Communist Party votes in the hamlets in 1969 was completely disproportionate. This requires an explanation, especially as the vote decreased in the following 1973 elections.

It seems that Fauzīyya's devotion to her son's medical education should be considered the decisive factor in the increase of votes for Raqaḥ in the hamlets. Her work concentrated on a "two-step flow" communication system. She explained her need to her close female relatives who in turn persuaded their sisters, daughters, mothers and other women. Thus, one woman actually had a decisive influence on the results of the Knesset elections—for definitely non-ideological and non-political reasons. Fauzīyya, having strong motivation as well as strong character was able to develop and use channels of influence within the village to accomplish her objective.

WOMAN'S DEFINITION OF HER ROLE AND STATUS

Woman's *own* view of her role, status and tasks is set out in Table 41. The answers given for woman's preferred or ideal occupation clearly illustrate the different attitudes of women in different age categories. Clearly, changes in society have left their mark on the role of woman, giving her new behavioral norms. Of the female newlyweds, sixty-five percent thought that woman should work outside her home (housewife also employed indicates working on the family farm): An additional fifteen percent believed that a woman should be full-time employed or undergoing higher education. It is interesting to note that almost all women, of whatever age group they belonged, emphasized educational work (teaching) as the most desirable outside occupation for a married woman.

Table 41

Preferred or Ideal Occupation for Women: The Woman's View

		Ideal Occupations/Activities (in percentages)			
Woman's Age	*No. of Women*	*Housewife only*	*Housewife also employed*	*Employed only*	*Higher Education*
to 30	121	19	65	6	9
31-50	124	34	56	3	7
51 and over	66	54	35	5	6
ALL AGES	311	33	55	5	7

While the male aspires to status, the female regards influence as her prime objective. In those cases when a woman decisively influences her husband, she does not usually display her power openly. By giving up the show of power, she receives a fair measure of influence. How much of woman's influence is due to her changing role is difficult to assess. It would seem that, *de facto*, women in Arab rural society has never been so low in the pecking order as the ideological view might indicate. It may be assumed with certainty, that women do have a considerable impact on decision making. The more opportunity that arises for woman to enhance her status may induce her to make her influence more openly felt, but it remains to be seen whether this development will take place and the consequent changes in Arab social activity that such a development would bring.

The power of the ideology of woman's inferiority and low status has not been borne out by my observations in the hamlets. The role of women in the village social structure is an aspect of Arab culture as yet inadequately comprehended, but toward an understanding of which the present work has hopefully made some contribution.

NOTES

1. See Victor W. Turner, *The Ritual Process* (Chicago, I11.: Aldine, 1969).

2. Peter Gubser, *Politics And Change In Al-Karak Jordan: A Study of a Small Arab Town and its District* (London: Oxford University Press, 1973), p. 70.

3. Aharon Layish, *Women and Islamic Law in a Non-Muslim State: A Study Based on Decisions of the Shari'a Courts in Israel* (New York and Tel Aviv: John Wiley and Israel Universities Press, 1975), p. 98.

4. Ibid., p. 98.

5. Ibid.

6. Hajji Shaykh Yusuf, "In Defence of the Veil," in *The Contemporary Middle East*, ed. Benjamin Rivlin and Joseph S. Szyliowicz (New York: Random House, 1965), p. 375.

7. Richard T. Antoun, "On the Modesty of Women in Arab Muslim Village: A Study in Accommodation of Traditions," *American Anthropologist* 70 (1968): 671.

8. Ibid., p. 678.

9. Hilma Granqvist, *Marriage Conditions in a Palestinian Village*. Vol. 2. Commentationes Humanarum Litterarum, Vol. 6, no. 8. (Helsingfors, Finland: Societas Scintiarum Fennica, 1935), p. 137; Taufik Canaan, "Unwritten Laws affecting the Arab Women of Palestine," *Journal of the Palestine Oriental Society* 11 (1931): 172-203.

10. Canaan, p. 174.

11. Henry Rosenfeld, "On Determinants of the States of Arab Village Women," *Man* 40 (May 1960): 66-70; Rosenfeld, "Change, Barriers to Change and Contradiction in the Arab Village Family," *American Anthropologist* 70 (December 1968): 732-52.

12. Questionnaire items are open-ended. The figures in the table are compiled from the contents of answers received.

13. A man or woman is addressed as the eldest son's father or mother, rather than by his/her Christian name. Accordingly, Jamīl addressed his neighbor as Umm Jalāl, meaning "the mother of her eldest son Jalāl." The father would be addressed as Abū Jalāl (abū meaning literally, "father of").

14. Antoun, p. 671.

15. Yolanda and Robert F. Murphy, *Women of the Forest* (New York: Columbia University Press, 1974), p. XI.

16. Laurel Bossen, "Women in Modernizing Societies," *American Ethnologist* 2 (1975): 599.

17. John P. Mason, "Sex and Symbol in the treatment of women: the wedding night in a Libyan oasis Community", *American Ethnolgoist* 2 (1975): 659.

18. Safia K. Mohsen, "Aspects of the Legal Status of Women among Awlan 'Ali," in *Peoples and Cultures of the Middle East, Vol. 1: Depth and Diversity*, ed. Louise E. Sweet (Garden City, N.Y.: The Natural History Press, 1970), pp. 220-33.

19. Susan Carol Rogers, "Female forms of power, and the myth of male dominance: a model of female/male interaction in peasant society," *American Ethnologist* 2 (1975): 729.

20. Ibid.

21. Aḥmad's half-brother (the son of $C_1 1$ and $C_1 2$, not shown on the chart) and his sons had cut off relations with Aḥmad.

22. Abner Cohen, *Arab Border Villages in Israel: A Study of Community and Change in a Social Organization* (Manchester, England: Manchester University Press, 1965), p. 122.

23. Emrys L. Peters, "The Status of Women in Four Middle East Communities," p. 28. I wish to thank Professor Peters for a copy of his Paper which will be published in *Beyond the Veil*, edited by N. Keddie and Lois Beck. (Cambridge, Mass.: Harvard University Press).

24. Rosenfeld, *Arab Village Women*, p. 69.

25. Canaan, Arab Women, p. 193. See also Laila Shukry Hamamsi, "The Changing Role of the Egyptian Woman," in *Readings In Arab Middle Eastern Societries and Cultures*, ed. Abdulla M. Lutfiyya and Charles W. Churchill (The Hague, Netherlands: Mouton, 1970), p. 593.

26. Peters, *Status of Women*, p. 29.

27. The term *za'alana* used by the Bedouin, has the same meaning as *ḥardane*. See Alios Musil, *The Manners and Customs of the Rwala Bedouins* (American Geographic Society, Oriental Explorations and Studies, No. 6, 1928), p. 235. The term is also used in the hamlet region. For a discussion of the usage of *za'alana* among peasant communities, see Rosenfeld, *Change*, p. 67.

28. When a bride is led out of her father's house, her father's brother (*'amm*) holds her by one arm and her mother's brother (*khal*) by the other. This indicates the strong influence the *khal* can have on marriage arrangements. See Granqvist, p. 76.

29. In the village of Ṭaybe there are several cases (six to the author's knowledge) in which the bride's family demanded that the land or the house should be registered in both names of the couple. In two out of the six cases there was a further precondition that the property be registered under the bride's name only. In one case the bride's family insisted that the couple should set up home some distance away from the groom's parents. This involved the groom's family in much additional expense, for although the family owned land near their home they did not own land in the area stipulated by the bride's parents in the marriage contract. It was possible to ask for such conditions because the girl's families were of a higher status than the families of their prospective husband. The men were accepted by these families because of their achieved status resulting from higher education. Ṭaybe has a tradition of emphasizing the importance of education. Such conditions are a very new attitude, as yet unknown in the surrounding villages, the first case occuring only in 1977.

30. Granqvist, *Marriage Conditions, Vol. II*, p. 257.

31. Aharon Layish, "The Social Status of the Muslim Woman in

Israel as Reflected in the Proceedings and Decisions of the Shari'a Courts." Ph.D. dissertation (Hebrew University; Jerusalem, 1972), p. 152.

32. Ibid.; p. 146. See also Granqvist, *Marriage Conditions, Vol. II*, p. 257.

33. For details on the different possibilities of woman to initiate divorce proceedings, see Layish, *Social Status of Muslim Women*, p. 182-224.

34. Granqvist, *Marriage Conditions, Vol. II*, p. 244, reports the case of a woman who chose to be *ḥardane* three times within the course of one year.

35. Raphael Patai, *Sex and Family in the Bible and in the Middle East* (New York: Doubleday, 1959), p. 117.

36. Patai, p. 117.

37. Granqvist, *Marriage Conditions, Vol. II*, p. 254.

38. Ibid., p. 255.

39. Ahmed Abou Zeid, "Honour and Shame among the Bedouin of Egypt," in *Honour and Shame*, ed. J.G. Peristiany (London England: Weidenfeld and Nicolson, 1965), p. 256.

40. Mason, pp. 649-50.

41. See Antoun, pp. 678-79.

42. Mason, p. 658.

43. Cohen, p. 126.

44. Antoun, p. 684.

45. Ibid.

46. This is another aspect of woman's status—her influence on her husband. In this case the influence led to a split between brothers, climaxed by a murder attempt with a nephew as the intended victim.

47. The murder took place on August 1, 1973. In court, Ḥusnī and his younger son Sa'id (E6), Lea's brother, were sentenced to life imprisonment. Sa'id claimed to have been in a cafe at the time of the murder and to have rushed home on hearing his mother's screams. At first he told the police that it was he and not his father who killed Lea. He made an official confession to this effect, evidently wishing to spare his father the imprisonment. The villagers, however, were convinced that Lea's father killed her without an accomplice.

48. Peter C. Dodd, "Family Honor and the Forces of Change in Arab Society," *International Journal of Middle East Studies* (January 1973): 40-54.

49. Bronislaw Malinowski, *Crime and Custom in Savage Society* (Paterson, N.J.: Littlefield and Adams, 1959), p. 78.

50. Howard S. Becker, *Outsiders: Studies in the Sociology of Deviance* (Glencoe, Ill; The Free Press, 1963), p. 15.

51. Malinowski, p. 80.

52. See Granqvist, *Marriage Conditions, Vol. II*; Hamed M. Ammar, *Growing Up in an Egyptian Village: Silwa, Province of Aswan* (London: Routledge and Kegan Paul, 1954); Peters, *Aspects of Family*; Rosenfeld,

Change; Fredrik Barth, "Role Dilemmas and Father-Son Dominance in Middle Eastern Kinship Systems," in *Kinship and Culture*, ed. Francis L.K. Hsu (Chicago, Ill: Aldine, 1973).

53. Granqvist, ibid; Antoun, *Modesty of Women*; Rosenfeld, *Arab Village Women*; Barbara C. Aswad, "Property Control and Social Strategies: Settlers on a Middle Eastern Plain," *Anthropological Papers*, No. 44 (Ann Arbor, Michigan: University of Michigan, 1971).

54. Granqvist, ibid; Rosenfeld, *Change*; Aswad, *Property Control*.

55. Peters, *Aspects of Family*.

56. Aswad, *Property Control*.

57. Rosenfeld, *Change*, p. 741.

58. Abdulla Luṭfīyya, *Baytin, A Jordanian Village* (The Hague, Netherlands: Mouton, 1966), p. 129.

59. Ibid.

60. See Peters, *Aspects of Family*, p. 134.

61. Emrys L. Peters, "Some Structural Aspects of the Feud among the Camel Herding Bedouin of Cyrenaica", *Africa* 37 (1967): 272.

62. Ibid., pp. 272-73.

63. Yolanda and Robert F. Murphy, pp. 138-39.

64. Faṭma was much younger than her husband and his second wife. At his first wife's funeral her uncle told 'Abd al-Latīf that after the forty days of mourning, he would let him marry his daughter. A wife promised under such circumstances is called *'aṭiyet el qaber* (literally, a gift from the grave). Faṭma was the only one in the hamlets married in this manner. Granqvist reported that only two men had *'atiyet el qaber* wives in Artas. Granqvist, *Marriage Conditions, Vol. I*, p. 110. See also Ibid., p. 108; and Granqvist, *Marriage Conditions, Vol. II*, p. 294.

65. According to Ammar, the patrilineal relations are the *'aṣaba* ("backbone") of the family and the matrilineal *laḥma* ("flesh"). See Ammar, p. 56. Though *'aṣaba* is perhaps best translated as "sinews."

66. Peters, *Aspects of Family*, p. 123, describes customs following a Bedouin wedding and refers to a father-son relationship: "Each morning, soon after daybreak and before camp is astir, the groom must leave his bride and repair to his father's tent to lie at his father's side as he always had done in the past, as if he had not left him."

67. Emrys L. Peters, "The Proliferation of Segments in the Lineage of the Bedouins of Cyrenaica [Libya]," in *Peoples and Cultures of the Middle East, Vol. I, Depth and Diversity*, ed. Louise E. Sweet (Garden City, N.Y.: The Natural History Press, 1970), p. 364.

68. Gideon M. Kressel, *Individuality against Tribality: The Dyanmics of a Bedouin Community in a Process of Urbanization* (Tel Aviv, Israel: Hakibbutz Hameuchad, 1976), p. 74 (Hebrew).

69. Emanuel Marx, "The Tribe as a Unit of Subsistence: Nomadic Pastoralism in the Middle East," *American Anthropologist* 79 (1977): 253. See also Marx, "The Ecology and Politics of Nomadic Pastoralists in the Middle East." In *The Nomadic Alternative*, ed. W. Weiss Leder (The Hague: Mouton, 1978).

70. For another example regarding relationships between full and half-siblings, see Antoun, pp. 65-66.

71. Emanuel Marx, "The Organization of Nomadic Groups in the Middle East," in *Society and Political Structure in the Arab World*, ed. Menahem Milson (New York, Humanities Press, 1973), pp. 306-36. See also Marx, *The Tribe*, p. 26.

72. Antoun, p. 692.

73. Ann H. Fuller, "The World of kin in Lebanon," in *Readings on the Family and Society*, ed. William Josiah Goode (Englewood Cliffs, N.J.; Prestice-Hall, 1964).

74. Fuad I. Khuri, "Parallel Cousin Marriage Reconsidered: A Middle Eastern Practice that Nullifies the Effect of Marriage on the Intensity of Family Relationships," *Man* (December, 1970): 609.

75. Granqvist, *Marriage Conditions, Vol. II*, p. 146.

76. Residence in the hamlets, as in most Arab rural communities, is patrilocal. Ammar says, that after the wedding ceremony, the couple temporarily lived at the bride's parental home, until the birth of the first child: ". . . [the man's] ultimate home will be his patrilineal house to which he eventually takes his wife." Ammar, p. 198.

77. Ian G. Cunnison, *Baggara Arabs; Power and the Lineage in a Sudanese Nomad Tribe* (Oxford Clarendon Press, 1966), p. 116. See also Cyntia Nelson, "Public and private politics: Women in the Middle Eastern World", *American Ethnologist* 1 (1974): 551-63.

78. In 1968 the bride of a resident of the Ibn Sina descent group (of another village) had to return to her father's home when she was found not to be a virgin. Her father repaid the bride price, but in the winter of 1969 the husband was persuaded to take her back receiving compensation equivalent to half of the original bride price. Although this was known to the whole hamlet, no one harmed the girl.

79. A *qaṭi'a* (a "cut-off woman"—whose male relatives are all dead) is to be pitied. See Granqvist, *Marriage Conditions, Vol. II*, p. 144.

80. See Robert Paine, "What is Gossip About?: An Alternative Hypothesis," *Man* 2 (1967): 280.

81. Max Gluckman, "Psychological, Sociological and Anthropological Explanations of Witchcraft and Gossip; a Clarification", *Man* 3 (1968): 29.

82. Paine, p. 287.

83. Bruce A. Cox, "What is Hopi Gossip About? Information Management and Hopi Factions," *Man* 5 (1970): 89.

84. Don Handelman, "Gossip In Encounters: The Transmission of Information In A Bounded Social Setting," *Man* 8 (1973).

85. See Gluckman, *Witchcraft and Gossip*, p. 33.

86. Max Gluckman, "Gossip and Scandal", *Current Anthropology* 4 (1963): 308.

87. Roger D. Abrahams, "A performance-centered Approach to Gossip," *Man* (1970): 290.

88. Elaine Baldwin, *Differentiation and co-operation in an Israel*

veteran moshav (Manchester: Manchester University Press, 1972), p. 184.

89. In rural societies young single men sometimes consort with animals, due to lack of opportunities for premarital sex, see Luṭfiyya, p. 151. According to Patai, such relations are only tolerated with single males. See Patai, *Sex and Family*, p. 176. Ammar mentions that bestiality is frequently the subject of jokes among male adolescents and unmarried young men. See Ammar, p. 192.

90. Gluckman explains this inclination of directing gossip at deceased persons by saying that "to be able to gossip properly, a member has to know . . . also about . . . forbears." See Gluckman, *Gossip and Scandal*, p. 309. Gluckman also claims that "one can 'hit one another' through their ancestors, and if you cannot use this attack . . . then you are in a weak position." Ibid.

91. Baldwin, p. 184.

92. These figures are confirmed by Hilma Granqvist, *Birth and Childhood Among the Arabs: Studies in a Muhammadan Village in Palestine* (Helsingfors, Finland: Söderstrom, 1947), p. 184. Granqvist mentions several circumcisions at the age of nineteen. In one case two adult brothers were circumcised secretly. Furthermore, one resident of the same village ". . . went to Jerusalem and had himself circumcised and this was after his marriage. And the father of Salem Othman was circumcised as he lay on the death board. When there was a quarrel in the village this fact was thrown in the face of his family". Ibid., pp. 206-207. It is very rare that a man is circumcised after his marriage, for without circumcision he is considered unclean. For example, he is not allowed to slaughter an animal served as food. Ammar, p. 116, states that circumcision in Egyptian villages takes place between the ages of three to six. Kennedy gives similar figures of between three to five. See, John G. Kennedy, "Circumcision and Excision in Egyptian Nubia," *Man* 5 (1970): 176. Marx gives the ages between two and twelve. Emanuel Marx, "Circumcision Feasts Among the Negev Bedouin," International Journal of Middle East Studies 4 (October, 1973).

93. See Granqvist, *Birth and Childhood*, pp. 187-93. Among the Bedouin, on the other hand, there are feasts which last more than a week. Marx, ibid., p. 417, reports that the circumcision feast he attended ". . . lasted ten days to a fortnight and was designed to reach its final climax on the day of the operation."

94. Granqvist, Ibid., p. 207. See Taufik Canaan, *Mohammedan Saints and Sanctuaries in Palestine* (London, England: Luzac, 1927), p. 218; Gilsenan describes in his study of Sufism that it is "at the *mulid* (the celebration of the day of the birth or death of a saint) that a vast number of small boys are circumcised. . ." Michael Gilsenan, *Saint and Sufi in Modern Egypt: An Essay in the Sociology of Religion* (Oxford: Clarendon Press, 1973), p. 51.

95. "The *mōlad* is the legendary story of the Prophet's birth and is a poem which describes not only the birth of the Prophet, but names his

ancestors "all of the prophets, and his own acts". A great part of the *mōlad* is devoted to the praise of Muḥammad." Canaan, ibid., p. 179.

96. In Nubia, the boy's mother takes care that his face is averted so "that he would not look at his wound and thereby become sterile," John G. Kennedy, "Circumcision and Excision in Egyptian Nubia," *Man* 5 (June 1970): 187.

97. Regarding both the actual ceremony and the presenting of gifts my observations do not tally with those of other researchers. See Marx, *Circumcision Feasts*; Ammar, p. 118; and Granqvist, *Birth and Childhood*, p. 205.

98. Peters, *Bedouin of Cyrenaica*, p. 372.

99. The refrain is the same as the one sung by the Bedouin. See Marx, *Circumcision Feasts*, p. 424. *Muṭaher* refers to the performer of the circumcision; *ṭuhūr* (Literally, "cleaning") applies to the circumcision itself, though the term *shalabi* (Literally, "handsome") is also used in the hamlets. The circumciser's family name is Shalabi. He has inherited the profession from his father and grandfather.

100. Max Gluckman, *Custom and Conflict in Africa* (Oxford: Blackwell 1956. [Reprint]), pp. 110, 117.

101. Rogers, p. 747.

102. Ibid., p. 748.

103. See Marx, *Circumcision Feasts*; Ammar, pp. 75, 116-23.

104. Hilma Granqvist, *Child Problems among the Arabs: Studies in a Muhammadan Village in Palestine* (Helsingfors, Finland: Söderston, 1950), p. 76.

105. Granqvist, *Marriage Conditions, Vol. II*, p. 244. For additional information on the status of barren women see Granqvist, *Vol. I*, p. 117; *Vol. II*, pp. 116, 246, and *Child Problems*, pp. 73-74.

106. Usually it is the woman who is blamed for sterility. However, one West Bank witchdoctor claimed that he could detrmine which marriage partner was at fault, thus hinting that it might be the male who was sterile. He would examine the husband's sperm. If it sank to the bottom of a glass of water, the wife was barren, but if it floated on the surface, the husband required treatment.

107. Granqvist, *Child Problems*, p. 78.

108. All these women were married for more than five years, and eight of them for more than ten years. Gossip claimed the husband was responsible in seven cases. Six instances were of three pairs of brothers, and residents attributed their sterility to inbreeding. The seventh husband divorced his wife and married a West Bank woman but had no children with her either. (His second wife was not included above, since the couple were married less than five years.)

109. Granqvist, *Birth and Childhood*, p. 196.

110. Ammar, p. 123.

111. Moshe Shokeid (Minkovitz), "Immigration and Factionalism; An Analysis of Factions in Rural Israeli Communities of Immigrants," *British Journal of Sociology* 19 (1968): 385.

112. Ibid.

113. Firth says that factionalism "tends to become activated on specific occasions, not as a regularly recurring feature." Raymond Firth, "Factions in India and Overseas Indian Society," *British Journal of Sociology* 8 (1957): 292. This view is supported by Pocock. See, David Francis Pocock, "The Basis of Factions in Girjerat," *British Journal of Sociology* 8 (1957): 296. Bailey, too, insists that a faction has no ideology and is usually recruited by a leader with whom the members have what he calls a "transactional relationship." See Fredrik George Bailey, *Strategems and Spoils: A Social Anthropology of Politics* (New York: Schocken Books, 1969), p. 53. The relationships between leader and led is analyzed by Nicholas who maintains that the leader "must have greater control over resources . . . than any of his supporters," and that he distributes them "in return for political support." Ralph W. Nicholas, "Factions: A Comparative Analysis," in *Political Systems and the Distribution of Power*, ed. Michael Banton. Association of Social Anthropologists of the Commonwealth Monographs, no. 2. (London: Tavistock, 1965), p. 56. Abu Gosh who studied a village in the same region (located south of the hamlets), distinguishes two types of factions, neither of which aims at accumulating political power only. Instead they concentrate on organizing the younger generation, better educated than their fathers and grandfathers, to rebel against traditionalism. See Subhi Abu Gosh, "The Politics of an Arab Village in Israel." Ph.D. dissertation (Princeton University, 1969), p. 165. Rosenfeld, on the other hand thinks that the *ḥamūlas* formed factions struggling for local influence. See Henry Rosenfeld, *They were Peasants: Social Anthropological Studies on the Arab Village in Israel* (Tel Aviv, Israel: Hakibbutz Hameuchad, 1964), p. 164 (Hebrew). To Barth, the term faction means "alignments of the younger men of small lineage segments around an older leader," Frederik Barth, "Father's Brother's Daughter Marriage in Kurdistan," *Southwestern Journal of Anthropology* 10 (Spring 1954): 168.

114. Khalil A. Nakhleh, "Shifting Patterns of Conflict in Selected Arab Villages in Israel." Ph.D. dissertation. Indiana University, 1973, p. 254.

115. The elections took place in November 1969. Data was collected for the preliminary study at the end of 1969 and the beginning of 1970.

116. In August 1965 there was a split in the communist party, one group assuming the name Raqaḥ, the other retaining the original name Maqi. Raqaḥ identified with the Arab minority in Israel and appeared as its champion." Jacob M. Landau, *The Arabs in Israel: A Political Study* (London, England: Oxford University Press, 1969), p. 254. For further information on the split see Ibid., pp. 81-92.

117. In the election year of 1961, Ahdut Havodah and Mapam were still independent parties. In 1965 Ahdut Havodah and Mapai formed an alignment with Mapam remaining independent. In 1969, Mapai and the Rafi party (that had earlier seceded from Mapai) merged into one party

with Ahdut Havodah, called the Labor Party. Mapam formed an alignment with the Labour Party and this alignment presented itself to the voters as one ballot.

In Table 40, the votes of the parties still not merged or aligned, are added up with the votes given to the two allied Arab lists of Mapai (later to become part of the Labor Party). In 1961 Maqi was still the name of the then united Communist Party. One of the two splinter groups adopted it as its name, while the other became known as Raqah. (In 1965 and 1973 Maqi did not receive even a single vote; in 1969 it obtained only one vote in all four hamlets). The Labour Party and its allied Arab lists, Mapam and Raqah, were the only permanent parties in the hamlets. All the others were "election-eve parties," see Landau, p. 153. The votes of all other parties have been totaled in the table.

In both 1965 and 1973 there was a marked increase in the votes given to the remaining parties. In 1965 Rafi set up an allied Arab list which appeared as an independent party and received eighty-six votes (18.9 percent of the 24.4 percent given to the "rest of the parties." Rafi obtained only three votes. In 1973 one of the two allied Arab lists appeared as an independent party and received 104 votes (19.7 percent) which were included in the 26.1 percent of the votes given to the "rest of the parties."

118. Yehiel Harari, *The Elections for the Seventh Knesset in the Arab Sector-1969* (Givat Haviva: Center for Arab and Afro-Asian Studies, 1971), pp. 31-4 (Hebrew).

119. Jacob M. Landau, *The Arabs in Israel*: A Political Study (Tel Aviv(Ministry of Defence, 1971), pp. 245-262 (Hebrew). See also Harari.

Epilogue

Adaptation to a technological economy has led to changes in the social, political and economic structures of Arab society in general, and Arab society within Israel in particular. Although there is limited contact between Arab farming communities and the farming settlements of their Jewish neighbors, the high standard of living and modern agricultural techniques have impressed the Arab peasants and have influenced them. For the hamlets, representation in the Regional Council has brought an even closer contact with Jewish farmers whose pattern of life is very different from their own.

Wherever unusually swift changes occur, the gap between ideology and actual fact tends to increase. This is particularly important in relation to the obtaining of information. While the ideals of the past have often ceased to be ideals, lip service continues to be paid to them. In this way, informants may give misleading information. They do not so much deceive the researcher, but themselves. They say what they wish to believe is still true even though their conduct may no longer be guided by the norms they proclaim. Participant observation is a *sine qua non* in this type of research. Participation by the researcher reveals not only what people aspire to, their ideologies, norms and beliefs, but also how they behave in various situations.

Even when changes occur that require modifications of basic values, the effects are often slow to come. To deny long established norms and ideals cannot be easy. Belief in them is part of the sense of identity of members of any society. Ideology prescribes conduct and often relieves from the necessity of decision. When man finds that he can no longer blindly obey norms or even strive to live up to them, this creates a sense of insecurity, the feeling that the world is no longer familiar. Such infamiliarity harbors dangers and challenges for which one is not prepared. This in turn makes declarations of loyalty to the ideology of male superiority, for instance, more emphatic than before, sometimes creating the impression that the informant who stresses it wishes to convince himself or herself above all. Peasants whose life used to be confined to their villages and their closest environment, must feel puzzled and upset by this unfamiliarity. It is as if they were facing a completely unchartered, new reality and being forced to live in terra incognita.

The hamlets possess special characteristics resulting from the separation from the parent village and their consequent functioning within a larger society. They had to learn how to negotiate with a bureaucracy of different character and to adjust to other norms and mores in their wider environment. The laws too, except those of personal status based on religion, were motivated by a different sociolegal conception. In sum, the residents came into contact with a heterogeneous and different society.

Taking into consideration the unique situation of the hamlets, it is not surprising that Fakhouri, who investigated a four-cluster rural community near Cairo at about the same time I did fieldwork, obtained different results, in spite of several extraneous similarities. His description stresses "patrilineal descent, patrilocal residence, patriarchical authority and preferred kingroup endogamy."[1] In the hamlets, the cohesion of the lineage and the descent group is decreasing, or, at least, there is a shift of allegiances which seems not to have occurred in the past. Loyalties are no longer entirely focussed on one group. Membership in many organizations and groups is now common. As long as each nuclear family occupied one room in the multi-generation household and the courtyard was the focus of common activities such as cooking and exchange of gossip, this extended family monopolized loyalty. But the multi-generation household of the extended family is no longer the order. Individual residential units have brought exposure to different influences and attachment to different individuals and groups, which has greatly reduced descent group allegiance.

School has introduced a new element into the lives of the younger generation. The peer group rather than the *ḥamūla* has become the dominant focus and children spend much of their time within its framework. The young child and teenager learns to function within a multiplicity of groups and is no longer entirely dependent on any one of them. New social and emotional links develop, coexisting with family loyalty. School, with its competitive value system, introduces achieved status as an important factor in their lives.

Achieved status, especially if combined with an independent income through wages or salaried employment, reduces paternal dominance and power. This new development often expresses itself in independent selection of marriage partners. The criteria which determine choice often include formal education and sociability, with personal preference coming to the fore. With growing individualism, patrilocal residence is inevitably on the wane. In the hamlets, it is almost normative that a son should receive a house of his own where he and his new wife will reside. This means, *inter alia*, that the male becomes a pater familias after his wedding. While patrilocal residence has almost disappeared in the hamlets (and in most of the Arab rural communities in Israel), it is still the rule for a son to live in close proximity with his parents. This may partly be ascribed to the fact that the site on which he builds is usually part of his father's property. Also, a man who has not yet received his heritage perhaps prefers to remain close to his father's residence. Thus, patrilocal residence in the strict sense of the term is no longer the norm but neither is it correct to speak of neo-local residence. In some villages where this pattern is not followed, the reason is lack of land. There, young couples move into housing projects, not for ideological reasons or due to the desire to live a more individualist existence but for purely practical considerations.

The new housing arrangement also greatly increases the power of the young bride. If she chooses to be a *ḥardane* in a household where she is the only adult female, such an action is more keenly felt than if there are elders to look after the children in a multi-generation household. This is a powerful sanction to be brought into play against a husband. This further reduces the power of influence of the elders, as does the fact that every nuclear family has its own *diwān*, unlike in the past when it was accommodated in the house of the head of the lineage.

As to preferred kingroup endogamy, unmistakable predilection for in-group marriage has been found in the hamlets, including patrilateral parallel first cousins' marriage. In-group marriage is a tendency strengthened by what Khuri calls the "myth of origin." That is, the creation of a shared family history that "may be entirely unfounded, historically, sociologically, however, they provide the idiom by which individuals and groups create relationships and form alliances."[2] Khuri explains preference for endogamy by "family structure and organization, legal rights and relationships."[3] Above all, he emphasizes the key role of the sister in her brother's marriage, an observation not confirmed in the hamlet study. There was only one case — where a sister provided her brother with background data about a young school teacher he met in a taxi.

Fakhouri describes the type of villager he studied as "an urbanite by day and ruralite during the evening hours."[4] Hamlet residents can be defined as farmers even when they are gainfully employed outside their villages and temporarily live in urban centers. Fakhouri uses the term "urbanite" as a synonym for "industrial worker," and assumes that anyone working in a factory is best defined as "urbanite." He classifies his subjects of study in a suburb of Beirut as suburbians but stresses their rural ancestry and roots, which the title of his investigation brings out: "From Village to Suburb." The young hamlet males consider their work outside the rural community as a temporary occupation. While gaining their independence in this way they are also waiting to receive their inheritance in the form of property and land they can cultivate. Their work outside the village does not qualify them as "urbanites," rather they remain villagers who wait for their time to come to own the fields which they will cultivate to earn their living.

Much of the data collected refers to both men and women. Since men are less restricted in their movements they absorb new ideas more easily and adopt new customs more quickly than women. Nevertheless, the role of woman has changed considerably. In cases where the husband takes on employment outside the village, his wife may become the manager of the family property. This role of accepting responsibility for the cultivation of fields and the organization of the farm is in addition to shouldering the task of raising children and running the house. Such extra activity considerably helps women acquire status within their families, their economic contribution being recognized and highly regarded. This new role does not clash with accepted norms. Their increased self-confidence sometimes results in their participation in public affairs, though they often prefer the "power of the weak," that is, they exercise their influence behind the scenes and are content with the results without parading their power. The men are fully aware of their wives' contribution and where so much is given, compensation in one form or another cannot be withheld.

However, much as the role and status of woman in Arab rural society has changed, ideology is slow to recognize the new reality and remains male-centered. Nor is it the men who insist most that the myth of male dominance be preserved. Evans-Pritchard rightly points out "that in some societies women crawl in the presence of their husbands or that people never eat in the presence of the other sex,"[5] but warns that this should not be taken at face value and interpreted as "abject subservience."[6] Rogers explains that "male dominance persists in peasant society as a 'myth' acting to maintain a non-hierarchical power balance between the categories, male and female. . ."[7] In other words, women, as one of the case histories demonstrates, know when to speak out and when to keep their own counsel in order to obtain what they desire. They are prepared to leave their husbands with the feeling of their undisputed dominance as long as the males submit to their wives' suggestions. The myth is partly based on Islamic tradition that proclaims women's inferiority and in addition labels them as tempters of male virtue. Labeling woman as a potential sinner who endangers man's virtue need not clash with respect for her if she conforms at least externally to the myth.

In Arab rural society, woman's conduct is a criterion of her agnate's honor. Her sexuality, so says the Quran, renders her dangerous. She must be both protected and watched. The result in everyday life is that she has to disappear when visitors enter the house and generally be kept at a safe distance from the male world. Prior to marriage, a woman's chastity is her male relatives' honor. A breach of modest conduct violates the norm and stains her agnates' honor the moment her deviant behavior becomes public knowledge. If man wishes to preserve his status in his community, some form of action is required. The weaker his position in the social hierarchy, the more quickly will he take recourse to punitive measures. Once a woman is married, modesty is her finest quality. Both her agnates and her family of reproduction ascribe great value to her reputation. Thus woman, even in an ideology that describes her as weak and dependant, greatly influences her family's social standing by her conduct.

It is almost self-evident that Arabic should have two words for honor. One refers to actions committed by a man himself — *sharaf*. For instance, a man can increase or decrease his *sharaf* according to his behavior as a host and in his general attitude towards helping others. The second word for honor refers to an action committed by a female relative — *'irḍ*. While women can neither augment nor diminish a man's *sharaf*, a woman cannot by exemplary conduct add to her agnates *'irḍ*, though by misbehaving, she can detract from it. It may be stained and reduced through the immodest conduct of any one of a man's close female relatives, once her actions become known in the community. Illicit sexual relations before marriage as well as adultery or indecorous behavior of the females of his family, all taint a man's *'irḍ*. He loses status in the eyes of others and can often only repair the damage by killing the woman responsible. One of the case histories emphasizes how much the conduct of a daughter reflects on her father's social position. He felt compelled to kill her because, being a relative newcomer in the hamlet, he could not afford to defy the accepted norms.

Woman's status used to be entirely dependent on that of her natal family. Even her husband's status was determined by that of her father since negotiations would usually not be opened unless there was some affinity of social position and economic power between the two families. Exceptions occurred, of course, but those were usually explained by physical or mental defects of one of the partners, or by some event that lowered the prestige of a family. Through school and university, women now acquire achieved status which is especially important to those males who have themselves received high school or higher education and want wives who match it. Men who have university degrees or diplomas, look for wives with at least a high school education. They pick their own partner and do not accept paternal orders. In one of the case histories, the young man pointed out that a younger brother, who possessed minimum formal education could enter into *badal* while he himself, because of his superior academic qualifications, had the right to make his own selection.

Status may perhaps best be measured through comparison. But with whom? The male of her own society. Very often, woman does not apply the same status symbols and criteria. Her pride derives from achievements other than those of the male. Is her status to be measured by that of women in the neighboring Jewish agricultural settlements? We possess a thorough description of life in a moshav by Baldwin who made a social anthropological study of a veteran settlement in the region of the hamlets. But these women are motivated by a very different ideology. Perhaps they do not *de facto* live up to it any more than the Arab peasant woman lives up to hers, but neither can its influence be entirely disregarded. Also, in a moshav there are elected offices and a kind of village hierarchy which cannot be found in the Arab village. The author has applied the yardstick of woman's participation in terms of decision making and her influence on the family, the *ḥamūla*, village affairs and on politics. However, it should be remembered that some of the women who are most emphatic in their acknowledgement of their inferior status due to their sex, are those who most often skilfully manipulate their males. They do this by not insisting on outward recognition of their power. A woman who may persuade her husband with a few words during an informal chat in their bedroom may outwardly demonstrate subservience that can mislead the casual observer. Not even a researcher who enjoys the confidence and to a degree, the friendship of his informants, will be aware of what happens between husband and wife. He may perhaps watch the husband do his wife's bidding, but may never know what brought about the change in his conduct. It is not easy, even for the fieldworker who has established a relationship of trust, to penetrate into the depth of personal relationships and to distinguish between make belief and actual happenings.

Some scholars claim that the general trend towards female equality may be more apparent than real. Confinement to the home may be a function of technical conditions and need not be synonymous with low status within the family. Evans-Pritchard has given this explanation by saying that "running the home is a whole-time occupation for primitive woman."[8] He finds that the adult primitive woman is above all "a wife whose life is centered in her home and family,"[9] since otherwise there would be no home and no family. Bossen doubts modern woman's status by claiming that "to the extent to which women are integrated into the modern, capitalist economy, this tends to occur in the low-paid sector."[10] In other words, the fact that woman is employed outside her home, need not mean that she has achieved equality and high status. Not always are the apparently objective criteria of woman's status really to be deemed as such. Evans-Pritchard says that one may measure it by "whether in homicide a woman's life is indemnified by as large a compensation as a man's, or whether both sexes have equal facilities for divorce."[11] Equal pay for equal work might be added to this.

Yolanda and Robert Murphy state that ". . . we must go back to certain sociological premises. First, people are more than just people; they are social personages, acting in certain ways that can be anticipated by others who must live with them and cooperate with them."[12] The Murphy's pinpoint precisely how the role and status of women should be considered. The male-female relationship cannot be just viewed through an ideological perspective. Women have always had the "power of the weak," which cannot be underestimated; and more recently, power resulting from making a significant contribution to family income. In both cases cooperation between husband and wife is an important factor. This cooperation is not achieved through prevailing ideological norms but is the result of the interaction of two different personalities. That women are aware of the ideology and of its importance to their males, is clearly illustrated in the following case history which occured in Spring 1979.

A teacher, in reprimanding a pupil, accidentally broke the boy's hand. Apart from the resulting enquiries made by the education authorities, this event created tension between the families of the boy and the teacher. The father of the teacher, as would be expected, sent an emissary to the boy's father in order to make amends. The father rejected this and similar requests to bring about a reconciliation. A *ṣulḥa* (peace agreement) was achieved only when the father of the teacher turned to an influential woman in the village, who spoke to the injured boy's mother. What several men could not arrange in weeks of negotiations, the women achieved by quickly arranging a meeting between males and females of both concerned families. The *ṣulḥa* took place in the evening. As the teacher's father pointed out to the author it was the women themselves who decided to have the ceremony in the evening so as not to demonstrate, in the words of the teacher's father, "what man with big moustache could not achieve." This unfortunate circumstance was not settled through set ideological ways of going about effecting a *ṣulḥa*, but by cooperation between women who recognized the importance of keeping their active role in as low a profile as possible.

To bring this study right up-to-date, one final item. At the beginning of 1979 the hamlets were connected to the national electricity grid. There was one exception however. In the northern section of Yamma, a resident objected to the wooden electricity poles being cited on his property. This caused a serious series of quarrels between the man and his neighbor brother. As a result this section of the hamlet is not yet connected to the electricity supply.

NOTES

1. Hani Fakhouri, *Kafr el-Elow, An Egyptian Village in Transition* (New York: Holt Rinehart and Winston, 1972), p. 55.

2. Fuad I. Khuri, *From Village to Suburb: Order and Change in Great Beirut* (Chicago, I11.: The University of Chicago press, 1975), p. 23.

3. Ibid., p. 125.

4. Fakhouri, p. 21.

5. Edward Evan, Evans-Pritchard, "The Position of Women in Primitive Societies and in our own," *The Position of Women in Primitive Societies and Other Essays in Social Anthropology*, ed. Edward Evans, Evans Pritchard (London: Faber and Faber, 1965), pp. 40-41.

6. Ibid., p. 41.

7. Susan Carol Rogers, "Female Form of Power and the Myth of Male Dominance: A Model of Female (Male Interaction in Peasant Society)." *American Ethnologist* 2 (November 1975): 747-8.

8. Evans-Pritchard, p. 45.

9. Ibid.

10. Laurel Bossen, "Women in modernizing Societies," *American Ethnologist* 2 (November 1975): 595.

11. Evans-Pritchard, p. 41.

12. Yolanda Murphy and Robert F. Murphy, *Women of the Forest* (New York: Columbia University Press, 1974), pp. 68-9.

Appendixes

Appendix A
Informant Questionnaires

The following are translations of the questionnaires used in the informant interviews. As noted, separate forms were designed for men and women. Questionnaires were completed by (or for) all male hamlet residents aged eighteen or over and all married women.

INFORMANT QUESTIONNAIRE: MEN (AGE EIGHTEEN AND OVER)

1. Full name. Full name of mother.
2. Name as it appears on official Identification Card.
3. Has name on Identification Card been changed since 1949? If so, why?
4. Exact birthplace. Mother's birthplace.
5. Current address. (If you have moved, indicate place names and dates). If married, place of residence immediately after your wedding.
6. In what kind of house were you born? TENT, SHACK, BRICK HOUSE, AQED, CINDER BLOCK HOUSE, POURED CONCRETE HOUSE, OTHER (specify).
   Have you moved from one type of house to another? If so, indicate house type(s) and date(s).
7. Age (as exact as possible).
8. Have you been divorced, widowed, remarried? If so, give dates. If widowed, give deceased wife's full name.
9. Are you related to your wife by birth? If so, give exact relationship.
10. Number and sexes of children. (If children from previous marriage, specify.)
11. Where did you attend school? How many grades did you complete?
12. What is your present occupation? Are you an independent farmer or employed?

13. Are you both a farmer and a wage earner? If so, indicate whether part-time wage earner. List all occupations in addition to farming.
14. How long have you been employed at your present occupation?
15. What was your previous employment?
16. Why did you change your place of work?
17. If your present work is seasonal, how many months are you employed per year?
18. Are you satisfied with your present work? If not, what kind of work would you rather have?
19. Monthly income as independent farmer? As employed farmer worker? (If income is seasonal, state monthly average for period of work).
20. Number of sons under age eighteen not working on your farm.
21. Nature of sons' employment and approximate income.
22. Amount of agricultural land owned and distribution as to crop types. (Give types of crops and number of *dūnams* allotted to each).
23. Number of leased *dūnams* being farmed.
24. From whom have you leased land? LANDS AUTHORITY, ARAB RESIDENT IN ONE OF THE FOUR HAMLETS, RESIDENT OF ANOTHER ISRAELI ARAB VILLAGE, ARAB RESIDENT OF WEST BANK, JEWISH FARMER.
25. Form of payment for leased land: CASH, SHARE OF PRODUCE, BOTH, OTHER SYSTEM OF PAYMENT. State amount and kind of payment per *dūnam*; indicate whether payment is for season or full year.
26. Number of *dūnams* with growth permits for vegetables (reference to permits required to raise tomatoes, cucumbers, etc.).
27. How many *dūnams* do you cultivate (give details for the last four years).
28. Were you ever fined? If so, give amount of fine and number of *dūnams* illegally worked (for the last four years).
29. Do you receive a water allocation (irrigation)? If so, how much (for the last four years).
30. Give details of crops raised prior to irrigation and crops raised in the past three years.
31. Give details as to any domestic stock you own: cows, sheep, calves for fattening, chickens, etc.
32. Did you have herds of any kind? If so, when did you liquidate them?
33. Are you a member of the Histadrut? If not, why?
34. Now, after several years' experience, are you pleased with the affiliation to the Regional Council?
35. Do you have any suggestions regarding specific issues to be handled by the Regional Council?

36. Would you prefer to have a local council serving all four hamlets, rather than being affiliated to the Regional Council?
37. Has any change occurred in the structure of the *ḥamūla* within the last twenty-five years? Have there been conspicuous changes in the last eight to ten years? suggesting that this period has seen more decisive changes than previous periods?
38. Are there any differences in the structure of the *ḥamūla* on the West Bank, as compared with those in Israel in general? In your village in particular?
39. Has any change occurred in the status of women in the past twenty-five years? Can you point out any marked changes in the last ten years? Has any change occurred in the status of women since contact with the West Bank was reestablished? If so, what kind(s) of change?
40. Is there any difference between the status of women in Israel and on the West Bank?
41. Have any negative changes taken place in Israel-Arab society? (Would you prefer previous conditions)?
42. What, in your opinion, are the factors that have brought about those changes?
43. Do you want additional changes? In all spheres of life? Or in some of them? If so, which ones?
44. Have you taken out life insurance? Is anyone else in your family insured?
45. Is your house or any other portion of your property insured?
46. How many rooms are there in your present house?
47. Do you have toilet facilities inside your house?
48. Does anyone besides your immediate family live in your house? If so, give details.
49. Do you have a car or other vehicle? If so, what kind? (State whether truck, pickup truck, private car, Jeep, or motor bike.)
50. What is the approximate monthly budget for your family (total, including clothing, and all current expenses for the house and its inhabitants)?

INFORMANT QUESTIONNAIRE: MARRIED WOMEN

1. Full maiden name.
2. Approximate age.
3. Husband's full name.
4. Approximate ages at time of marriage.
5. Name of birthplace.
6. Is the *ḥamūla* structure different than it was twenty-five years ago? If so, what is/are the difference(s)?
7. Has the status of woman changed as compared with that twenty-five years ago? If so, what is/are the difference(s)?
8. Which tasks do you think women should fulfill? What is your preferred/ideal occupation?
9. Number of sons.
10. Number of daughters.
11. Number of births. Age(s) of deceased child(ren) at time of death and place in birth order.
12. Number of miscarriages and place in birth order.
13. Full name of married daughters' husband and of son's wives (maiden name).
14. Address of son or daughter. (Indicate whether he or she lives with parents or others or has a separate house).
15. Are you related to your husband by birth? If so, give exact relationship.
16. Are your married son(s) or daughter(s) related to their husband(s) and wive(s) by birth? If so, give exact relationship.
17. How and by whom was the marriage of your son/daughter planned?
18. How was your own marriage planned? Who, in your opinion, decided? What was your attitude?
19. Have you bought any property with your money (with money you received on festivals or other events from members of your natal family)? Did you buy land? Domestic animals? Any other property?
20. Which members of your natal family visit you and how frequently? When did the last visit take place?
21. Do you visit your natal family? Which of its members? When did the last visit take place?
22. What was your share in decisions such as (a) New house for the nuclear family, (b) Additional rooms for the old family building, (c) New houses for sons being married, (d) Agricultural crops, (e) Acquisition of agricultural implements, (f) Various other purchases such as furniture? Were there any purchases you initiated? Initiated in consultation with you? After you had been asked to agree?

23. Have you friends who are not members of your natal family? Do mutual visits occur? How often? When was the last visit (yours with your friends or hers with you)? Are there meeting places other than in your or her home? How often do you meet? When did you meet last at this place?
24. Do you know how to read and write? If so, how many classes did you finish? Do you read the newspaper and how often?
25. Do you go to town? To which town(s)? How often? With whom do you go? For what purposes? Shopping, visits, medical or any other reasons? When did you go last?
26. What equipment do you have in your kitchen? Gas stove? Refrigerator? Other gadgets?
27. Have you a solar water heater?
28. To what extent does your husband help you with household chores?
29. To what extent do your sons help you with household chores?

Appendix B
Supplementary Agricultural Data

The income and expense data on the following pages demonstrates the differences in agricultural income (net profit) derived from various crops grown in the hamlets by using different agricultural techniques. The figures, provided by the hamlet farmers, are adjusted to indicate average costs per *dūnam* of land under cultivation. Both conventional, and intensive farming techniques are represented, as are a variety of crops for comparison. Dates are indicated for each listing and should be taken into account when costs and receipts are viewed in terms of progressing currency devaluation (figures cited are actual figures for the year in question, unadjusted to compensate for devaluation).

Tomatoes (Summer Planting, without plastic)—1972

Expense Item		*Amount*
Deep plowing		IL 11.00
Discing		5.00
Manure and application		60.00
Chemical fertilizer		33.00
Application (labor)		13.00
Ammonia		34.00
Cultivation (raking)		5.00
Tomato plants (1,500)		45.00
Planting (women @ IL 10/day, men @ IL 20/day)		90.00
Hoeing		40.00
Plant supports (materials: posts and wires)		95.00
Installation (labor)		60.00
Spraying (materials)		70.00
Labor		40.00
Irrigation equipment		20.00
Water		60.00
Harvesting (labor)		150.00
Packing, transport and marketing		511.00
TOTAL EXPENSES		IL 1,342.00
Crop yield (300 boxes)	IL 1,800.00	
NET PROFIT	IL 458.00/*dūnam*	

Tomatoes Winter Planting (under plastic)—1972

Expense Item	*Amount*
Cultivation and discing	IL 16.00
Sub-soiling	5.00
Manure and application	110.00
Ridge sectioning	4.00
Plowing (horse)	15.00
Plastic coverings	
Wire supports	70.00
PVC sheeting (plastic)	250.00
Brick weights	24.00
Chemical fertilizer	33.00
Tomato plants	75.00
Planting (2 days @ IL 10/day)	20.00
Installation of plastic coverings (labor)	60.00
Hoeing (2 days @ IL 10/day)	20.00
Weeding (3 times)	30.00
Insecticides and pesticides	105.00
Application (labor)	30.00
Water	35.00
Maintenance of sprinklers	10.00
Harvesting (12 days @ IL 10/day)	120.00
Marketing, packing and shipping	534.00
TOTAL EXPENSES	IL 1,566.00

Crop Yield (200 boxes)	IL 3,000.00/*dūnam*
NET PROFIT	IL 1,434.00

Cucumbers Winter Planting (under plastic)—1973

Expense Item	*Amount*
Plowing (tractor)	IL 10.00
Discing	5.00
Sub-soiling	5.00
Manure	50.00
Application (labor)	10.00
Poultry dropping and application	10.00
Ridge sectioning	4.00
Plowing (horse)	15.00
Plastic coverings	
Wire supports	70.00
PVC Sheeting (plastic)	250.00
Brick weights	24.00
Chemical Fertilizer (3 sacks)	33.00
Ammonia	9.00
Seeds	35.00
Sowing	10.00
Installation of plastic coverings	50.00
Hoeing (2 woman days @ IL 10/day)	20.00
Miscellaneous labor	30.00
Insecticides and pesticides	150.00
Application (labor)	40.00
Sprayer (rental and fuel)	16.00
Water	30.00
Maintenance of sprinklers	10.00
Harvesting (20 days, 2 laborers)	400.00
Packing, transport and marketing	647.00
TOTAL EXPENSES	IL 1,933.00

Crop yield (250 boxes)	IL 3,250.00/*dūnam*
NET PROFIT	IL 1,317.00

Cucumbers (Greenhouse Crop)
Greenhouse Construction and One Year Operation—1973

Expense Item	*Amount*
Greenhouse construction (1st year expense)	
Water pipes	IL 6,380.00
Concrete	200.00
Assembly (labor)	1,000.00
PVC (plastic) sheeting	1,200.00
Lumber	6,450.00
Overhead (drip) sprinkler system	2,330.00
Water	100.00
Trellis wire	300.00
Nails	50.00
Manure	500.00
Chemical fertilizer	250.00
Seeds	430.00
Plastic plant ties	140.00
Cultivation (labor)	50.00
Soil sterilization	50.00
Spraying	1,000.00
Other labor (men @ IL 40/day, women @ IL 20/day)	5,000.00
TOTAL EXPENSES	IL 25,430.00

Crop yield, gross	IL 25,457.91
NET PROFIT, FIRST YEAR	IL 25,27.91/*dūnam*
ESTIMATED 2ND YEAR PROFIT	IL 15,000.00/*dūnam*

Onions (for Export) Winter Crop (December planting)—1972

Expense Item	*Amount*
Deep plowing (2 times)	IL 10.00
Chemical fertilizer (2 sacks)	24.00
Amoniated sulphur (30 kg.)	7.00
Ridge sectioning	4.00
Seedlings (40,000 plants)	200.00
Planting (6 woman days @ IL 10/day)	60.00
Water	20.00
Use and maintenance of sprinklers	10.00
Weed killer	20.00
Dusting (materials and labor)	60.00
Harvesting and topping (4 days)	40.00
Sorting and grading	150.00
TOTAL EXPENSES	IL 605.00

Crop yield (3,000 tons)	IL 1,005.00
NET PROFIT	IL 400.00/*dūnam*

Olives (For Oil)—1972

Expense Item	*Amount*
Plowing (2 times)	IL 30.00
Hoeing (labor, 1/2 day)	6.00
Weeding	5.00
Fertilizer (materials and labor)	55.00
Picking	40.00
Use of local olive press	20.00
TOTAL EXPENSE	IL 156.00

Crop yield (olive oil)	IL 360.00/*dūnam*
NET PROFIT	IL 204.00

NOTE: One olive crop per twelve month period. Trees produce, on average, one full crop on alternate years only. Accordingly, figures represent two year profit average.

Sesame*—1955

Expense Item	*Amount*
Plowing and sowing	IL 10.00
Seeds (1/2 kg.)	1.00
Weeding and thinning (twice; 3 days @ IL 2/day)	6.00
Harvesting (2 days @ IL 2/day)	4.00
TOTAL EXPENSES	IL 21.00

Crop yield (75 kg.)	IL 112.50/*dūnam*
NET PROFIT	IL 91.50

NOTE: Growing season = 6 to 7 months.

* Sesame was a common crop in the area as a dry-farming crop until the late 1950s when irrigation was introduced.

Appendix C
Kinship Charts

Chart I
MUHAMMAD'S LINEAGE OF THE YAZĪD DESCENT GROUP

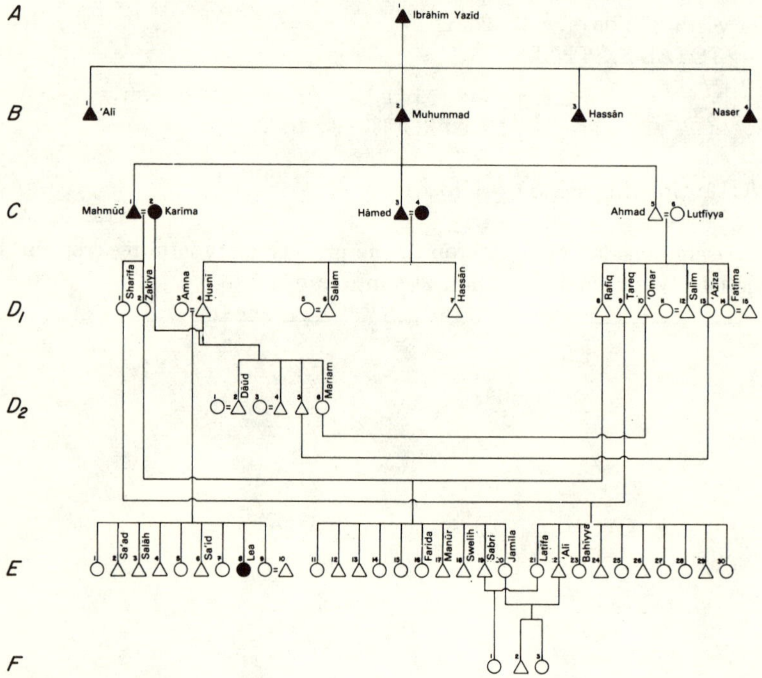

Chart 2

THE LINEAGES OF IBN-JABĀR AND ṢAQER ATTACHED TO THE AMĪN DESCENT GROUP BY MARRIAGE

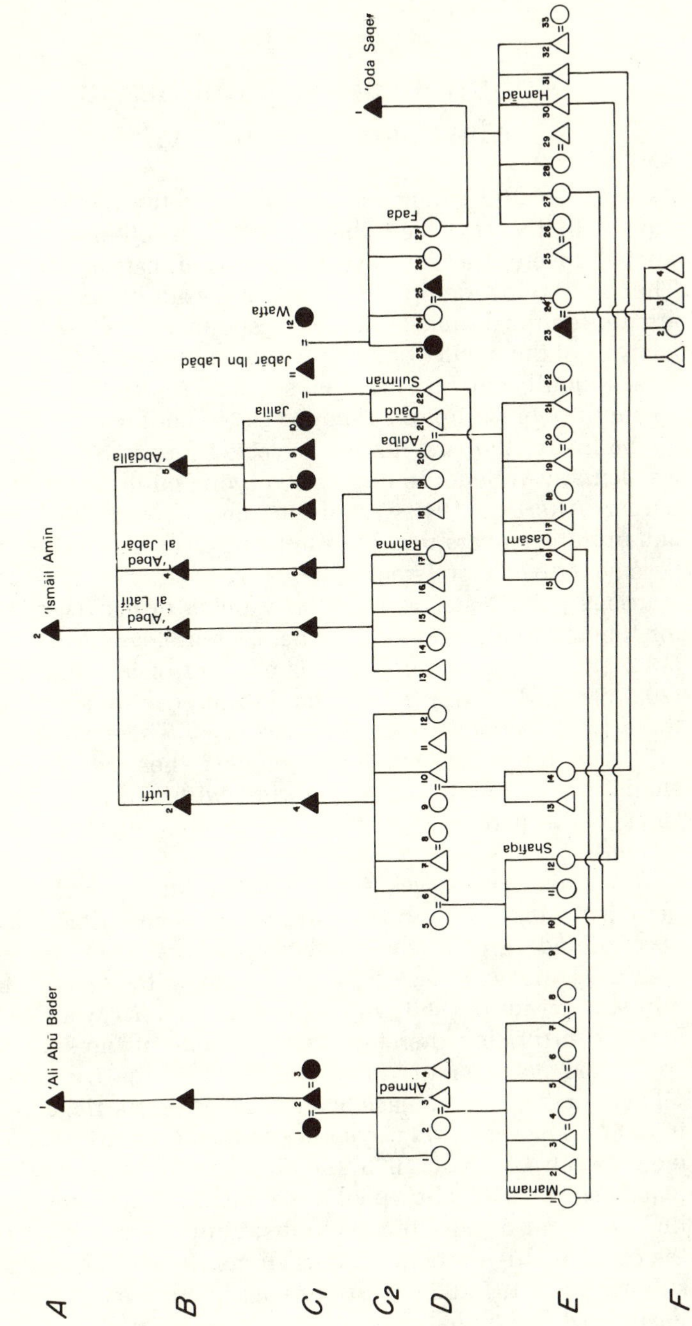

Appendix D
Supplementary Studies in Marriage Pattern Analysis

As a test of the general applicability of the methodology employed in the text (see chapter 4), three other separate communities were used for the test analysis of marriage pattern data. The sub-periods identified for each of the additional communities are not identical, nor do they correspond with those used in the analysis of the hamlet data. Rather, the sub-periods are defined by locally significant external events which, logically, vary from one community or group of communities, to another.

The first of the communities selected for the test analysis was a sedentarized Bedouin population living on the Israeli-Lebanese border. After the 1948 War the border divided the tribe, about half of the members remained in Lebanon, while the second half became citizens of Israel. The latter were the subject of the marriage pattern study. The total number of marriages recorded for the community was 108. There were eleven FBD marriages (10.2 percent); and thirty-two other cases of in-group marriages (29.6 percent) within the descent group, making a total of forty-three (39.8 percent) in-group marriages. There were sixty-five (60.2 percent) out-group marriages and these were distributed among the following sub-categories: within the tribe, fifty-one cases (47.2 percent); outside the tribe, fourteen cases (13.0 percent).

The year 1948 serves as a dividing line between two sub-periods for the community. However, since the tribe's settlement was located directly on the border, there were few changes regarding movement restrictions imposed by the military administration until 1966 when these restrictions were abolished. It is not surprising therefore that only one of the six marriages contracted between the Israeli segment of the tribe and other villages or tribes took place before 1965 (this marriage took place in 1959). The remaining five out-of-village unions were contracted between 1965 and 1973, the other eight unions having taken place before 1948. The "pool of candidates," determined by the limited "field of possibilities" outside the community, dictated the observed high rate of intra-tribal marriages. In this regard the sub-period of 1948-65 is best compared with the third sub-period designated for the hamlets.

The second community is the village Qalandia, located near Jerusalem airport, on the northern edge of the area incorporated into the Jerusalem juridicial district after the Six Day War. Ninety-three marriages were recorded for Qalandia distributed in the following categories: Thirty-four (36.6 percent) in-group, of which seventeen were FBD and seventeen within the broader descent group category. There were fifty-nine out-group marriages (63.4 percent); twenty-two of which were within the village (23.6 percent) and the remaining thirty-seven (39.8 percent) contracted with women outside the village.

Between June 1967 and the end of 1968, there was not a single wedding in Qalandia. In the six months immediately preceding the Six Day War, three marriages were contracted, two of them with women outside the village, and the third between members of unrelated families within the village. There were nine marriages between 1969 and 1973 – including one FBD marriage, and two with women of neighboring West Bank villages. Thus, June 1967 and the beginning of 1969 should be considered the dividing lines for sub-grouping. After June 1967 the residents of Qalandia felt that they were living in an enclave. They had become Israeli residents, whereas their neighboring villages, with which they had had most of their social and economic interactions, remained under West Bank administration.

The eighteen months between June 1967 and the end of the 1968 sub-period were a time marked by uncertainty for the villagers. There were rumors that the annexation was only temporary, and this dictated a "wait and see policy" for those concerned. If the marriages after 1968 are examined, it is found that only two out of the nine were with women out of the village, but these were with women from villages very close to it. In Qalandia it was not the actual "field of possibilities" that affected the distribution of marriages, but rather the "field of eligibles" that showed the effects of the situation. One characteristic required of a candidate for marriage was her being a resident of Qalandia.

The third community chosen to demonstrate the validity of the methodology used, was the Samaritan community.[1] The four hundred and sixty Samaritans are divided equally between two places. Two hundred and thirty live in Nablus (Shechem) on the West Bank, close to their religious center on Mt. Gerizim; while the other half live in a residential location, – in Holon, a small town bordering on Tel Aviv.

The Samaritans are only allowed to marry members of their own religion or Jews who agree to become Samaritans. Out of the total of 128 cases of marriages recorded for Samaritans,[2] there were only six cases in which the wife was Jewish, and only one case in which a Jewish male became a Samaritan. However, this marriage ended in divorce and the man dissociated himself from the community.[3] Forty-one marriages were FBD (thirty-two percent); fifty were with other members of the descent group (thirty-nine percent); and thirty-seven were with members of other descent groups (twenty-nine percent). That is twenty-nine marriages were contracted within the six descent groups which compose the entire community, and six with Jewish women from outside it (making thirty-seven). Bonné reported an increase in FBD marriages after 1933 and noted a preference for FBD partners.[4]

Between 1948 and 1952 there were no contacts between the two groups of Samaritans. Only from 1952 were the Israeli Samaritans (the residents of Holon) permitted to cross the border for their Passover ritual sacrifice on Mt. Gerizim. Not one marriage took place among the Holon community between 1949 and 1952 since it was cut off from the other half of the Samaritan group and from its most important religious center, although there were four marriages within the Shechem group in 1949. In this year its members were informed by the Jordanian authorities that the Israeli Samaritans would be permitted to join them for the Passover sacrifice in 1950 and after. In fact, Passover 1952 was the first time the Jordanians actually allowed the Israeli group to cross the border for the celebrations on Mt. Gerizim. On the same occasion in the following year, the first marriage was contracted between a resident of Shechem and a woman living in Holon. During the years 1950-3 there were no marriages among members of the Shechem group; while between 1953 and 1967 there were ten marriages between partners from opposite sides of the border. In nine cases the woman was a member of the Shechem group and only in one case a resident of Holon. All ten couples chose to live in Holon. Between 1967 and 1974 six marriages of the total of nineteen within the entire community were between mates not belonging to the same residential group. Four were male members of the Shechem group and five out of these six couples live in Holon. As only one male from the Shechem group remained in Holon, residence is uxorilocal for three couples. The distribution of marriages within each of the residential groups show seventeen within the Shechem group, as opposed to six within the Holon group. One of the latter was between a Samaritan male and a Jewish woman who became a Samaritan.

For the Samaritans, the dividing lines of the sub-periods should be 1948 and 1953 respectively. Their "field of eligibles" is restricted by prohibition against marriage outside the religious community. The "field of possibilities" of this small community was influenced by the closed borders during the 1948-1953 sub-period. The avoidance of marriage during the years of separation between the two congregations prevented an increase of in-group marriages. If the Jordanians had not permitted the Israeli Samaritans to celebrate their Passover sacrifice on Mt. Gerizim, an increase in the in-group marriages category would have seemed likely due to the demarcation of the "field of possibilities."[5]

Analysis of these three different communities serves to reinforce the approach put forward earlier. The dividing lines between the subperiods are usually determined by external events which influence the statistics of planned marriages as opposed to those dictated by exigency.

Notes

1. The Samaritans are a religious sect that broke away from the mainstream of Judaism sometime around the fifth century B.C.

"The beginnings of the Samaritans are viewed by Jews and Samaritans from two opposite standpoints. According to Biblical sources, the Samaritans are the descendants of the settlers that were transplanted into Palestine in 722 B.C. by the Assyrian King Sargon (Kings II, 17:5) . . .

The settlers included people from Babylon, Hamath Kuth (or Kutah) after which the Samaritans were called 'Kuthim' in Jewish sources. . . The Samaritans on the other hand deny vehemently their foreign origin and regard themselves as pure Israelites. . . According to the Samaritans their history begins with the settlement of the tribes in the Holy Land." Batsheva Bonné, "Are there Hebrews Left?" *American Journal of Physical Anthropology*, 24 (1966): 135-36.

The Samaritans claim to be the descendants of three tribes: Ephraim, Menashe and Levi. According to the Samaritans, Mt. Gerizim was chosen as the Holy Place for building the Temple. "The choice of Jerusalem as the religious and political center by David and Solomon is deeply resented by the Samaritans who saw in it a definite break with God's decrees." Ibid., p. 236.

2. I would like to take this opportunity to thank Mr. Benyamin Tsedaka (Editor of the biweekly Samaritan newspaper, based in Holon)

for his assistance in collecting the data concerning the Samaritan marriages.

3. Personal communication from Mr. Benyamin Tsedaka.

4. "There was an increase from 21.4 percent of first cousin mating among those married previous to 1933 to 41.2 percent among those married after 1933. Preference for first cousin is demonstrated and may be an additional factor in delay of marriage and age discrepancy between mates." Batsheva Bonné, The Samaritans: A Demographic Study, *Human Biology* 35 (1963): 87.

5. For further information on marriages among the Samaritans, see: Batsheva Bonné, "Genes and Phenotypes in Samaritan Israelis," *American Journal of Physical Anthropology*, 24 (1966): 1-19. For background regarding the community, see: Benyamin Tsedaka, J. McDonald and A. Loewenstamm, Vol. 14, pp. 726-57. *Encyclopaedia Judaica* (Jerusalem: Keter Publishing House, 1971).

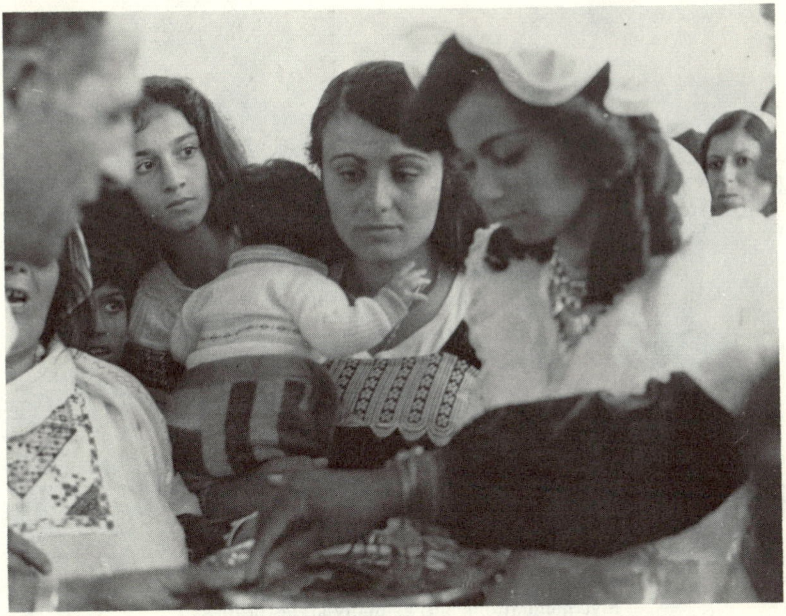

Bride receiving key of new house from the groom's father — a new development in the wedding ceremony

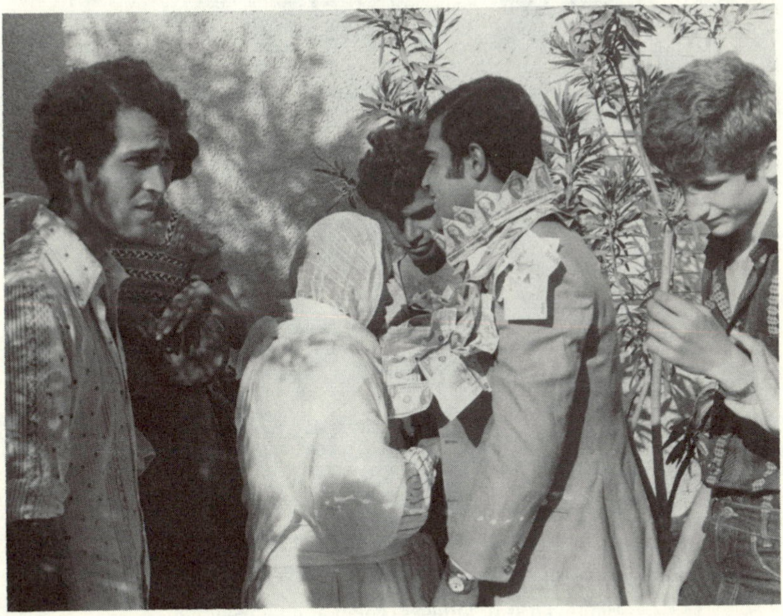

The groom, dressed in dollars, being blessed by his mother before meeting his bride.

Five generations and as many styles of dress.

Happy faces of villagers celebrating a wedding.

Bibliography

Abrahams, Roger D. "A Performance-centered Approach to Gossip." *Man* 5 (June 1970): 290-301.

Abramovitz, Zeev and Guelfat, Itzhaq. *The Arab Economy*. Tel Aviv, Israel: Hakibbutz Hameuchad, 1944 (Hebrew).

Abu-Gosh, Subhi. "The Politics of an Arab Village in Israel." Ph.D, dissertation, Princeton University, 1969.

Abou Zeid, Aḥmed. "Honour and Shame among the Bedouin of Egypt." In *Honour and Shame*, edited by J.G. Peristiany, pp. 243-59. London, England: Weidenfeld and Nicholson, 1965.

Amiran, David H.K. "The Patterns of Settlements in Palestine." *Israel Exploration Journal*, 3 (March 1953): 65-78.

Ammar, Hamed M. *Growing Up in an Egyptian Village; Silwa, Province of Aswan*. London, England: Routledge and Kegan Paul, 1954.

Antoun, Richard T. "On the Modesty of Women in Arab Muslim Villages: A Study in the Accommodation of Traditions." *American Anthropologist* 70 (December 1968): 671-97.

Antoun, Richard T. *Arab Village: A Social Structural Study of a Trans-Jordanian Peasant Community*. Bloomington, Indiana: Indiana University Press, 1972.

Aswad, Barbara C. *Property Control and Social Strategies: Settlers on a Middle Eastern Plain*. Anthropological Papers, No. 44. Ann Arbor, Michigan: University of Michigan, 1971.

Ayoub, Millicent R. "Parallel Cousin Marriage and Endogamy: A Study in Sociometrry." *Southwestern Journal of Anthropology* 15 (Autumn 1959): 266-75.

Baer, Gabriel. *Population and Society in the Arab East*. London, England: Routledge and Kegan-Paul, 1964.

Bailey, Fredrick, George. *Strategems and Spoils: A Social Anthropology of Politics*. New York: Schocken Books, 1969.

Baldenspeeger, Philip J. "Women in the East." *Palestine Exploration Fund, Quarterly Statements* 32 (April 1900): 171-90.

Baldwin, Elaine. *Differentiation and Co-operation in an Israeli Veteran Moshav*. Manchester, England: Manchester University Press, 1972.

Barth, Fredrik. "Father's Brother's Daughter Marriage in Kurdistan." *Southwestern Journal of Anthropology* 10 (Spring 1954): 164-71.

Barth, Fredrik. *Nomads of South Persia: The Basseri Tribe of the Khamseh Confederacy*. Boston, Mass.: Little, Brown and Little, 1961.

Barth, Fredrik. "Role Dilemmas and Father-Son Dominance in Middle Eastern Kinship Systems." In *Kinship and Culture*, edited by Francis L.K. Hsu, pp. 87-95. Chicago, Ill.: Aldine, 1973.

Barth, Fredrik. "Descent and Marriage Reconsidered." In *The Character of Kinship*, edited by Jack Goody, pp. 3-20. Cambridge, England: Cambridge University Press, 1973.

Bates, Daniel G. *Nomads and Farmers: A Study of the Yörük of Southwestern Turkey*. Anthropological Papers, No. 52. Ann Arbor, Michigan: University of Michigan, 1973.

Beattie, John. *Understanding an African Kingdom: Bunyor*. New York: Holt, Rinehart and Winston, 1965.

Becker, Howard S. *Outsider: Studies in the Sociology of Deviance*. Glencoe, Ill.: The Free Press, 1959.

Ben-Zvi, Itzaq. *Eretz-Israel Under Ottoman Rule: Four Centuries of History*. Jerusalem, Israel: Bialik Institute, 1955. (Hebrew)

Bergheim, Samuel. "Land Tenure in Palestine: Answer to Questions." *Palestine Exploration Fund, Quarterly Statements* 26 (April 1894): 191-99.

Black-Michaud, Jacob. *Cohesive Force: Feud in the Mediterranean and the Middle East*. Oxford, England: Basil Blackwell, 1975.

Bonné, Batsheva. "The Samaritans: A Demographic Study." *Human Biology* 35 (February 1963): 61-89.

Bonné, Batsheva. "Genes and Phenotypes in Samaritan Israelis." *American Journal of Physical Anthropology* 24 (January 1966): 1-19.

Bonné, Batsheva. "Are there Hebrews Left?" *American Journal of Physical Anthropology* 24 (March 1966): 135-45.

Bossen, Laurel. "Women in modernizing Societies." *American Ethnologist* 2 (November 1975): 587-601.

Bott, Elizabeth. *Family and Social Network: Roles, norms and external relationships in ordinary urban families.* London, England: Tavistock Publications, 1964.

Bromlei, Iu. V. "Ethnos and Endogamy." *Soviet Anthropology and Archeology* 13 (Summer 1974): 55-69.

Canaan, Taufik. *Mohammedan Saints and Sanctuaries in Palestine.* London, England: Luzac, 1927.

Canaan, Taufik. "Unwritten Laws affecting the Arab Woman of Palestine." *Journal of the Palestine Oriental Society* 11 (1931): 172-203.

Chelhood, Joseph. "Le Marriage Avec La Cousine Parallelle Dans Le Systeme Arabe." *L'Homme* 5 (Juillet-Decembre 1965): 113-73.

Cohen, Abner. *Arab Border Villages in Israel: A Study of Community and Change in a Social Organization*. Manchester, England: Manchester University Press, 1965.

Cohen, Eric. "Mixed Marriages in an Israeli Town." *The Jewish Journal of Sociology* 11 (June 1969): 41-50.

Conder, Claude Reignier. *Tent Work in Palestine*, Vol. 2. London, England: R. Bentley and Son, 1879.

Conder, Claude Reignier, and Horatio Herbert Kitchener. *The Survey of Western Palestine: Memoirs,* Vol. 2. London, England: The Committee of the Palestine Exploration Fund, 1882.

Cox, Bruce A. "What is Hopi Gossip About? Information Management and Hopi Factions." *Man* 5 (March 1970): 88-98.

Cuisinier, Jean. "Endogamie et Exogamie dans le Marriage Arabe." *L'Homme* 2 (Mai-Aout 1962): 80-105.

Cunnison, Ian. *Baggara Arabs*. Oxford, England: Calderon Press, 1966.

Dalman, Gustaf Hermann. *Arbeit und Sitte in Palestina*, Vol. 6. Zeltleben Hildesheim, Germany: George Olms, 1964 (1939 Reprint).

Danin, Ezra. *Documents and Figures*. Tel Aviv, Israel: Hamagen Haivry (Hebrew).

Dodd, Peter, C. "Family Honor and the Forces of Change in Arab society." *International Journal of Middle East Studies* (January 1073): 40-54.

Dumont, Louis, and Pocock, David. "For a Sociology of India." *Contributions to Indian Sociology* 4 (1960): 82-89.

Evans-Pritchard, Edward Evan. "The Position of Women in Primitive Societies and in our Own." In *The Position of Women in Primitive Societies and Other Essays in Social Anthropology*, edited by Edward Evan, Evans-Pritchard, pp. 37-58. London, England: Faber and Faber, 1965.

Fadida, Michael; Pat-El, Uri and 'Athamma, Said. "Arab Co-operation: Socio-economic Study." Tel Aviv, Israel: Israeli Institute for Research and Information, 1972 (Hebrew).

Fakhouri, Hani. *Kafr El-Elow: An Egyptian Village in Transition*. New York: Holt, Rinehart and Winston, 1972.

Firth, Raymond. "Factions to India and Overseas Indian Society." *British Journal of Sociology* 8 (December 1957): 291-95.

Freeman, Linton C. "Marriage without Love: Mate Selection in Non-Western Societies". In *Selected Studies in Marriage and the Family*, edited by Robert Francis Winch, Robert McGinnis and Herbert R. Barringer, pp. 439-55. New York: Holt, Rinehart and Winston, 1962.

Fuller, Ann H. "The World of Kin in Lebanon." In *Readings on the Family and Society*, edited by William Josiah Goode, pp. 176-80. Englewood Cliffs, N.J.: Prentice-Hall, 1964.

Gertz, Abraham. "The Settlements and their Inhabitants." In *'Emeq Hefer: An Historical, Demographic and Economic Survey*. Kfar Vitkin, Israel: 'Emeq Hefer Regional Council, 1970 (Hebrew).

Gilsenan, Michael. *Saint and Sufi in Modern Egypt: An Essay in the Sociology of Religion*. Oxford, England: Clarendon Press, 1973.

Gilbert, John P., and Hammel, E.A. "Computer Simulation and Analysis of Problems in Kinship and Social Structure." *American Anthropologist* 68 (February 1966): 71-93.

Ginat, Joseph. "The Bedouin of the Negev in the Ayalon Basin." In *The Western Ayalon Basin*, edited by Shlomo Marton, pp. 240-48. Tel Aviv, Israel: Hakibbutz Hameuchad, 1970 (Hebrew).

Ginat, Joseph. "Cooperation in the Arab Sector in Israel." In *The Cooperation in the Arab Sector in Israel*, edited by Yehuda Don, pp. 74-75. Tel Aviv, Israel: International Research Center on Rural Communities, 1974 (Hebrew).

Ginat, Joseph. "Marriage Patterns and Political Structure." Paper presented at graduate seminar, April 1970, Department of Sociology and Anthropology. Tel Aviv University.

Gluckman, Max. *Custom and Conflicts in Africa*. Oxford, England: Blackwell, 1956 (Reprint).

Gluckman, Max. "Political Institutions." In *The Institutions of Primitive Societies*, edited by Edward Evan Evans-Pritchard, pp. 60-80. Oxford, England: Blackwell, 1956.

Gluckman, Max. "Gossip and Scandal." *Current Anthropology* 4 (June 1963): 307-15.

Gluckman, Max. "Psychological, Sociological and Anthropological Explanations of Witchcraft and Gossip: A Clarification." *Man* 3 (March 1968: 20-34.

Goffman, Erving. *The Presentation of Self in Everyday Life*. New York: Doubleday, 1959.

Golany, Gideon. "Geography of Settlements of Eron Valley Region: Determining Factor in the Formation of Branch Villages." Ph.D. dissertation. The Hebrew University, 1966 (Hebrew).

Goldberg, Arlette. "Le Changement social dans un village musulman d'Israel." Ph.D. dissertation, Sorbonne University, 1974.

Goldberg, Harvey. "FBD Marriage and Demography Among Tripolitanian Jews in Israel." *Southwestern Journal of Anthropology* 23 (Summer 1967): 176-91.

Goode, William Joshia. *The Family*. Englewood Cliffs, N.J.: Prentice-Hall, 1964.

Granott, Abraham. *The Land System in Palestine: History and Structure*. London, England: Eyre and Spottiswoode, 1952.

Granqvist, Hilma. *Marriage Conditions in a Palestinian Village, Vol. 1*. Commentationes Humanarum Litterarum, vol. 3, No. 8. Helsingfors, Finland: Societas Scintiarum, Fennica, 1931.

Granqvist, Hilma. *Marriage Conditions in a Palestinian Village, Vol. 2.* Commentationes Humanarum Litterarum, vol. 6, no. 8. Helsingfors, Finland: Societas Scintiarum Fennica, 1935.

Granqvist, Hilma. *Birth and Childhood Among the Arabs: Studies in a Muhammadan Village in Palestine.* Helsingfors, Finland: Söderström, 1947.

Granqvist, Hilma. *Child Problems among the Arabs: Studies in a Muhammadan Village in Palestine.* Helsingfors, Finland: Söderström, 1950.

Gubser, Peter. *Politics and Change in Al-Karak, Jordan: A Study of a Small Arab Town and Its District.* London, England: Oxford University Press, 1973.

el Hamamsy, Laila Shukry. "The Changing Role of the Egyptian Woman." In *Readings in Arab Middle Eastern Societies and Cultures*, edited by Abdulla M. Luṭfīyya and Charles W. Churchill, pp. 597-601. The Hague, The Netherlands: Mouton, 1970.

Hammel, E.A. and Goldberg, Harvey. "Parallel Cousin Marriage." *Man* 6 (September 1971): 488-89.

Handelman, Don. "Gossip in Encounters: The Transmission of Information in a Bounded Social Setting." *Man* 8 (June 1973): 210-27.

Harari, Yehiel. *The Elections for the Seventh Knesset in the Arab Sector – 1969.* Givat Haviva, Israel: Center for Arab and Afro-Asian Studies, 1971.

Harris, Marvin. *The Rise of Anthropological Theory: A History of Theories of Culture.* New York: Thomas Y. Cromwell, 1970.

Histadrut Executive Body. "Budget Proposal for 1974." Tel Aviv, Israel: Va'ad Hapo'el, 1974 (Hebrew).

Israel. Central Bureau of Statistics. Statistical Abstract of Israel. Jerusalem, Israel: 1967.

Israel. Central Bureau of Statistics. Census of Agriculture 1971: Manpower Employment Series, no. 2. Jerusalem, Israel. 1973.

Israel. Government of Official Gazette. no. 2353. Jerusalem, Israel: The Government Press, 1969.

Israel. Ministry of Housing. *For Better Living*. Tel Aviv, Israel: Japhet Press, 1964.

Jaussen, Joseph Antonion. *Coutumes des Arabes en pays de Moab*. Paris, France: Adrien-Maisonneuve, 1908.

Kennedy, John G. "Circumcision and Excision in Egyptian Nubia." *Man* 5 (June 1970): 175-91.

Keyser James M.B. "The Middle Eastern Case: Is There a Marriage Rule?" *Ethnology* 13 (July 1974): 293-309.

Khuri, Fuad I. "Parallel Cousin Marriage Reconsidered: A Middle Eastern Practice that Nullifies the Effect of Marriage on the Intensity of Family Relationships." *Man* 5 (December 1970): 597-618.

Khuri, Fuad I. *From Village to Suburb: Order and Change in Great Beirut*. Chicago, Ill.: The University of Chicago Press, 1975.

Kressel, Gideon M. "The Dynamics of Israeli Arab Community in a Process of Urbanization." Ph.D. dissertation, Tel Aviv University, 1972 (Hebrew).

Kressel, Gideon M. *Individuality against Tribality: The Dynamics of a Bedouin Community in a Process of Urbanization*. Tel Aviv, Israel: Hakibbutz Hameuchad, 1976 (Hebrew).

Landau, Jacob M. *The Arabs in Israel: A Political Study*. London, England: Oxford University Press, 1969.

Landau, Jacob M. *The Arabs in Israel: A Political Study*. Tel Aviv, Israel: Ministry of Defence, 1971 (Hebrew).

Layish, Aharon. "The Social Status of the Muslim Women in Israel as Reflected in the Proceedings and Decisions of the Shari'a Courts." Ph.D. dissertation. The Hebrew University, 1972 (Hebrew).

Layish, Aharon. *Women and Islamic Law in a Non-Muslim State: A Study Based on Decisions of the Shari'a Courts in Israel*. New York and Tel Aviv: John Wiley and Israeli Universities Press, 1975.

Leach, Edmond Ronald. *Rethinking Anthropology*. Monographs on Social Anthropology, no. 22. London, England: London School of Economics, 1966.

Lévi-Strauss, Claude. *The Elementary Structure of Kinship*. London, England: Eyre and Spottiswoode, 1969.

Luṭfīyya, Abdulla. *Baytīn; A Jordanian Village*. The Hague, The Netherlands: Mouton, 1966.

Malinowski, Bronislaw. *Crime and Custom in Savage Society*. Paterson, N.J.: Littlefield and Adams, 1959.

Malinowski, Bronislaw. "Avenues to the Trobrianders." In *The Family: Its Structure and Function*, edited by Rose Laub Coser, pp. 216-25. New York: St. Martin's Press, 1964.

Mar'i, Sami and Abraham, Benjamin. *The Attitude of Arab Society in Israel Towards Technological-Vocational Education*. Haifa, Israel: University of Haifa, School of Education, Research Institute for Arab Education and its Development, 1975 (Hebrew).

Mar'i, Sami, and Zaher, Nabiyya. *Facts and Trends in the Development of Arab Education in Israel*. Haifa, Israel: University of Haifa, School of Education, Research Institute for Arab Education and Its Development, 1976 (Hebrew).

Marshall, Gloria A. "Marriage". In *International Encyclopedia of Social Sciences*, editd by David L. Sills, pp. 10-12. Vol. X. New York: Macmillan and the Free Press, 1968.

Marx, Emanuel. *Bedouin of the Negev*. Manchester, England: Manchester University Press, 1967.

Marx, Emanuel. "The Organization of Nomadic Groups in the Middle East." In *Society and Political Structure in the Arab World*, edited by Menahem Milson, pp. 305-35. New York: Humanities Press, 1973.

Marx, Emanuel. "Circumcision Feats among the Negev Bedouin." *International Journal of Middle East Studies* 4 (October 1973): 411-27.

Marx, Emanuel. "The Tribe as a Unit of Subsistence: Nomadic Pastoralism in the Middle East." *American Anthropologist* 79 (1977): 352.

Marx, Emanuel. "The Ecology and Politics of Nomadic Pastoralists in the Middle East." In *The Nomadic Alternative*, edited by W. Weiss Leder. The Hague: Mouton, 1978.

Mason, John P. "Sex and Symbol in the Treatment of Women: the wedding rite in a Libyan oasis community." *American Ethnologist* 2 (November 1975): 649-61.

Merton, Robert K., Intermarriage and Social Structure: Fact and Theory. In *The Family: Its Structure and Function*, edited by Rose L. Coser, pp. 128-52. New York: St. Martin's Press, 1964.

Mills, Eric. *Census of Palestine: Population of Villages, Towns and Administration Areas*. Jerusalem, Palestine: Greek Convent and Goldberg Presses, 1932.

Mohsen, Safia K. "Aspects of the Legal Status of Women Among Awlad 'Ali." In *Peoples and Cultures of the Middle East, Vol. 1, Depth and Diversity*, edited by Lopuis E. Sweet, pp. 220-33. Garden City, N.Y.: The Natural History Press, 1970.

Murphy Robert F. and Leonard Kasdan. "The Structure of Parallel Cousin Marriage." *American Anthropologist* 61 (February 1959): 17-29.

Murphy, Robert F. and Leonard, Kasdan. "Agnation and Endogamy: Some Further Considerations." *Southwestern Journal of Anthropology* 23 (Spring 196): 1-14.

Murphy, Yolanda, and Robert, F. Murphy. *Women of the Forest*. New York: Columbia University Press, 1974.

Musil, Alios. *The Manners and Customs of the Rwala Bedouins*. Oriental Exploration and Studies, no. 6, New York: American Geographic Society, 1928.

Nakhleh, Khalil A. "Shifting Patterns of Conflict in Selected Arab Villages in Israel." Ph.D. dissertation, Indiana University, 1973.

Nelson, Cynthia. "Public and Private Politics: Women in the Middle Eastern World." *American Ethnologist* 1 (November 1974): 551-63.

Nicholas, Ralph W. "Factions: A Comparative Analysis." In *Political Systems and the Distribution of Power*, edited by Michael Banton, Association of Social Anthropologists of the Commonwealth Monographs, no. 2, pp. 21-61. London, England, Tavistock, 1965.

Paine, Robert. "What is Gossip About? An Alternative Hypothesis." *Man* 2 (June 1967): 278-85.

Palestine, Government of. *Village Statistics*. Jerusalem, Palestine: The Government Press, 1938.

Palestine, Government of. *Village Statistics*. Jerusalem, Palestine: The Government Press, 1945.

Parsons, Talcott. *The Social System*. Glencoe, Ill.: The Free Press, 1949.

Patai, Raphael. "Cousin-Right in Middle Eastern Marriage." *Southwestern Journal of Anthropology* (Winter 1955): 371-90.

Patai, Raphael. *Sex and Family in the Bible and the Middle East*. New York: Doubleday, 1959.

Patai, Raphael. "The Structure of Endogamous Unilineal Descent Groups." *Southwestern Journal of Anthropology* 21 (Winter 1965): 325-50.

Patai, Raphael. *Golden River to Golden Road: Society, Culture and Change in the Middle East*. Philadelphia, Penn.: University of Pennsylvania Press, 1969.

Peres, Yochanan. *Ethnic Relations in Israel*. Tel Aviv, Israel: Sifriat Hapoalim and Tel Aviv University, 1976 (Hebrew).

Peters, Emrys L. "Aspects of the Family among the Bedouin of Cyrenica." In *Comparative Family Systems*, edited by M.F. Nimkoff, pp. 191-46. Boston, Mass.: Houghton-Mifflin, 1965.

Peters, Emrys L. "Some Structural Aspects of the Feud among the Camel Herding Bedouin of Cyrenaica." *Africa* 37 (July 1967): 262-82.

Peters, Emrys L. "The Proliferation of Segments in the Lineage of the Bedouin of Cyrenaica [Libya]." In *Peoples and Cultures of the Middle East, Vol. 1, Depth and Diversity*, edited by Louise E. Sweet, pp. 363-98. Garden City, N.Y.: The Natural History Press, 1970.

Peters, Emrys L. "Aspects of Rank and Status among Muslims in a Lebanese Village." In *Peoples and Cultures of the Middle East, Vol. 2: Life in the Cities, Towns and Countryside*, edited by Louise E. Sweet, pp. 76-123. Garden City, N.Y.: The National History Press, 1970.

Peters, Emrys L. "The Status of Women in Four Middle East Communities." In *Beyond the Veil*, edited by Nikki R. Keddie and Lois Beck. Cambridge, Mass.: Harvard University Press.

Pocok, David Francis. "The Basis of Faction in Girjerat." *British Journal of Sociology* 8 (December 1957): 295-306.

Randolph, Richard R. "The Social Structure of the Qdiirat Bedouin." Ph.D. dissertation. University of California, 1963.

Randolph, Richard R. and Allan D. Coult. "A Computer Analysis of Bedouin Marriage." *Southwestern Journal of Anthropology* 24 (Spring 1968): 83-99.

Robinson, Edward, and Eli Smith. *Biblical Researches in Palestine Mount Sinai and Arabia Petrea: A Journal of Travels in the Year 1838*. London, England: J. Murray, 1841, 3 vols.

Rogers, Susan Carol. "Female Forms of Power and the Myth of Male Dominance: A model of Female/Male Interaction in Peasant Society." *American Ethnologist* 2 (November 1975): 727-56.

Rosenfeld, Henry. "An Analysis of Marriage and Marriage Statistics for a Muslim and Christian Arab Village." *International Archives of Ethnography* 48 (Summer 1957): 32-62.

Rosenfeld, Henry. "On Determinants of the Status of Arab Village Women." *Man* 40 (May 1960): 66-70.

Rosenfeld, Henry. "From Peasantry to Wage Labor and Residual Peasantry: The Transformation of an Arab Village." In *Process and Pattern in Culture: Essays in Honor of Julian Steward*, edited by Robert A. Manners, pp. 211-34. Chicago, Ill.: Aldine, 1964.

Rosenfeld, Henry. *They were Peasants: Social Anthropological Studies on the Arab Village in Israel*. Tel Aviv, Israel: Hakibbutz Hameuchad, 1964 (Hebrew).

Rosenfeld, Henry. "Change, Barriers to Change and Contradictions in the Arab Village Family." *American Anthropologist* 70 (December 1968): 732-52.

Rosenfeld, Henry. "Patrilineal Endogamy in the Arab Village in Israel." *Social Research Review* 1 (1973), pp. 41-62 (Hebrew).

Schrift, Ruth. "Interethnic and Interracial Marriage: A Comparative Study between Israel, the U.S.A. and South Africa." M.A. dissertation, Tel Aviv University, 1975 (Hebrew).

Shaykh Yusuf, Hajji. "In Defence of the Veil." In *The Contemporary Middle East*, edited by Benjamin Rivlin and Joseph S. Szyliowicz, pp. 355-52. New York: Random House, 1965.

Shepher, Joseph. "Mate Selection Among Second Generation Kibbutz Adolescents and Adults: Incest Avoidance and Negative Imprinting." *Archives of Sexual Behavior* 4 (Summer 1971): 293-307.

Shimoni, Yaacov. *Arabs in Palestine*. Tel Aviv, Palestine: Am Oved, 1947 (Hebrew).

Shokeid, Moshe (Minkovitz). "Immigration and Factionalism: An Analysis of Faction in Rural Israeli Communities of Immigrants." *British Journal of Sociology* 19 (December 1968): 385-406.

Smelser, Neil. *Theory of Collective Behavior*. New York: Free Press of Glencoe, 1963.

Smith, William Robertson. *Kinship and Marriage in Early Arabia*. Edited by Stanley A. Cook 2nd ed. 1907. Reprint Oosterhout, The Netherlands: Offsetbedrijf H. Zopfi, 1966.

Sweet, Louise E. "Camel Raiding of North Arabian Bedouin: A Mechanism of Ecological Adaptation." In *Peoples and Cultures of the Middle East, Volume 1: Depth and Diversity*, edited by Louise E. Sweet, pp. 265-89. Garden City, N.Y.: The Natural History Press, 1970.

Tsafrir, Jenni, and Isaac Halbrecht. "Consanguinity and Marriage Systems in the Jewish Community in Israel." *Annual of Human Genetics* 35 (Spring 1972): 343-47.

Tsedaka, Benyamin; McDonald, John and Loewenstumm, Ayala. "Samaritans." *Encyclopaedia Judaica*, Vol. 14, pp. 726-57. Jerusalem, Israel: Keter Publishing House, 1971.

Turner, Ralph H., and Killian, Lewis M. *Collective Behavior*. Englewood Cliffs, N.J.: Prentice Hall, 1957.

Turner, Victor W. *The Ritual Process*. Chicago, Ill.: Aldine, 1969.

United Nations. The Rhodes Agreement: Armistice Agreements Between Israel and the Hashemite Kingdom of Jordan. Security Council, Official Records: Fourth Year, Special Supplement no. 1, 1949 New York.

Viteles, Harry. *A History of the Co-operative Movement in Israel. Vol. 1: The evolution of the Co-operative movement, a sourcebook*. London, England: Vallentine and Mitchell, 1966.

Volney, Constantin Francqis. *Voyage en Egypte et en Syrie pendant les anneés 1893, 1784 et 1785*. Paris, France: Desenne, 1787.

Westermarck, Edward. *The History of Human Marriage*. Vol. 1. 5th ed. London, England: Macmillan, 1921 (3 Vols.).

Williams, Thomas Rhys. *Field Methods in the Study of Culture*. New York: Holt, Rinehart and Winston, 1967.

Winch, Robert F. *Mate Selection*. New York: Harper and Row, 1958.

Yaqir, Yair. "Problems in Management and Supervision on Arab Co-operatives." In *The Cooperation in the Arab sector in Israel*, edited by Yehuda Don, pp. 31-34. Tel Aviv, Israel: International Research Center on Rural Communities, 1974 (Hebrew).

INDEX

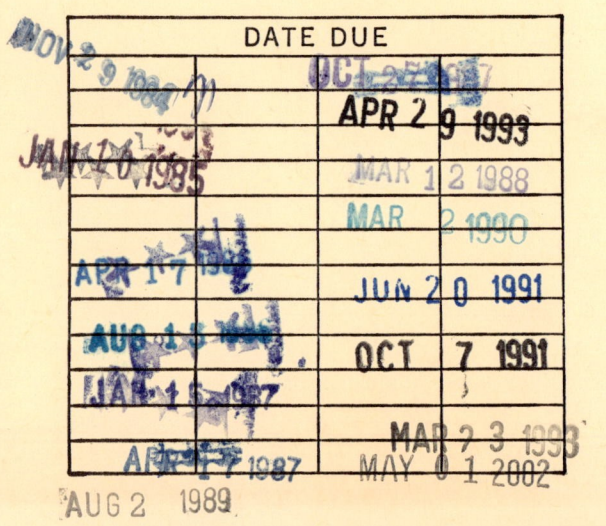